The Shambhala Guide to Sufism

Ibn 'Arabi, a Sufi for All Ages.

THE SHAMBHALA GUIDE TO SUFISM

Carl W. Ernst, Ph.D.

SHAMBHALA

Boston & London

1997

Shambhala Publications, Inc.
Horticultural Hall
300 Massachusetts Avenue
Boston, Massachusetts 02115
http://www.shambhala.com

© 1997 by Carl W. Ernst

9 8 7 6 5 4 3 2 1

First Edition
Printed in the United States of America
⊗ This edition is printed on acid-free paper that meets
the American National Standards Institute Z39.48 Standard.
Distributed in the United States by Random House, Inc.,
and in Canada by Random House of Canada Ltd

Library of Congress Cataloging-in-Publication Data
Ernst, Carl W., 1950–
The Shambhala guide to sufism / Carl W. Ernst.
p.   cm.
Includes bibliographical references and index.
ISBN 1-57062-180-2 (pbk.: alk. paper)
1. Sufism.   I. Title.
BP188.48.E76   1997   97-10189
297.4—dc21   CIP

To Annemarie Schimmel

with gratitude and affection

Contents

List of Figures

Preface

TEN YEARS AGO, I went to Pakistan on a Fulbright research grant, with the aim of writing a book on South Asian Sufism. It was an extraordinary year, in which my family and I experienced the remarkable hospitality and cultural richness of the people of Lahore. But a peculiar thing happened whenever Pakistani acquaintances questioned me about my work. Sometimes, when informed that I was studying Sufism, the questioner would sit back and observe in a dismissive way, "Well, you should know that Sufism has nothing to do with Islam." On other occasions, my interlocutor would lean forward enthusiastically and say something like, "You're working on Sufism! Wonderful! Let me tell you, my grandfather was a *pir* [master], and I can take you to visit his tomb if you wish." These two attitudes reflect an ambivalence about the term *Sufism,* and its relation to Islam, that is deeply written into contemporary Muslim societies around the world.

In most Muslim societies today one can find a current of dogmatic piety that is quite critical of many of the practices and beliefs associated with Sufism. This tendency, which has come to the fore mainly since the year 1800, is often described by its followers in terms of the "revival" or "reform" of the Islamic faith. In its most ideological and political manifestations, this attitude is best known to the mass media under the term *fundamentalism,* or *Islamism*; for those who have had no contact with actual Muslim men and women, the media's politicized concept of Islam is all that there is. Specialists prefer to use the term *fundamentalism* to describe the ideology of antimodernism that has taken hold among approximately twenty percent of the adherents of all major religious traditions. In this respect, Islamic fundamentalism has a role and strength comparable to Christian, Jewish, Hindu, and Buddhist fundamentalisms. Most observers have been impressed with the way in which fundamentalists have concentrated their wrath on denunciations of the secularism and moral corruption associated with "the West," now a code word for the governing political, economic, and scientific authority invested in European and American countries and, to a lesser extent, in their former colonies. Thus to some extent the rhetoric of fundamentalism in Muslim countries is a polemical response to the vast colonial enterprise of conquest carried out by Western countries. In that process, from the time of Napoleon's invasion of Egypt in 1793 to the breakup of the Ottoman empire in 1920, nearly every Muslim country was conquered and colonized by foreign powers. So it should not be surprising that resistance to "Western" dominance continued to be a major theme on the part of ideologues like Iran's Ayatollah Khomeini.

The political focus of the Western media obscures the other main obsession of fundamentalist rhetoric, which is directed within at what are seen as internal threats to Islam. Chief among these threats to Islam, in the fundamentalist perspective, is Sufism. It is considered to be a survival of medieval superstition, idolatry, and corruption. Sufism, in their view, is derived from the idolatrous practices of saint-worshipping Christians and from the heretical doctrines of pantheistic Greek philosophers. They see in it such abominations as worship of tombs, pagan music borrowed from Hindus, and the fleecing of credulous believers by greedy and fraudulent Sufi masters. The seriousness with which fundamentalists take Sufism is indicated by the Wahhabi movement in Arabia in the early 1800s, considered the progenitor of today's fundamentalist movements; when their tribal alliance first came to power, one of their first actions was to destroy all the stately tombs of Sufi saints and Shi'i imams in Arabia and Iraq. These were regarded as idolatrous creations, which raised some human beings above others as demigods; hence they had to be destroyed. Even the popular veneration of the Prophet Muhammad is decisively rejected by many fundamentalists. Adept at the manipulation of mass media, fundamentalists have tried to monopolize the rhetoric of religious legitimacy, both in their home countries and in the West. Their authoritarian tendencies, couched in the language of submission to God, permit no competing visions of religious truth.

Ironically, as a result of strategic successes by fundamentalist movements in certain key regions like Arabia, and the massive oil wealth that fell into the lap of the Saudi regime, many contemporary Muslims have been taught a story of the Islamic religious tradition from which Sufism has been rigorously excluded. It is ironic because as recently as the late eighteenth century, and for much of the previous millennium, most of the outstanding religious scholars of Mecca, Medina, and the great cities of the Muslim world were intimately engaged with what we today call Sufism. It is doubly ironic because the fundamentalist story is belied by the religious practices of more than half of today's Muslim population. Veneration of the Prophet Muhammad and the Sufi saints is found as a major theme in every Muslim country from China to Morocco. On a more specialized level, millions have sought initiation in the multiple Sufi orders, which trace back a sacred teaching, generation after generation, all the way to the Prophet Muhammad. Techniques of meditation and chants of the names of God, sometimes in combination with music and dance, continue to be practiced as disciplines under the supervision of Sufi masters. Poetry, songs, and stories in dozens of local languages convey the lives and teachings of Sufi saints to a huge public. Despite the attempts of many postcolonial governments to regulate Sufi shrines and orders, because of their large followings and potential political clout, much of the activity connected with Sufism goes on regardless of attempts at interference.

The polemical attacks on Sufism by fundamentalists have had the primary goal of making Sufism into a subject that is separable from Islam, indeed hostile to it. This strategy permits fundamentalists to define Islam as they wish by selective use of certain scriptural texts. The novelty of this project has so far escaped the notice of most journalists and diplomats, since the study of Islamic cultures has not played a significant part in most Euro-American education. The Arabic term *islam* itself was of relatively minor importance in classical theologies based on the Qur'an; it literally means submission to God, and it denotes the minimal external forms of compliance with religious duty. If one looks at the works of theologians such as the famous Abu Hamid al-Ghazali (d. 1111), the key term of religious identity is not *islam* but *iman*, or faith, and the one who possesses it is the *mu'min* or believer. Faith is one of the major topics of the Qur'an, mentioned hundreds of times in the sacred text. In comparison, *islam* is a relatively uncommon term of secondary importance; it only occurs eight times in the Qur'an. Since, however, the term *islam* had a derivative meaning relating to the community of those who have submitted to God, it became practically useful as a political boundary term, both to outsiders and to insiders who wished to draw lines around themselves.[1]

Historically, the term *Islam* was introduced into European languages in the early nineteenth century by Orientalists like Edward Lane, as an explicit analogy with the modern Christian concept of religion; in this respect, *Islam* was just as much a neologism as the terms *Hinduism* and *Buddhism* were. Before that time Europeans used the term *Muhammadan* or *Mahometan* to refer to the followers of the Prophet Muhammad. The use of the term *Islam* by non-Muslim scholars coincides with its increasing frequency in the religious discourse of those who now call themselves Muslims. That is, the term *Islam* became popular in reformist and protofundamentalist circles at approximately the same time, or shortly after, it was popularized by European Orientalists. Both the outside "scientific" observers and the internal ideologues had found an ideal tool in the term *Islam*. Treated simultaneously as a set of changeless religious doctrines and as a sociological unit (now usually assimilated to the Arab minority), Islam became the eternal other, opposing European civilization. The fact that much of Islamic history and culture was left out of the picture was not too great a price to pay for either of these constituencies. In this book, I try to avoid referring to *Islam* as a changeless monolithic religion that somehow homogenizes hundreds of millions of people from different times and places. I use *Islamic* to refer to an orientation in which the primary scriptural focus is the Qur'an and the leading personal model is the Prophet Muhammad, without insisting on any particular authoritative structure beyond this simple formulation. Following Marshall Hodgson, I use *Islamicate* to describe civilizational and cultural practices accepted by Muslims and non-Muslims alike, which are associated with Islamic religious tradition but which do not themselves derive from the primary Islamic scriptural sources.

The term *Sufism* has a complicated history, which will be explored in the opening chapter of this book. Like *Islam*, the term *Sufism* was introduced to European languages by Orientalists, but the two terms were believed to be essentially different. Premodern Muslim societies knew no such distinction. For them, the multifarious activities that we subsume under the terms *Sufism* and *Islam* were not spheres of existence separate or separable from religious life in general. It would not have been possible to formulate the statement "Sufism has nothing to do with Islam" prior to the nineteenth century. While some readers may wish to jump directly into the subsequent chapters that describe different aspects of the Sufi tradition, this first chapter is recommended in order to provide a basis for identifying the issues at stake in the interpretation of Sufism today.

But the modern mania for identity definition has led to new conflicts and new ironies undreamed of in previous eras. Recently I gave a public lecture on Sufism and art at a museum in Washington, D.C., attended by well over a hundred people. In the question period following the lecture, I expected to get inquiries about the topics I had discussed in the lecture. Instead, I was confronted by several people, rising in sequence, who passionately denounced the idea that Sufism could have anything to do with Islam. It became evident that these men were Iranians and Afghans, exiled from their homelands, who blamed fundamentalist interpreters of Islam for all the horrors they had suffered. Yet they were deeply attached to the great Sufis whom they continued to revere, especially the Persian poet Rumi. They could not conceive that their beloved Rumi could have any connection with the hated leaders of the Islamic revolution in Iran or the fanatical faction leaders of Islamist militias in Afghanistan. Thus, for those who had become alienated by fundamentalism, Islam had become the symbol of authoritarian oppression, while Sufism was the way to freedom and universality. The fundamentalist definition had been stood on its head.

I have no intention of trying to announce any final definition of the terms *Sufism* and *Islam* in this book. The point is that these are highly contested terms. If one wishes to give either term some kind of authoritative definition, that kind of statement has meaning primarily in political confrontations of an ideological character, or in the self-definition of groups that draw upon the Sufi tradition. In other words, Sufism is not a thing that one can point to; it is instead a symbol that occurs in our society, which is used by different groups for different purposes. While Orientalists were interested in *Sufism* as a descriptive term for a body of religious beliefs and practices, Muslim mystics traditionally used the term *Sufi* in a prescriptive way to convey certain ethical and spiritual ideals; the multiple forms of activity actually practiced by Muslim mystics all had distinct names and terminologies. Modern Sufi leaders who wish to legitimate their own perspective sometimes discredit other versions as "pseudo-Sufism," particularly in the cases of groups that deemphasize Islamic practices and identity. Fundamentalists decry Sufism as a perversion of Islam, while secular modernists object to Sufism as medieval superstition.

Normally one finds that scholarly writings with a historical emphasis describe Sufism as the mystical aspect of Islam. This kind of description suggests that Sufism involves a personal contact with the Divine, through the inner meaning of Islamic religious practice, and that certainly communicates something. Still, such an explanation contains a number of unstated problems. That is, the very language of the description is assumed to be clear and accurate when it is not. For one thing, mysticism carries the connotations of private and personal experience, so that it fails to account for some of the corporate and political activities of Sufi groups. In addition, a term such as *mysticism* is itself subject to debate and confusion, which has led some leading scholars of Sufism to reject the word *mysticism* altogether as a description of Sufism.[2] And, as suggested above, the term *Islam*, which is generally assumed to be a global and total explanation, is certainly one of the more opaque terms in the contemporary religious vocabulary. People end up taking these terms to mean whatever they wish.

In contrast, nonacademic sources, including some published by Sufi orders, describe Sufism as the universal spirit of mysticism that is at the heart of all religions. From this perspective, Islam is incidental at best (and perhaps an obstacle) in any discussion of Sufism. In this book, I use the term *Sufism* in the broadest descriptive sense, to include not only those people who describe themselves or are described by others as Sufis but also the whole range of historical traditions, texts, cultural artifacts, and practices connected with Sufis. By using such a "family resemblance" approach to Sufism, I am deliberately shelving any attempt to decide who is a "true Sufi," or what is the proper relationship of Sufism and Islam. In terms of Sufi rhetoric, such formulations have meaning only in relation to the spiritual authority of a Sufi master, which I make no pretense to claiming. While I am critical of some of the political attitudes underlying old-fashioned Orientalist scholarship, I believe it is possible to study and sympathetically appreciate a tradition such as Sufism without mystification, from the viewpoint of the study of religion. The only authority asserted in this book is the ability to make judgments and arguments on the basis of historical evidence; this book is, in short, a descriptive essay in interpretation.

This book is not aimed at experts or specialists in Middle Eastern or Islamic studies, and I am forgoing here the diacritical marks, used in the transliteration of foreign names and terms, that are so beloved by specialists. This is instead a broad treatment of the subject which is designed both to describe Sufism and to point out the contentious issues that currently surround it. Today in any music store one can buy fine recordings of music that originated in Sufi circles, which has now been transformed into "world music" performances. The Pakistani *qawwali* singer Nusrat Fateh Ali Khan and the Moroccan musicians from Jahjouka have obtained the sponsorship of major recording labels and the enthusiastic support of successful European and American musicians, and their music has appeared on recent motion picture soundtracks (*Dead Man Walking*). The Persian poet Rumi in multiple English versions is now the best-selling poet in America. The Whirling Dervishes from Turkey regularly perform tours in major concert halls in the West. There are dozens of Internet Web sites linked to Sufi groups based in America. High-quality literary periodicals, with glossy photographs and well-written articles, are being produced by groups such as the Iranian Nimatullahi Sufi order, now based in London. How is one to evaluate all these manifestations of Sufism? By providing an overview of the contexts from which modern Sufism emerged, this book will give the reader a basic background, with the help of which current expressions of Sufism can be understood more clearly.

Keeping in mind the problematic character of our terminology, this book begins with a brief cautionary discussion of how Sufism came to be a subject of interest in the West, and how the term *Sufism* has functioned in the languages of the West. After that introduction, I wish to explore the practices, teachings, and personalities associated with Sufism, both in its historic phases and in the present day. This book does not pretend to be exhaustive; specialists will doubtless detect in my presentation a bias for examples from the Muslim East, particularly the Persian and Indian sphere, in comparison with Turkish, Arab, or Southeast Asian regions. The range of the subject is immense, and a full discussion of the history, literature, philosophy, art, institutions, and practices associated with Sufism would require many volumes and the expertise of scholars conversant with many languages.[3] Instead, this guidebook takes the form of a broadly sketched interpretive essay based on themes that provide an overview of the Sufi tradition in varied contexts.

The interpretive approach of this book will probably be seen as a radical departure from the standard historical and doctrinal studies of Sufism, because I do not take it for granted that any term under discussion has a clear definition agreed upon by everyone. I am also much more concerned to explain what it means to participate in the practices and teachings of Sufism than to explicate abstract philosophical doctrines. Unlike most earlier surveys of Sufism, this book does not treat Sufism primarily as a traditional phenomenon of the past; while the study of historical Sufism is essential for an understanding of the topic, this needs to be juxtaposed with the exploration of Sufism's current manifestations to reveal its contemporary significance. By acknowledging and clarifying the arguments and conflicting points of view that are at stake in current interpretations of Sufism, I hope to perform the genuine service of a guide for the reader who wants to assess the uses to which Sufism is put today. At the same time, I have provided for the reader, in the bibliography and notes, suggestions for some of the best and most accessible translations of Sufi writings and studies of Sufism.

After the opening chapter on the concept of Sufism, I discuss the

origin and development of Sufism through a series of themes, which
gradually move from the earlier periods to the present day. The topics begin with the sacred sources upon which Sufism draws, particularly the Qur'anic revelation and the model of the Prophet
Muhammad. A discussion of the nature of saints and sainthood is
followed by an overview of meditation practices focusing on the repetition of the word of God. Next comes a description of the spread
of Sufi orders and their institutions and rituals. Then Sufi poetry
and music are taken up, with comments on their presentation in
contemporary culture. The final chapter deals with the peculiar di-
lemmas faced by Sufism in the contemporary world, where the question of the relation between Sufism and Islam has been answered in
many different ways. Some Sufi teachers today insist that Sufism is
nothing different from the true practice of Islam in its fullest sense.
Other Sufis have dropped any effort at following Islamic law or ritual,
and they present Sufism as a universal spirituality beyond the limits
of religion. Both points of view are described here, but it is beyond
the scope of a book like this to tell the reader which to follow. Sufi
metaphysics has been more frequently studied than any other aspect
of the subject; if I give this topic short shrift here, it is because I wish
to emphasize practical Sufism, which has not been given adequate
treatment in most previous surveys.

This book is based on my pursuit of Sufi studies in Arabic, Persian,
and Urdu over the past twenty years, in graduate study at Harvard
University, and then as a professor, first at Pomona College and now
at the University of North Carolina at Chapel Hill. It has been en-
riched by long research tours in India and Pakistan and by travel in
Turkey and Iran. My greatest debt is owed to my former teacher,
Professor Annemarie Schimmel, the single most influential scholar
in Sufi studies over the past half-century; this book is dedicated to
her, in gratitude for the immense service she has performed for all
who are interested in Sufism. I have learned much over the years
from many scholars from South Asia, the Middle East, Europe, and

North America. I have benefited in particular from the generosity and comradeship of my two colleagues at Duke University, both of whom are specialists in Sufism. Vincent Cornell, an acute critic and a great conversation partner, read an earlier draft of the book and made a number of valuable suggestions. Bruce Lawrence, with whom I have collaborated over the past decade and a half in research and teaching about Sufism and Islam, has been an unfailing source of helpful insight and keen wit; without the benefit of his company and his example, this book would not have come about. I owe a special debt to the students who have taken my classes over the years, whose enthusiasm and candid responses have helped me formulate this approach to Sufism. Thanks also to research assistant Jennifer Saunders for her efficient and thorough collection of materials. Photographer Gerald Blow of the Ackland Art Museum did an expert job in preparing figures 1, 4, 6, and 10. I would also like to express my thanks to the Sufi leaders who have kindly shared their insights with me and who have freely offered their hospitality; in particular I would like to thank the late Capt. Wahid Bakhsh Sial Rabbani, of the Sabiri Chishti order (Pakistan), and Dr. Javad Nurbakhsh, head of the Ni-matullahi order (Iran). I of course remain responsible for all the views expressed here. I especially thank Kendra Crossen of Shambhala, who suggested this volume. As always, I am grateful to my wife, Judith Ernst, for her understanding and support.

Note: The Qur'an is cited by *sura* and verse of the standard Egyptian edition. Dates are in the Common Era (CE) of the Gregorian calendar except in the notes, where publication dates are given in the Islamic *hijri* calendar followed by a slash and the Gregorian equivalent.

THE SHAMBHALA GUIDE TO SUFISM

1
What Is Sufism?

Go, soar with Plato to th' empyreal sphere,
To the first good, first perfect, and first fair;
Or tread the mazy round his followers trod,
And quitting sense call imitating God;
As Eastern priests in giddy circles run,
And turn their heads to imitate the Sun.
Go, teach Eternal Wisdom how to rule—
And turn into thyself, and be a fool!

—ALEXANDER POPE, ESSAY ON MAN (1734), 2:23–30

"Dervish" and "Fakir": The Outsider's View of Sufism

THE SUBJECT OF SUFISM is difficult to approach. Like any other complex of non-European religious phenomena, what we today call Sufism was not a primary object of interest to Europeans before modern times. It is only during the past two centuries that Europeans (and Americans) turned their attention to the religions of the world as a subject worth investigating seriously. The very concept of religion that they took for granted was in large part based on their understanding of Christianity, particularly of the Protestant variety. The European interest in non-Christian religions grew out of the situation of world conquest and colonialism which became the chief policy goals of European nations. Colonial administrators needed to know something about the religion of "the natives" in order to rule over them effectively. Scholarship on these religions was carried out by specialists in the languages and cultures of the East—Orientalists, who produced many volumes of studies and translations dealing with Oriental religions. For Americans today, *Oriental* is a quaint term for what we now call Asian, a term associated primarily with China and Japan; we forget that for Europe, the closest region of the East lay in the domains of the Turks, the Arabs, and the Persians. Considerable debate has raged in recent years about the politics of Oriental scholarship, particularly since the publication of Edward Said's *Orientalism* in 1978. Some still defend the Orientalist enterprise as a pure and disinterested search for knowledge, while others contend that Orientalists have been accomplices in colonial oppression. Without advocating a simplistic solution to this debate, I would like to point out that scholars who work on non-European studies, particularly in relation to cultures of the Middle East, sooner or later find that their studies have political relevance. The news media, Euro-American foreign policy officials, and heads of Middle Eastern and Asian governments all make use of religious terms and concepts, often for the crudest of political reasons. Studies produced by Euro-American scholars are read with interest in Middle Eastern and Asian countries. The study of Sufism is no different. For this reason, I would like to analyze the terminology that has been used for Sufism, both in European and non-European contexts, with particular attention to the rhetorical implications of disapproval or acceptance that characterize each term. In this way it will be possible to bring out the conflicting tendencies that underlie the modern debate about Sufism.

The beginnings of the modern study of Sufism lie in the colonial period (roughly 1750–1950), when many of the basic concepts and categories that govern our understanding of the term were first invented. Since the very concept of Sufism is hotly contested among both Muslims and non-Muslims today, it is important first of all to examine briefly the historical development of the European study of Sufism, in order to disentangle the issues underlying the current debate. The modern concept of Sufism emerged from a variety of European sources, including travelers' accounts of exotic lands and Orientalist constructions of Sufism as a sect with a nebulous relation to Islam. When this picture of Sufism is compared with the internal documentation of Sufi tradition, a number of mismatches appear. Outsider terminology for Sufism stressed the exotic, the peculiar, and behavior that diverges from modern European norms; in the context of colonialism, this terminology emphasized the dangers of fanatic resistance to European rule.

The two terms that best sum up early European attitudes to Sufism are *fakir* (Arabic *faqir*) and *dervish* (the Turkish pronunciation of Persian *darvish*). Both words mean more or less the same: *faqir* is the Arabic word for "poor man," and *dervish* (probably derived from a term meaning "standing by the door") is the Persian equivalent. European travelers from the sixteenth century onward have given incidental descriptions of dervishes as mendicants equivalent to Catholic monks or friars, known for their solitary way of life. For Protestants, this comparison alone was enough to convict the dervishes of a gross religious error. By the eighteenth and nineteenth centuries, however, dervishes became known in a new and more sensational way. European observers, particularly those traveling in Ottoman territories, made much of the groups of dervishes who could be seen publicly performing their rituals. These groups now became known as the dancing, whirling, and howling dervishes—terms that reflect their most obvious external behaviors; in the absence of any context or explanation, the Europeans could only view these as exotic Oriental customs. In the sarcastic verses quoted above from Alexander Pope, the "Eastern priests," who "in giddy circles run, / And turn their heads to imitate the Sun," are undoubtedly the whirling dervishes, members of the Sufi order known in Turkey as the Mevlevis. Pope obviously regarded them as deluded followers of Plato, insofar as they were believed to reject the body for the sake of the soul. Books written by travelers and diplomats, such as *The Dervishes; or, Oriental Spiritualism*, written in 1868 by American diplomat and translator John P. Brown, featured illustrations of the strange customs of dervishes as a staple of the wonders of the Orient (see figure 2, pages 6–7).

The term *faqir* has a more complicated history, because Persian-writing officials of the Mughal empire in India used the term to describe non-Muslim ascetics, such as yogis, along with Sufi ascetics and wayfarers. The British inherited this terminology when they conquered most of India, and in nineteenth-century English, *fakir* (or *fakeer*) was used almost exclusively for Hindu ascetics, whether of the organized monastic fraternities or those whom the British described as "wandering rogues." The accidental resemblance of the term to the English word *faker* seems to have encouraged the impression that these ascetics were all frauds and mountebanks.

In contrast to these outsiders' impressions, in their original contexts, both *dervish* and *fakir* were terms that signified spiritual poverty, being poor in relation to God, and hence being dependent upon him. As in other religious traditions, poverty for the Sufis was a sign of turning away from the world and focusing on the divine reality. "Poverty is my pride," the Prophet Muhammad is reported to have said. Yet the reports of travelers concerning the fakirs and dervishes of the East created a totally different portrait of bizarre behavior that was already a cultural icon over a century ago. Popular American songs of the nineteenth century refer to the dancing dervish as an image of wild and frantic activity. Magazine cartoons today still preserve the image of the fakir lying on a bed of nails. Travelers' reports were based on fragmentary information, so that the fakir or dervish might sometimes appear to be a solitary figure but at other times was part of a strange brotherhood with peculiar rituals. To be sure, the negative portrait of the dervish had its analogues in some Muslim countries, such as Persia, where the rise of Shi'ism put organized Sufism into disrepute.

In the nineteenth century, European colonial rule over Muslim countries began in earnest. The curiosity of travelers about solitary fakirs or groups of dervishes engaged in strange rituals was superseded by the more pressing concerns of colonial administrators. The indigenous aristocratic elites of Mughal India, Mamluk Egypt, Algeria, and Java were being displaced by British, French, and Dutch colonial bureaucracies. Centers of traditional learning that had been dependent on the patronage of Muslim rulers lost their support. In many Muslim regions, the Sufi orders, often referred to as brotherhoods or confreries by Europeans, were the only local organizations to remain intact after the onset of colonial rule. In North Africa, French officials paid close attention to "marabouts" (from Arabic *murabit*, a resident in a Sufi lodge known as a *ribat*), fearing charismatic leaders who might organize local tribes. In places like the Indian Punjab, the descendants of Sufi saints were caretakers of what had become popular pilgrimage sites, and the British concocted a strategy of co-opting them into the system as influential landlords. In other cases, Sufi leaders who had extensive followings led resistance to European conquest. In Algeria, the Emir 'Abd al-Qadir fought the French for years until his defeat in 1847; in his exile in Syria, he wrote extensively on Sufism and supervised the publication of important Arabic Sufi texts. In the Caucasus, Shaykh Shamil of the Naqshbandi Sufi order set up an independent state that frustrated Russian attacks until 1859. The messianic movement of the Sudanese Mahdi, destroyed by British forces in 1881, originated from a Sufi order; British accounts of the defeat of the "dervishes" at the battle of Omdurman formed one of the high points of colonial triumphalism.

By the end of the nineteenth century, the study of the brotherhoods had become a necessary subject for European colonial administrators. In these circles the study of Sufism became a cross between the assembly of police dossiers and the analysis of dangerous cults. Sufi leaders like the Pir Pagaro in Sind were described as hypnotic demagogues whose fanatic followers would kill themselves at a hint

a. A Mevlevee Dervish of
Damascus

b. An Abdal Marabout, or Holy
Man, in a Crazed State

c. A Rufa'ee Dervish in an
Ecstatic State

d. Another Rufa'ee Dervish in
an Ecstatic State

Figure 2. Illustrations of Sufis in *The Dervishes; Or, Oriental Spiritualism* (London, 1868), by American diplomat and translator John P. Brown, with original captions.

e. A Sheikh of the Nakshibendees Subduing a Lion by his Spiritual Powers

f. Mevlevee Dervishes undergoing Penance

g. A Bektash Dervish inhaling Hasheesh

from the master. In Somalia, the British dismissed the conservative Sufi leader Shaykh Muhammad 'Abd Allah Hasan as "the mad mulla," though he was neither mad nor a mulla (traditional religious scholar); he is remembered today by his countrymen as the father of the Somali nation. Probably the most remarkable example of governmental conflict with Sufism occurred in modern Turkey, which banned all dervish orders in 1925; in a case of the internalization of European political anxieties, secular nationalism had apparently eliminated a potential rival with strong claims on the loyalties of Turkish citizens.

The Orientalist "Discovery" of Sufism

Travelers and administrators had been concerned about the social and political behavior of dervishes and fakirs. The term *Sufism* first came into circulation through much more literary channels. Nearly two hundred years ago, several British Orientalists discovered a surprising religious phenomenon that significantly changed their understanding of the East. These eminent scholars, associated with the British East India Company, particularly Sir William Jones (d. 1794) and Sir John Malcolm (d. 1833), were well versed in Persian, the language of international diplomacy and government in Persia, Afghanistan, Central Asia, and most of India. In their historical and literary studies of "the Orient," which from Europe was viewed as all very much the same, these scholars began to comment on a mystical form of religion that was somehow associated with the followers of Muhammad (or "Mahometans"). The so-called Sooffees appeared wherever the mosque and minaret were found, but they were much more attractive than the hated Ottoman Turks, who a century earlier had threatened to conquer all of Christian Europe. These Sooffees were poets, after all, and they composed odes to the joys of wine-drinking, something no pious "Mahometan" would do. Furthermore, they were fond of music and dance, they were great lovers, and their bold declarations were an open affront to the Qur'an. Malcolm and Jones saw them as freethinkers who had little to do with the stern faith of the Arabian Prophet. They had much more in common, so went the argument, with true Christianity, with Greek philosophy, and with the mystical speculations of the Indian Vedanta. Literary Sufism had little to do with the scruffy vagabond dervishes and fakirs who disfigured the landscapes and cities of the East. Thus the term *Sufi-ism* was invented at the end of the eighteenth century, as an appropriation of those portions of "Oriental" culture that Europeans found attractive. The essential feature of the definitions of Sufism that appeared at this time was the insistence that Sufism had no intrinsic relation with the faith of Islam.

In retrospect, the unusual perspective of the British Orientalists on Sufism can be partially explained by the eccentric sources to which they were exposed. Jones relied in particular on a Persian text called the *Dabistan*, in which a seventeenth-century Zoroastrian author had presented a complex vision of the religious history of India and Persia, predicated on the notion of imbedding all major philosophical and mystical breakthroughs in ancient Persian history. On this basis, Jones wrote the following description of Sufism:

> I will only detain you with a few remarks on the metaphysical theology, which has been professed immemorially by a numerous sect of *Persians* and *Hindus*, was carried in part into *Greece*, and prevails even now among the learned *Muselmans*, who sometimes avow it without reserve. The modern philosophers of this persuasion are called *Sufi's*, either from the *Greek* word for a sage [i.e., *sophos*], or from the *woollen* mantle [Arabic *suf*], which they used to wear in some provinces of *Persia*: their fundamental tenets are, that nothing exists absolutely but GOD: that the human soul is an emanation from his essence, and, though divided for a time from its heavenly source, will be finally re-united with it; that the highest possible happiness will arise from its re-union, and

that the chief good of mankind, in this transitory world, consists in as perfect an *union* with the Eternal Spirit as the
incumbrances of a mortal frame will allow; that, for this purpose, they should break all *connexion* (or *taalluk*, as they call
it), with extrinsick objects, and pass through life without *at-
tachments,* as a swimmer in the ocean strikes freely without
the impediment of clothes; that they should be straight and
free as the cypress, whose fruit is hardly perceptible, and not
sink under a load, like fruit-trees *attached* to a trellis; that, if
mere earthly charms have power to influence the soul, the
idea of celestial beauty must overwhelm it in extatick delight; that, for want of apt words to express the divine perfec-
tions and the ardour of devotion, we must borrow such
expressions as approach the nearest to our ideas, and speak
of *Beauty* and *Love* in a transcendent and mystical sense.
. . . Such in part (for I omit the minuter and mure subtil
metaphysicks of the *Súfi's,* which are mentioned in the *Dabi-
stàn*) is the wild and enthusiastick religion of the modern
Persian poets, especially of the sweet HAFIZ and the great
Maulavi [i.e., Rumi]: such is the system of the *Védánti* philosophers and best lyrick poets of *India*; and, as it was a system of the highest antiquity in both nations, it may be added
to the many other proofs of an immemorial affinity between
them.[1]

In later years. nineteenth-century scholars reacted against the unusual historiography of the *Dabistan* and rejected it as a fraud. Recent scholarship has again begun to take this text seriously as part of
an important intellectual trend in early modern Persianate thought,
but most scholars today would not consider it a basic source for
Sufism. Nevertheless, the universal tone of this work fit the mood of
romantic enthusiasm that led Jones to master Persian, Arabic, and
Sanskrit, on his way to founding the Asiatic Society in Calcutta in
1784. For him, all profoundly mystically doctrines were ultimately

the same; they are expressed in "a thousand metaphors and poetical figures, which abound in the sacred poems of the *Persians* and *Hindus*, who seem to mean the same thing in substance, and differ only in expression as their languages differ in idiom!"[2] The Indian origin of all mysticism became a widely accepted hypothesis in Romantic circles. The universalizing impulse in Jones's interpretation of Sufism made Islamic connections interesting but incidental.

The detachment of Sufism from Islam took a more explicit form in the work of Sir John Malcolm. As ambassador of the British East India Company to the Persian court in 1800, he had formed a congenial relationship with a leading religious authority of the city of Kermanshah, whom he calls Aga Mahomed Ali. Mahomed Ali was a representative of the Shi'i hierarchy and was totally opposed to the Sufi groups that had recently begun to attract large followings in Persia. He and other Shi'i scholars persuaded the king of Persia to mount a campaign of persecution against the Sufi leaders, on the grounds that they represented moral corruption and the destruction of religion. As an aside, it is necessary to explain that the rise of Shi'ism in Persia since 1500 created a highly ambiguous situation for Sufism, in which the theoretical and practical sides of the movement were radically separated, for largely political reasons. Theoretical mysticism, known as *'irfan* or gnosis, has retained a very high reputation in Iran to this day; leading scholars such as Ayatollah Khomeini and Ayatollah Mutahhari are well known for their writings on philosophical and theoretical mysticism. On the other hand, anyone who actually practices mysticism in a social context is known instead under the name *darvish*, which in Iran has become a term of contempt suggesting idleness, drug use, immorality, and every other sort of evil. This distinction permitted the religious hierarchy of Iran to eliminate possible rivals to their authority while appropriating those Sufi doctrines which they admired.

In any case, although Malcolm recognized that his Persian contact was biased, in his 1815 *History of Persia* he nonetheless reproduced the latter's extremely hostile view towards Sufism. Concerning the "Sooffees," he wrote:

> We discover, from the evidence of Mahomedan authors, that these enthusiasts were co-existent with their religion. Their rapturous zeal, perhaps, aided in no slight degree its first establishment; but they have since been considered among the most dangerous of its enemies.[3]

Following Jones, Malcolm accepted the notion of an Indian origin for Sufism:

> It is in India, beyond all other climes, that this delusive and visionary doctrine has most flourished. There is, in the habits of that nation, and in the character of the Hindoo religion, what peculiarly cherishes the mysterious spirit of holy abstraction in which it is founded; and we may grant our belief to the conjecture which assumes that India is the source from which other nations have derived this mystic worship of the Divinity.[4]

Yet in his account of Sufism, Malcolm was satisfied to set forth at length the enumeration of its twenty heretical sects according to his priestly informant. They are ultimately dangerous to religion, he claimed, because of their assertion that they attain to union with God:

> [They] are also accused by orthodox Mahomedans of having no fixed faith, but of professing a respect which they do not feel for religion, that they may smooth the path of those whom they desire to delude. They pretend, their enemies state, to revere the prophet and the Imaums, yet conceive themselves above the forms and usages which these holy personages not only observed, but deemed of divine inspiration.[5]

From this extensive early account, derived from a hostile Shi'i leader, one could only conclude that Sufism had only the most tangential relation with Islam. Other British ambassadors came to similar conclusions. Mountstuart Elphinstone in an 1808 mission to Afghanistan observed that "the Soofees . . . consider the peculiar tenets of every religion as superfluities, and discard all rites and religious worship, regarding it as a matter of little importance in what manner the thoughts are turned to God, provided they rest at last in contemplation on his goodness and greatness."[6]

Up to this point, discussions of Sufism were brief observations in the context of remarks on Persian history and culture. The first separate treatment of Sufism in a European language was an article by an officer on the staff of Malcolm, Lt. James William Graham; it was originally delivered as a lecture in 1811 and later published in the *Transactions of the Literary Society of Bombay* in 1819. Graham was conscious that he was embarking on new territory by attempting to describe "the celebrated though little known subject of Sufiism," and he paid due compliments to the essays of Jones and Dr. John Leyden (d. 1811) that had touched upon the subject.[7] In Graham's article, entitled "A Treatise on Sufiism, or Mahomedan Mysticism," he exhibited the same universalizing tendency to abstraction shown by his predecessors. Indeed, Graham went even further; he saw Sufism as an attractive system precisely to the degree that it denies the law of Muhammad and approaches Christianity:

> With regard to the religion (if it can be so termed in the general acceptation of that word) or rather doctrine and tenets of the sect of Sufis, it is requisite to observe, first, that any person, or a person of any religion or sect, may be a *Sûfi*: the mystery lies in this;—a total disengagement of the mind from all temporal concerns and worldly pursuits; an entire throwing off not only of every superstition, doubt, or the like, but of the practical mode of worship, ceremonies, &c. laid down in every religion, which the Mahomedans term *Shĕryat*,

being the law, or canonical law; and entertaining solely mental abstraction, and contemplation of the soul and Deity, their affinity, and the correlative situation in which they stand: in fine, it is that spiritual intercourse of the soul with its Maker, that disregards and disclaims all ordinances and outward forms, of what sect or religion soever; such as observances of feasts, fasts, stated periods of prayer, particular kinds of meat to be eaten, ablutions, pilgrimages, and suchlike other rites and ceremonies which come under the head of practical worship (*Jismani amul*), being the deeds of the law, in contradistinction to mental or spiritual worship (*Roohâni âmul*), that is, as I take it to be, grace or faith.[8]

Graham takes this alleged lack of concern with religious law and ritual to be identical with the teaching of Paul's Epistle to the Romans in the New Testament. Further, the Sufi is described as disdaining the material world and as contemplating his own soul as an emanation of God: "This is the wonderful system of the *Yōgēē* or Indian Ascetic, and *Dnani* or person possessing divine wisdom or omniscience; from whom the Sûfis are supposed by some to have borrowed their doctrine." Throughout his discussion, Graham insists on explaining Sufi concepts as identical with Indian, Christian, and Greek ones (the Greek epigraph for the article is the Delphic motto *gnothi seauton*, "Know thyself," and there are extensive quotations of the Hindi poetry of Kabir). Graham does not conceal the fact that he finds the Sufis attractive, as when he observes: "Through my colloquial intercourse with natives of different classes, I have heard with some degree of pleasure many anecdotes of this wonderful order." Perhaps the most remarkable of Graham's statements is when he suggests that the British themselves are regarded as Sufis by their Indian subjects: "We are, generally speaking, at least in this country, looked upon as a species or one kind of *Sûfi*, from our nonobservance here of any rites or forms, conceiving a worship of the Deity in mind and adherence to morality sufficient. In fine, the present free-thinker or modern philosopher of Europe would be esteemed as a sort of Sufi in the world, and not the one retired therefrom." Graham actually provides much more than his predecessors in the way of descriptions of Sufi teachings and stories, based on Persian treatises that he had gained access to in Western India, although the sources that he used would be considered quite obscure by most scholars today. Nonetheless, the overwhelming impression one would gain from reading this article was that Sufis were wonderful mystics but that they had little if anything to do with the Islamic faith.

The first European book on Sufism, a Latin treatise published in 1821 by a German theologian named Tholuck, freely acknowledged the critical role of the British Orientalists in the discovery of Sufism. Tholuck also indicated what Europeans may have expected from the discovery of such an interesting group, apparently only lightly attached to the Islamic faith; he cites a report from the *Missionary Register* of 1818 claiming "that there is a number of about 80,000 persons in Persia, called Sophis, who about ten or twelve years ago, openly renounced Mahommedanism."[9] This report, which appears to be a missionary fantasy, still underlines the firm wish of Orientalists to isolate Sufism from Islam. The title of Tholuck's treatise, *Ssufismus, sive theosophia Persarum pantheistica* (Sufism, or the pantheistic theosophy of the Persians), indicates the intellectual categories of greatest importance for this analysis. *Pantheism* is a term for European philosophies (e.g., Spinoza) that consider God and nature to be identical, and *theosophy* (most recently associated with the German mystic Boehme) was used to describe the doctrine that humanity can attain divine wisdom; both terms were derogatory from the perspective of Protestant theology. However inexact the analogies, Tholuck further modified them by attributing Sufism mainly to the Persians; later, under the attraction of racial theory, this conclusion would turn into a theory of Sufism as "Aryan" mysticism overlaid on the "Semitic" legalism of the Arabs. Tholuck's study was quite substantial, however, and in over three hundred pages he undertook to summarize the origins and leaders of Sufism, with accounts of anthropology, cosmology, free will, prophetology, mystical terminology, and levels of teaching. He had access to a handful of Arabic, Persian, and Turkish manuscripts in the royal library in Berlin, which gave him a relatively wider base of knowledge than Jones or Malcolm had access to. Thus, in reply to the question of the Greek or Indian origin of Sufism, Tholuck was forced to acknowledge that among the earliest followers of Muhammad one can recognize the seeds and elements of what would later be known as Sufism. From its early simplicity, however, Tholuck concluded that Sufism degenerated into mere pantheism, contrary to the very principles of Muhammad. He observed that "the rest of the doctrines of the Sufis, that is, the theory of the divinity in men, the emanation of the world, the removal of discrimination between good and evil, and even the rejection of civil laws (for all these, as our argument shows, are found in later Sufism), derive from one teaching, the conjunction or union with God."[10] As an academic subject, Sufism was now fully established. The religious and political imperatives of modern Europe had created the term, which was duly entered in the list of doctrines and philosophies deserving the suffix -ism.

The most remarkable thing about the "discovery" of Sufism as described above is that it would have been unrecognizable to most Sufis. Although authors such as Graham were aware of major Sufi figures, such as Hallaj and Shams-i Tabriz, and Jones was certainly conversant with the great Persian Sufi poets, these British scholars relied primarily on either poetry or else obscure and biased sources. Tholuck added a few Arabic sources, but he also made more blatant the bias of Protestant theological dogma. By treating Sufism as an abstract mystical philosophy, these scholars entirely ignored the social context of Sufism as expressed in the Sufi orders, the institutions formed around saints' tombs, and the role of Sufis in politics—points that will be alluded to later in this book. Most importantly, by separating Sufism from Islam, the Orientalists denied the significance of the Qur'an, the Prophet Muhammad, and Islamic law and ritual for

Sufism; yet for most of the people who are called Sufis, all these elements were very much a part of their worldview and their practice. Writing in North Africa in the fifteenth century, the famous Muslim philosopher and historian Ibn Khaldun wrote as follows:

> Sufism belongs to the sciences of the religious law that originated in Islam. It is based on the assumption that the practices of its adherents had always been considered by the important early Muslims, the men around Muhammad and the men of the second generation, as well as those who came after them, as the path of truth and right guidance. The Sufi approach is based upon constant application to divine worship, complete devotion to God, aversion to the false splendour of the world, abstinence from the pleasure, property, and position to which the great mass aspire, and retirement from the world into solitude for divine worship. These things were general among the men around Muhammad and the early Muslims. Then, worldly aspirations increased in the second [eighth] century and after. At that time, the special name of Sufis was given to those who aspired to divine worship.[11]

This attitude towards Sufism was typical of most Muslim intellectuals up through the eighteenth century.

In the years that have passed since the "discovery" of Sufism by Orientalists, a considerable amount of progress has been made. Many more Sufi texts have become available through printed editions in their original languages, both in Muslim countries and in the West. A growing number of readable translations into European languages makes it possible for readers to approach Sufism for study or personal engagement. Nevertheless, we are still far from having the kind of access to Sufi writings that is possible with European literature; certainly less than ten percent of existing Arabic manuscripts have ever been printed, to say nothing of those in Persian,

Turkish, Malay, Berber, Swahili, Urdu, and a number of other languages used by Sufis. More importantly, a look at current studies of Sufism will show that many of the underlying assumptions of the early Orientalists are still active, despite the relatively much larger base of knowledge that is currently available. There are still scholars who cherish the notion that they can discover and announce the true "sources" of Sufism in terms of Hindu, Buddhist, or Christian "influence." There are many writers who uncritically accept Muslim fundamentalists as the true representatives of Islam, and hence they tacitly accept fundamentalist denunciations of Sufism as marginal to Islam. Preconceptions about the essentially legalistic character of Islam (formerly "Mahometanism") are used as criteria by which to judge Sufism as a separate enterprise that may be in conflict with religion as such. Writings of colonial officials from the nineteenth century (now free of copyright) are still reprinted in formerly colonized countries, and secularized elites regard these studies as authentic guides to history and culture.[12] Reformist and fundamentalist thinkers have not hesitated to appropriate the Orientalist tendency to venerate past "golden ages"; this strategy permits them to pay respectful homage to selected early Sufis who can be described as pious Muslims, and at the same time to complain bitterly of the decline of modern Sufism into corruption. Those who wish to avoid unwittingly committing themselves to any of these prejudices will be better prepared to do so by becoming aware of this complicated genealogy of the concept of Sufism in the West.

The Term Sufi *as a Prescriptive Ethical Concept*

How is it possible to tell what Sufism is, and who is a Sufi? In Arabic and Persian, there are dozens of terms for Muslim mystics with distinct and sometimes conflicting meanings, all of which are subsumed by the English word *Sufism.* As with other terms coined during the Enlightenment to describe religions, *Sufism* has now become a standard term, whether we like it or not. It is easy to assume that it is the primary reality or phenomenon that we are concerned with, and that any other terms are simply minor variations on this theme. This assumption is an outcome of the way social and intellectual history has developed in Europe and America. Terms constructed in the form of "isms" describe philosophies and social movements, so that ideally one can reduce them to descriptive definitions based on their essential qualities. This approach to classification, especially in the comparative study of religion, is based on the model of comparative zoology. The primary categories, corresponding to the biological genus, are considered to be the major religions, and sects and particular types of religious practices are viewed as different species or subspecies. There are a number of problems with this approach to the study of religion. It tends to assume that there is an unchanging essence for every religion, and so a sect or school of thought that seems to be in conflict with the dictionary definition of the religion can be dismissed as a deviation, probably due to "influence" from another religion. It is this kind of thinking that has created the bifurcation between Islam and Sufism in Orientalist literature. Islam is assumed to have the essential characteristic of harsh legalism, and Sufism is considered to be indifferent to matters of religious law; thus it becomes easy to posit an external origin for Sufism in India or elsewhere. The increasing stress on sociology and ideology in the study of religion results in the current picture of Sufism as a kind of mystical philosophy found in Muslim countries, which can include figures on the margins of society (dervishes and fakirs) along with politically important mass movements.

This descriptive approach to Sufism contrasts sharply with the use of the term *Sufi* in Sufi texts. There we find a prescriptive use of the term which sets forth goals of ethical and spiritual perfection. The historical origin of the word *Sufi* is fairly well established; it derives from the Arabic word for wool (*suf*), used in the rough garments worn by ascetics in the Near East for centuries. Some Sufi writers highlight this meaning of the word, and they suggest that wool was the preferred dress of most of the prophets as well. The world-denying attitude suggested by this etymology had a sharp significance in the early Islamic era, when the conquering Arab armies created an imperial court culture of lavish magnificence and self-indulgence. Sufis were able to point to the simple material lifestyle of the Prophet Muhammad (d. 632) and many of his companions as an important precedent to the ascetic way of life (another etymology, first suggested by the philosopher al-Biruni, links Sufi with the Greek word for wise man, *sophos*, and hence with Greek philosophy; this derivation has not played any role in Sufi literature, however, though it has been revived again by Orientalists beginning with Jones and Tholuck in their attempt to find extra-Islamic origins for Sufism). Despite the importance of clothing in later Sufi ritual, however, the etymological connection with wool was only of secondary importance for the term *Sufi*, compared with its prescriptive meaning.

The creation of the term *Sufi* in its prescriptive sense was largely an achievement of the fourth Islamic century (tenth century CE), though it drew on earlier precedents. If one theorist were to be singled out as the main formulator of this concept, Abu 'Abd al-Rahman al-Sulami (d. 1021) would be a good choice. Sulami, who lived in eastern Iran, wrote numerous works in Arabic, including the earliest major collection of lives of Sufi saints. He constructed a historical interpretation of the Sufis as the heirs and followers of the prophets, drawing a portrait of Muslim spirituality and mysticism that stretched over the previous three centuries. Sulami like other Sufi writers acknowledged that the term *Sufi* did not originate at the time of the Prophet Muhammad, but like other religious technical terms (in law and scriptural study, for example), it came into existence later on to reflect the increasing specialization of Muslim religious vocations. It was observed by Ansari (d. 1089) in his Persian translation of Sulami's biographical work that the first person who bore the name *Sufi* was a Syrian named Abu Hashim al-Sufi (d. 767), but he adds, "Before him there were saints characterized by asceticism, abstemiousness, and good deeds in the path of trusting God and the path of love. But this name *Sufi* was first used of him." [13] The Arabic term that we translate as Sufism is *tasawwuf*, literally "the process of becoming a Sufi." *Tasawwuf* is a verbal noun from the particular grammatical structure (fifth form verb) used in Arabic for assimilating or taking on a religious or ethnic identity; thus, *tanassur* means "to become a Christian [*nasrani*]," and *tafarnus* means "to become French." Even though the term was novel, the quotation from Ansari shows how it was used to cover a broad spectrum of spiritual qualities. The early biographies of Sufis by Sulami and others could thus include the lives of religious figures who were not known as Sufis in their own time. In a similar fashion, 'Umar al-Suhrawardi (d. 1234) observed, "God most high mentions in the Qur'an groups of the good and the pious, and he calls some the blessed people, and others the near ones, and there are also the patient, the sincere, the reciters, and the lovers. The name *Sufi* comprehends all distinctions in these names. This name did not exist in the times of the Messenger of God (God bless him and grant him peace), though it is said that it existed in the time of his followers."[14]

The literature of Sufism that began to be produced in the tenth century CE employed the term *Sufi* in a deliberate and self-conscious fashion to orchestrate the ethical and mystical goals of the growing movement. A series of writings, primarily in Arabic, expounded the ideals of the Sufis and explained their relationship to other religious groups in Muslim society. It is extremely difficult to reconstruct with confidence the earliest history of Islamic spirituality and mysticism, nor will I attempt such a project here—partly because most of the texts describing early Sufis were written at a later period and reflect contemporary concerns. Nevertheless, early writers on Sufism carry a strong sense of distinctive identity. They refer to the Sufis simply as the people (*al-qawm*), or the faction (*al-ta'ifa*). This sense of self-consciousness, already evident in the ninth century, was based on the slow formation of small informal groups of like-minded people, who traded comments with each other about their practice of the religious life. Those authors who formulated a comprehensive spiritual discipline around the term Sufi invoked these earlier Muslim devotees as their predecessors. The definitions of Sufism that they propose are historical only in the sense that history furnishes admirable examples of the religious life that may be used as models in Sufi literature. In this way, the term *Sufi* was linked with the Arabic word *suffa* or bench (source of the English word *sofa*), and in this sense it invokes the historical memory of the People of the Bench, a group of poor followers of the Prophet Muhammad who were homeless and slept on a bench in Medina, sharing their meagre belongings and supplies. This derivation clearly attempted to link the Sufis with an early group of ascetic followers of the Prophet, but just as importantly, it established the ideal of shared community as the basis of Sufi mysticism.

The term *Sufi* in this way took on a didactic rather than an informational purpose. Answers to the question "What is Sufism?" multiplied and began to take on a new importance, as they nearly always were placed prominently at the beginning of every new treatise on Sufism. Typically these definitions begin with additional etymologies that connect the term *Sufi* to other Arabic roots, especially *safa'* or purity, and *safwa*, meaning the chosen ones. In this way Qushayri (d. 1074) introduced the subject of the Sufis: "God made this group the chosen ones among his friends, and he honored them above the rest of his worshippers after his messengers and his prophets . . . and he purified them from all obscurities."[15] Qushayri was quite frank in stating that the term *Sufi* does not originate linguistically in any of the roots that have been proposed for it, since most of them stretch the rules of language. "This group is too well known to require definition by verbal analogy and etymological research," he stated. Nevertheless, the poetic and rhetorical effects of these derivations are clear. The linking of Sufism with purity allows it to be described as the purification of hearts (*tasfiyat al-qulub*), which means a rigorous ethical discipline based on meditative exercises. Introducing the notion of the chosen elite means that God's grace is all-important in any notion of holiness in human beings, in this way cultivating a sense of surrender to the all-powerful creator. So despite the disclaimers of linguistic definition of the term *Sufi*, Qushayri marshaled an impressive list of sayings from different early Sufi masters that create different prescriptive ethical and spiritual goals for those who are attracted to this ideal. Here are some examples that he gave:

> Sufism is entry into exemplary behavior and departure from unworthy behavior.
>
> Sufism means that God makes you die to yourself and makes you live in him.
>
> The Sufi is single in essence; nothing changes him, nor does he change anything.
>
> The sign of the sincere Sufi is that he feels poor when he has wealth, is humble when he has power, and is hidden when he has fame.
>
> Sufism means that you own nothing and are owned by nothing.
>
> Sufism means entrusting the soul to God most high for whatever he wishes.
>
> Sufism means seizing spiritual realities and giving up on what creatures possess.
>
> Sufism means kneeling at the door of the beloved, even if he turns you away.
>
> Sufism is a state in which the conditions of humanity disappear.
>
> Sufism is a blazing lightning bolt.[16]

Countless other examples of this type could be mentioned.[17] All these definitions are elusive from the perspective of descriptive history and social science. They do not have any clear reference to a defined group of people. Instead, they accomplish a powerful rhetorical transaction; the person who listens to or reads these definitions is forced to imagine the spiritual or ethical quality that is invoked by the definition, even when it is paradoxical. Definitions of Sufism are, in effect, teaching tools.

The creation of a self-conscious community based on these Sufi ideals had some negative consequences. Some of the most important psychological and ethical goals of the movement would be defeated by egotistical self-absorption in one's identity as a Sufi. From the very moment that the notion of the Sufi appeared, it seems that the idea of the fake Sufi was not far behind. Other examples Qushayri gave include the following:

> The sign of the sincere Sufi is that he feels poor when he has wealth, is humble when he has power, and is hidden when he has fame. The sign of the false Sufi is that he acts rich towards the world when he is poor, acts powerful when he is humble, and is famous among his followers.
> The foulest of all foul things is a greedy Sufi.

The ambiguity created by insincere and hypocritical pretensions to the Sufi ideal even led to some discomfort with the term. When Shibli was asked why Sufis were so called, he said, "They must still have some ego, otherwise they would not be connected to this term." Ironically, the unease with the term *Sufism* seems to have emerged almost as soon as the term itself became popular. When asked about Sufism, Hujwiri (d. ca. 1075) replied: "In our time this science has been in reality obliterated, especially in this region, for people are all occupied with pleasure, and have turned away from satisfying [God]. The scholars of the age and pretenders of the day have formed an impression of it that is contrary to its principles."[18] Thus lamenting its decline has been part of the definition of Sufism from the beginning, as an illustration of the tension between the ideals of mysticism and the realities of social practice. The most famous such formulation is attributed to an early Sufi named Abu al-Hasan Fushanja: "Sufism today is a name without a reality, whereas it was once a reality without a name."[19]

The formulators of Sufism were keen to emphasize the religious credentials of their movement. The works written to expound Sufism in the tenth and eleventh centuries take great pains to link Sufism first of all with the Qur'an and the Prophet Muhammad, to emphasize their close relationship with divine revelation and its messenger. Next, these Sufi authors (such as Sarraj, Sulami, Kalabadhi, Suhrawardi) placed great stress on their status not only as complementary to the masters of other Islamic religious sciences (such as law and the study of Muhammad's sayings) but also as superior to them. As an example, the anonymous author of a tenth-century Arabic work, called *The Manners of Kings*, portrayed the Sufis as the true kings of the world from the spiritual point of view. He described jurists, specialists in the sayings of Muhammad (*hadith*), Qur'an commentators, and literary scholars as all being deficient in comparison to the Sufis: "Each one of them is attached to the external form of knowledge, and they ignore its [inner] realities. . . . But I have seen no people more firmly connected to the prophetic example, both externally and internally, both secretly and openly, in terms of law, intention, and practice, than the society known by the name of Sufism."[20] In comparison with this Sufi ideal, it was possible to criticize conventional religious scholars as corrupt servants of unlawful secular regimes. This defensive and critical attitude arose partly as the result of the need for a recently self-conscious movement to justify and explain itself in terms of the central concepts of order in Islamic culture. Certain well-publicized heresy trials and attacks on individual Sufis also encouraged Sufi apologists to formulate their teachings with an insistence on widely accepted theological or legal teachings, such as the doctrines of Ash'ari theology or the Hanbali legal school. Descriptions of Sufism, like any other religious point of view in Islamic society, necessarily employed polemical arguments designed to appropriate the sources of religious authority and legitimacy.

The basic metaphor in Sufi rhetoric, which is also prominent in other major streams of Islamic culture, is the primacy of the inner reality. Using a phrase from the Qur'an (57:3), Sufis invoked the description of God as "the first, the last, the outer, the inner." Stressing the notion of God as the inner aspect (*batin*) of all things required an articulation of the relation between the inner and the outer. This was expressed most fully in a threefold rhyming structure commonly employed in oral instruction: the outward form is Islamic law (*shari'a*), the inner approach is the path (*tariqa*), while God is the reality (*haqiqa*). This kind of rhetorical formula permitted Sufis to position their distinctive practices as the internalization of the external rituals of Muslim religious life. Sufism was a way to proceed from ordinary external life to find the inner reality of God. This hierarchical grading of reality amounts to a theory of esotericism; as the Qur'an states (39:9), "Are those who know equal to those who do not know?" It is important to recognize that this pervasive metaphor of inner reality and knowledge requires the external forms of religion to make any sense at all. The self-articulation of Sufism has in this way presupposed the norms of Islamic tradition at the same time that it pointed beyond the limitations of those conventions.

Actual Terminology Used for Sufis

Despite its importance as a theoretical and symbolic term, the word *Sufi* was not very often applied to actual individuals. Partly this was because of the intrinsic tension between the ideal of selflessness and the egotism inherent in claiming such status. There was a sense, in other words, that a true Sufi would never claim that title. Derivative words were spun off to cover these contingencies, so that a *mutasawwif* was someone who legitimately aspired to be a Sufi, and this term could be happily adopted by many. Alternatively, someone who falsely claimed to be a Sufi was a *mustaswif*, a term used only pejoratively. But if one looks at literary works that describe the variety of different Muslim mystics, it is remarkable to see how infrequently the word *Sufi* is used. By the fourteenth century, to call someone a Sufi was commonly a sarcastic challenge to pretended sanctity; when the poet Hafiz uses the word *Sufi*, it almost always has this significance. For instance, regarding extravagant claims made by pretenders to mystical experience, Hafiz said:

> Come, let us take this Sufi cloak to the tavern,
> and take these ecstatic boasts to the fairy-tale bazaar.
> We should be ashamed of our stained woolen cloaks,
> if we call this kind of skill and art a miracle.[21]

The great Persian writer Sa'di (d. 1292) of Shiraz included an important chapter titled "The Morals of Dervishes" in his classic *Gulistan* (The Rose Garden), in which he employs a wide range of terms for different kinds of mystics, but he hardly ever uses the word *Sufi*. The actual terminology for different Islamic mystical vocations covers a wide range of semantic fields. A sampling of these terms (all Arabic unless otherwise noted) is given below, organized according to the general category of religious practice to which they belong. The abstract and generalizing character of the descriptive term *Sufism* should be evident from the widely varying connotations of the terms most frequently used to describe the many different kinds of Muslim mystics.

Worship. The basic concept of worship is found in the term *'abid* (also in the form *muta'abbid*), meaning devotee or pious worshiper; the term derives from *'abd*, slave, and has a connotation of total obedience and dedication to God. Persian also uses the word *parsa*, meaning pious and upright in behavior.

Ethics. The most ancient of the terms for ethical practice is *zuhd*, meaning asceticism and avoidance of the pleasures of the world; the ascetic or abstemious person was called the *zahid*. These ascetics were noted not only for their strong aversion to the world but also for their fear of hellfire; in later times the ascetic was criticized as dry and harsh in comparison with the lovers of God (see below). Ethical virtue and adherence to religious duty are the qualities associated with the *salih* or righteous one; the root is associated with right action, goodness, peace, and creating order. In some regions, particularly North Africa, *salih* is the preferred term for a holy man or saint. Sincerity and truthfulness are the virtues of the *siddiq* or sincere one. The epithet was most famously associated with Muhammad's companion Abu Bakr, who testified with full faith to the veracity of the Prophet's account of his ascension to paradise. *Wara'* or scrupulous observance in avoiding unlawful food and gifts emerges from the intense desire to follow God's commandments in all actions.

Knowledge. Sufism is frequently described in the early manuals as a form of religious learning (*'ilm*) alongside the familiar religious sciences of law and the sayings of the Prophet. A master of this kind of learning was known as an *'alim*, or scholar (plural *'ulama'*). Many of the most important religious scholars in Islamic history were simultaneously engaged in the practices of Sufism, so that titles of the learned such as *mawlana* (our master) are frequently applied to Sufis and religious scholars without any distinction. When mystical knowledge was emphasized over traditional learning, the preferred term was *ma'rifa* or *'irfan*, meaning a special knowledge or gnosis that transcended ordinary rationality. The possessor of this knowledge was known as an *'arif*, or gnostic. Many intellectuals combined their interest in mysticism with the metaphysical curriculum derived from Greek philosophy, which was highly developed in Arabic through translations of Plato and Aristotle as well as independent works by philosophers such as Ibn Sina, also known as Avicenna (d. 1037). The master of metaphysical wisdom or *hikma* was called a *hakim*, or sage.

Traveling. Other terms for Sufism invoke the metaphor of traveling, which is suggested by the common description of Sufism as a way or path (*tariqa*). Treatises on mystical experience describe their topic as traveling (*suluk*). The self-possessed wayfarer on the path was frequently described as a traveler (*salik*; Persian *rahrav*). The importance of this metaphor was heightened by the common Sufi practice of traveling to distant lands, either to seek religious knowledge or as a form of self-discipline.

Love. Perhaps the most common epithets for mystics were drawn from the vocabulary of love and intimate affection. It was a badge of honor for these Sufis to be known as lovers of God, of the Prophet Muhammad, and of their Sufi master. One frequently finds people who are called simply a lover (*muhibb*, *'ashiq*) or by one of the common terms for a friend (Persian *dust*, *yar*). The powers of affection were so central to mystical experience that Sufi masters were often known as "masters of the heart" (Persian *sahibdil*, *ahl-i dil*).

Intoxication. In contrast to the sober and self-possessed traveler, some souls were overpowered by the attraction (*jadhb*) of divine energies. Those "fools of God" lost normal rationality and could appear to be mad. Whether their condition was temporary or permanent, those who were ecstatically absorbed (*majdhub*, also known in Persian as *mast*, or intoxicated) were often regarded as holy, and they were cared for and respected by ordinary people.

Social Ambiguity. The very notion of religious authenticity that underlies the ideals of Sufism was bound to create serious social contradictions as Sufism became more widely spread in Muslim societies after the twelfth century. From early times a group of Sufis had deliberately courted the blame (*malama*) of others, operating from a strong sense of the limitations of conventional social values. These *malamati* or self-blaming Sufis were exceeded by groups who rejected both ordinary society and what they saw as the complacent corruption of mysticism in institutional Sufism. Wandering groups of ascetics wearing animal skins and occasionally iron chains, shaving all body hair, and generally acting in an outrageous fashion, began to be seen all over the Middle East and South Asia. Variously known as *qalandar, abdal* (substitutes), *baba* (father), *haydari, malang,* or *muwallih* (enraptured), these figures were often viewed as dangerous by political authorities. They have been associated with peasant uprisings, particularly in Anatolia.

Mastery and Discipleship. Among the more important designations for Sufis were those that describe the role of the spiritual master. The most common term was the Arabic word for old man (*shaykh,* Persian *pir*), used as a title of respect. Similar titles include teacher (*ustadh*) and guide (*murshid*). The master or teacher in some ways functioned along the same lines as teachers of standard Islamic religious sciences, with a similar reliance on chains of transmission going back to the time of the Prophet Muhammad. The disciple or aspirant (*murid*), is said to focus on the master as the object of aspiration (*murad*). Chief disciples are chosen to act as the successor (*khalifa*) or representative (*muqaddam*) of the master.

Sainthood. One of the central terms of Sufism is the Islamic doctrine of sainthood (*walaya* or *wilaya*), which denotes closeness and intimacy with God, as well as protection by God. The saint (*wali,* plural *awliya';* equivalent to Persian great man or *buzurg,* and Turkish man of God or *eren*) was a figure who could intercede with God, much as a feudal noble could intercede with the king. The saint's closeness to God and consequent authority are themes that go back to the earliest stage of Sufism with its prescriptive ideals and implicit critique of worldly power. Eventually the tombs of saints became centers of widespread pilgrimages, as people of all classes sought the ongoing living presence of the saint as a conduit to spiritual and material goals.

Spiritual Status. The concept of an invisible hierarchy of saints was the logical corollary of spiritual perfection and authority. From a very early period, terms and titles were in use to describe the various levels in this hierarchy, some of which were likened to the key implements used to hold up the universe as a kind of cosmic tent.

Thus we find the pegs (*awtad*) and the pole (*qutb*) among these titles, along with other offices such as the chiefs (*nuqaba'*), the pious (*abrar*), the good (*akhyar*), the substitutes (*abdal*), and the savior (*ghawth*). Out of these, the pole and the savior are both used to designate the single supreme figure of the hierarchy.

In view of the multiple vocations, experiences, and attitudes that underlie these different terms for Sufis, it must be admitted that the English word *Sufism* has to be pretty elastic to accommodate them all. More to the point, *Sufism* as it is used today means all of these internal ideals at the same time that it describes their external social and historical manifestations. We are forced to use *Sufism* both as an insider's term and as an outsider's term, and there will inevitably be tension between the two perspectives. The remainder of this book is an attempt to mediate between these two understandings of Sufism.

2
The Sacred Sources of Sufism

For you the messenger of God is a beautiful model, for those who
have hope of God and the last day, and who recall God much.

—QUR'AN 33:21

The Qur'anic Event as the Matrix of Mystical Experience

"TRULY WE CAUSED IT to descend on the Night of Power. And
what shall inform you of the Night of Power? The Night of Power is
better than a thousand months. On it descended the angels, and the
spirit, with the permission of their Lord, with every command. It is
peace, until the break of day." This is, in its entirety, the *sura* of
Power, numbered 97 out of the total of 114 *suras* (books or chapters)
in the Qur'an. It is reported that this passage records the moment
when the Prophet Muhammad experienced the totality of the
Qur'anic revelation while on retreat in a cave on Mount Hira outside
the town of Mecca sometime around the year 610. The revelations
would unfold over the next twenty-three years until the death of the
Prophet in 632. It is in this ongoing Qur'anic event that we find the
starting point of Sufism.

The revelation "descended" upon Muhammad on one of the last
nights in the month of Ramadan. The text indicates the accompani-
ments of revelation: the descent of the angels from heaven and the

spirit. Like certain other *suras* from the earliest part of Muhammad's prophetic career, this one conveys the strong impact of the initial experience. In this case, there is the overwhelming feeling of divine power, expressed through the commands of the Creator. The moment is suffused, however, with a peace that lasts through the night.

The sudden onslaught of divine power seems to be reflected in another Qur'anic passage (53:1–11), in which Muhammad's revelation is carefully distinguished from error and vain desire:

> By the star when it sets!
> Your companion does not err, nor is he deceived,
> And he does not speak from desire.
> This is nothing but revelation revealed,
> Which one mighty in powers taught him,
> One full of strength; and he stood erect,
> While on the highest horizon.
> Then he drew near and descended,
> So he was two bows' lengths distant, or nearer,
> And he revealed to his slave what he revealed.
> The heart did not lie about what it saw.

If this describes Muhammad's experience on Mount Hira, one can indeed imagine the drama of this encounter. The power of the account derives as much from what is not said as from that which is explicit. The figure who delivers the revelation is shrouded in mystery and is described only in terms of his overpowering presence, detected from the end of the universe until it suddenly descends into immediate proximity. The content of the revelation is not described here, either. The revelation is self-authenticating. Although convention typically portrays Muhammad as receiving the revelation through the medium of the angel Gabriel, the language here suggests that it is God whom Muhammad encounters; humans are slaves only to God, and that is the term that describes the relationship between the Prophet and the source of revelation that has come down to him.

Balancing this descent of divine power is the reverse movement of the Prophet's ascension, to which the Qur'an briefly alludes in several places. The ascension is usually understood as beginning with a night journey from Mecca to Jerusalem: "Praise be to him who brought his slave by night from the holy mosque to the farthest mosque, the environs of which we blessed in order to show him our signs" (17:1). From that point, from a spot traditionally located near the Dome of the Rock in Jerusalem, he ascended through the heavens to the divine presence:

> And he saw him by another place,
> By the lotus of the farthest edge,
> Near which is the paradise of refuge,
> When the lotus was veiled by what veiled it.
> His eye did not waver, nor did he transgress;
> He had seen one of the greatest signs of his lord.
>   (53:13–18)

This encounter too is hedged round by mysterious symbols that confirm the miraculous exchange while concealing its substance. The imagery of paradise and ultimate distance from the world did not overpower the Prophet, however, since his glance never wavered. Revelation, as the locus of the divine-human encounter, is not only the fundamental theme of the Qur'an but also the fact which the text demonstrates by its very articulation.

In the twofold motion of the descent of revelation and the ascent of the Prophet is contained the rhythm of the Qur'an. This remarkable document, dictated orally in pieces over the course of twenty-three years, is of such complexity and density that it will only be possible to allude to a few of its themes and structures here. For those who are not familiar with it, it is necessary to say something about what the Qur'an is not. Unlike the Hebrew Bible, the Qur'an does not contain extended narratives about the prophets and their roles in history. Except for the story of Joseph (*sura* 12), and brief episodes from the lives of the other prophets, nowhere do we find in the Qur'an the equivalent of the extended prophetic and patriarchal narratives of Genesis and Exodus. Instead, it is assumed that readers and listeners are familiar with all the main characters and themes.

Unlike the Gospels, which are a collection of different narratives about the actions and sayings of Jesus as gathered by key disciples, the Qur'an is instead the recorded revelations that Muhammad pronounced to his followers. The Muslim equivalent of the Gospels is better sought in the corpus of *hadith* literature, a vast number of discrete reports on Muhammad's sayings and deeds. The Qur'an is not a book of stories and traditions that one sits down and reads from start to finish (in fact, it is often recommended that one begin reading the shortest *suras* at the end of the Qur'an, which include the earliest revelations, and then work backward with the aid of a subject index, to start developing an acquaintance with the themes, style, and vocabulary of the text). Muslims do not approach the Qur'an as a literary work, but as the primary collection of the words of God; its anecdotes are important not as history but as teaching, above all illustrating the role of the Prophet as the conveyor of God's words. Its 114 *suras* are arranged roughly in order of size, starting with the largest, without regard to content or inner structure. Many *suras* contain passages that abruptly switch topics; detailed prescriptions of inheritance law may be followed by accounts of the Israelites rejecting Moses or vivid depictions of the afterlife. All this is conveyed in resonant lines that employ all the powerful resources of rhythm and rhyme that Arabic possesses. The Qur'an was viewed as a repository of the words of God, expressed with brevity and eloquence, which reflect primarily on the Prophet's mission to convey God's will to humanity.

In order to understand the importance of the Qur'an for Sufism, it is important to grasp the way in which it was studied. As with other scriptures, the Qur'an was frequently memorized, and this complete internalization of the sacred text permitted an intimate acquaintance with it as a kind of simultaneous event. It is recited in portions, minimally, during the five daily prayers required of all Muslims. Those who were especially motivated could continue, however, with additional recitations at the standard prayer times and in the five supererogatory prayer times that continued through the night. It is probably in this devotional recitation of the Qur'an that the mystical interpretation of the text originated. Scholars of law would have been most interested in the content of those sections that had clear applicability to legal practice—particularly in the fields of personal law (inheritance, marriage, and divorce) and ritual (purity, prayer, fasting, pilgrimage, alms), where the Qur'an has much to say (criminal and commercial law are touched upon by only a few verses). But those who responded to the emotional power of the text probed further to seek its deeper meanings.

Accounts of the life of Muhammad contain many cases in which the simple recitation of the Qur'an would bring his listeners to tears, but its ability to penetrate the heart had a cognitive dimension as well. From an early date, students of the Qur'an understood that it had multiple aspects. A number of passages were susceptible to varying interpretations. While the New Testament did not assume a definitive form until many years after the crucifixion of Jesus, the text of the Qur'an was fixed shortly after the death of Muhammad. Nevertheless, a variety of interpretations soon arose in the Muslim community concerning such issues as the nature of free will and predestination, the condition of the sinner, and the character of the just ruler. One of the chief theological issues that divided Muslims was the nature of the Qur'an itself. If it was the word of God, was it eternal and unchanging like God? Or was it God's speech in time, subject to interpretation according to the conditions of human existence?

In the debate over the nature of the Qur'an, there were political factors at work alongside theological ones, but even the most literalist reading of the Qur'an had to deal with the problem of interpreting certain verses metaphorically. In particular, the verses that described God in human terms, referring to the face or hand of God, for instance, had to be understood metaphorically if they were not to be anthropomorphic. How should one understand the description of God sitting on the celestial throne? Without attempting to explain the many different schools of thought in early Islamic history, one can point to an emerging mystical interpretation of the Qur'an as one of the basic sources of what would become Sufism. The Qur'an itself (3:7) alludes to the difficulty of interpreting the passages that contain symbolism, in contrast to the portions of the Qur'an that have clear instructions:

> He is the one who caused the book to descend upon you. Part of it is clearly defined verses, which are "the mother of the book," and others are symbolic. But those with error in their hearts follow the symbolic part of it, seeking dissension and seeking its interpretation. None knows its interpretation except God and those who are firmly rooted in knowledge. [Others] say, "We have faith in it; it is all from our lord." But none recalls except those who possess the inner heart.

This passage is itself an example of both the need and the difficulty of interpretation of the sacred text. Because of the lack of punctuation in the earliest Qur'anic manuscripts, it is possible to read the latter portion of the verse differently:

> None knows its interpretation except God. And those who are firmly rooted in knowledge say, "We have faith in it; it is all from our lord."

The first reading, preferred by Sufis, philosophers, Shi'is, and others, is found in some of the earliest Qur'an commentaries, and it indicates that there is a class of people "firmly rooted in knowledge" who are able to interpret the symbolic passages of the Qur'an. The second reading, which is favored in the most widely distributed version of the Qur'an today, states that only God can know the interpretation of the symbolic passages; all that the believers can do is have faith in it without asking further questions. Yet the typical balanced rhetoric of the Qur'an ends the verse with an important qualification, stating obliquely that only those "who possess the inner heart (*lubb*)" can heed and recall the message. For those who were attentive to the language of the Qur'an regarding human psychology, this invocation of "the inner heart" was itself a reminder that there is a special knowledge that permits access to the divine: "In the creation of the heavens and earth, in the alternation of night and day, there are signs for those who possess the inner heart" (3:190).

In contemporary debates among Muslims over the legitimacy of Sufism, it is remarkable how what amounts to the placing of a punctuation mark in this Qur'anic verse can open up a chasm between opposing positions. The literalism that is characteristic of fundamentalism everywhere accords divine authority to the text. By a peculiar and disingenuous form of transference, the fundamentalist denies that any interpretation is possible, even while demanding that others accept a coercive and authoritarian interpretation. By suggesting that some people are knowledgeable enough to interpret the scripture, Sufis and others who favor esotericism challenge the monopoly on control of the cultural capital of the Islamic tradition.

A potent example of mystical knowledge in the Qur'an is found in the story of Moses' encounter with an unusual "servant of God" who is commonly identified with the deathless prophet Khidr (or Khizr, "the green one"). In this episode (18:60-82), Moses and his cook were seeking for "the meeting place of the two oceans," a miraculous spot known in Near Eastern legend as the source of the fountain of life. They knew that they had reached the spot when the fish that was being cooked by the servant came back to life and swam away. At that point they encountered someone that God described as "one of our servants to whom we gave our mercy, and whom we taught knowledge from our presence" (18:65). Moses begged to accompany this personage, who at first refused on the grounds that Moses would not be able to understand his actions. Eventually giving in, the esoteric prophet led Moses on a series of strange actions: damaging a boat, killing a youth, and repairing a wall in a town inhabited by rude people. When Moses protested the seeming irrationality of these acts, Khidr explained that he had accomplished three hidden purposes: protecting fishermen from having a tyrant confiscate their boat, saving pious parents from a son who would have become a monster, and preserving the buried inheritance of two orphans from being discovered by the rude townspeople. "That," he said, "is the interpretation of what you were unable to bear." Here the great law-bringing prophet Moses is unaware of the interpretation that is accessible to the servant of God who has been privileged with divine knowledge. This ambiguous encounter will serve as the classical formulation of the tension between the public role of the prophet and the inner experience of the saint.

The reverberations of the Qur'anic word in the hearts of those who recited it with intensity began to accumulate and to form a tradition of mystical interpretation. The beginnings of this tendency can be found in comments given by Muhammad's companions on the meanings of particular Qur'anic verses. Probably the most important early commentary on the Qur'an for Sufism was that attributed to the sixth imam of the Shi'a, Ja'far al-Sadiq (d. 765), a widely revered figure. His explanations of Qur'anic passages stressed the notion that there are multiple interpretations of the Qur'an corresponding to the different levels of the listeners. He also exemplified a method of understanding the Qur'an as constantly capable of yielding meanings relevant to the quest for inner experience. In interpreting the verse, "When kings enter a city, they destroy it" (27:34), his commentary took this as a metaphorical description of the psychological effect of encountering God: "This alludes to the hearts of the believers. When mystical gnosis enters their hearts, their desires and longings cease altogether, so that no place remains in their hearts for anything except God."[1] The interpretations of Ja'far became part of a core of Qur'anic commentary amplified by Sufis such as Dhu al-Nun the Egyptian (d. 859). Generations of mystical interpreters, including such figures as Sulami, Qushayri, and Ruzbihan Baqli (d. 1209), expanded on this commentary by inserting the individual comments of important early Sufis on particular verses, and in some cases they added their own interpretations. Other influential mystical traditions of Qur'an interpretation are found in the large Persian commentary assembled by the students of Ansari under the title *The Unveiling of Secrets* (not to be confused with the work of the same title by Ruzbihan Baqli), and in a commentary produced by a series of masters in the Kubrawi Sufi order over several generations. Other exegetical traditions of a regional character have arisen among Sufis in Turkey, North Africa, and India. What is striking about this enterprise is its cumulative and nonexclusive character. Different insights into the sacred text were acknowledged as valid reactions and discoveries from the perspective of the particular experiences that inspired them. As long as the rules of grammar were observed, each interpretation could claim validity without superseding any other. The literature of mystical Qur'an interpretation forms a truly vast subject that is just beginning to be explored by scholars. It is certainly one of the most important underpinnings of Sufism.

Mystical Themes of the Qur'an

Even a cursory reading of the Qur'an will make certain themes jump out at the reader. One of these is God's creative power, as manifest in creation, but which is in no way limited to that creation. This power is praised in the majestic Throne Verse (2:255), which often adorns Muslim homes in calligraphic display:

God—there is no god but him, the living, the eternal. Slumber does not affect him, nor sleep. To him belongs what is in the heavens and earth. Who is able to intercede with him, except with his permission? He knows what lies before them and behind them, but they comprehend nothing of his knowledge, except as he wishes. His throne extends through the heavens and earth, but sustaining them does not burden him, for he is the lofty and mighty one.

God is the creator of both life and death, at once the source and the goal to whom all return. In comparison with him, nothing else is truly real: "Everything upon (the earth) is vanishing, but the face of your lord remains, full of majesty and glory" (55:26–27). God is described in enigmatic terms in the famous Light Verse (24:35):

God is the light of the heavens and earth. The likeness of his light is as a niche, in which there is a lamp. The lamp in a glass—the glass as though it were a shining star—is kindled from a blessed tree, an olive that is neither of the east nor west, the oil of which nearly lights up without fire touching it. It is light upon light. God guides by his light those whom he wishes. God speaks to humanity in similitudes; God is knowing with all things.

Passages like this, with their strong poetic imagery, challenge the reader to find the inner key to the similitudes and parables of the sacred text. Numerous other examples could be given of the Qur'anic insistence on the creative power of God, which made powerful impressions on the imaginations of careful readers.

Another theme that attracts close scrutiny is the intimate relation of closeness that can exist between God and humanity. "We created man, and we know what his soul whispers to him, for we are nearer to him than the jugular vein" (50:16). Worshippers meditated upon the character of those bound to God by love: "God shall bring a people who love him, whom he loves" (5:54). Other passages of the Qur'an opened up vistas on the human spirit as the field where access to the presence of God is possible. The omnipresence of God in creation was clearly announced in verses like the following: "To God belong both east and west; wheresoever you turn, there is the face of your lord" (2:115). God manifests simultaneously in nature and in the human heart: "We shall show them our signs on the horizons and in themselves, until it is clear to them that 'he is the truth'" (41:53).

But God is ultimately beyond the grasp of human perception: "Vision does not encompass him; he encompasses vision" (6:103). The Qur'an places great stress on God's uncompromising unity, in contrast to the polytheistic tendencies to which humanity is prone, when it worships anything less than God. "There is no likeness unto him" (42:11). The Qur'an provides on the one hand the affirmative description of God through many attributes, such as the merciful, the compassionate, and the knowing; these attributes mentioned in the Qur'an form the ninety-nine names traditionally ascribed to God. On the other hand, the succinct *sura* called Sincerity warns that he is beyond all characterization. "Say, he, God is one; God is everlasting. He has no offspring, nor is he begotten, and no other one compares to him" (112:1-4).

Matching the creation as a theme of ultimate importance is the last day, the final judgment of all souls. Some of the most visually arresting parts of the Qur'an are found in the vivid accounts of the garden of paradise and the fire of hell, the destinations of human beings following the resurrection of the dead. God describes "a day when we shall say to hell, 'Have you filled up?' and it will reply, 'Is there any more?'" (50:30). Early ascetics focused their attention on the fear of hellfire as the primary theme for meditation. Even when the emphasis for most Sufis was shifted from fear of God to divine love, the language of the Qur'an had penetrated so deeply into the vocabulary of Sufis that even a horrific scene from hell could become the template for the description of ecstatic states. Such was the case when two early Sufis were exchanging correspondence about their capacity for divine love, symbolized as wine.

> It is related that Yahya ibn Mu'adh (God's mercy upon him) wrote a letter to Bayazid, saying, "What do you say of someone who drinks a cup of wine and becomes intoxicated with pre-eternity and post-eternity?" Bayazid answered, "I don't know that, but I do know that there is a man here who day and night drinks oceans of pre-eternity and post-eternity, and he calls out, 'Is there any more?' " [2]

Just as influential was the description of the gardens of paradise in the Qur'an, which formed a focus for the devotions of many. Early meditation manuals give detailed directions for a series of forty-day retreats, focusing in succession on asceticism, fear of God, longing for paradise, and love of God (see chapter 4). The Qur'anic imagery of paradise features gardens with flowing rivers and beautiful youths and maidens who serve the souls of the blessed. Although Islamic law forbids wine, the Qur'an depicts the inhabitants of paradise with "a full cup" (78:34) or "a pure drink, sealed with a seal of musk" (83:25–26). This paradisal imagery is in part the source of the extensive wine symbolism employed in later Sufi poetry.

Perhaps the most distinctive Qur'anic theme developed by the Sufis was that of the primordial covenant, the pact that God made with the unborn souls of humanity, prior to the creation (7:172):

> When your lord brought out their offspring from the children of Adam, from their backs, and made them testify to themselves: "Am I not your lord?" They said, "Yes, we have borne witness."

It was in this pre-eternal moment that the destinies of all humanity were sealed, and the standard commentators view this as a statement of divine predestination. Those who answered yes would be the obedient servants of God, and those who did not reply would be rebels. The Sufi interpreters have gone further:

> Through understanding the language of reality, this verse has a different secret and a different taste. It is an allusion to the first states of the lovers, and the tying of the bond and covenant of love with them on the first day, in the pre-eternal covenant when the Truth was present and reality was attained. . . . What a fine day, for it is the day of laying the foundation of love! What a wonderful time, for it is the time of seizing the bond of love! Disciples never forget the first day of discipleship. The passionate know that the time of union with the beloved is the crown of life and the most worshiped moment.[3]

Mystical speculation focused on this moment as the first time when God's voice was heard by humanity; the reverberation of that divine voice is faintly recalled in all beautiful voices and in song. Thus, every session of Sufi music is fundamentally an attempt to return to that primordial moment of the first contact with God (see chapter 7). This whole complex of meaning, as with many of the themes of the Qur'an, could be recalled by a single word. When the Arabic word *alast[u]* ("Am I not?") appears in a Persian or Urdu poem, it acts like a gem that transforms its setting; the day of the primordial covenant (*ruz-i alast*) turns an ordinary love poem into the celebration of God's eternal love for humanity.

For the Sufi tradition, the Qur'an frames all of time and eternity into three days. Yesterday is the dawn of creation, when God created the universe and sealed the destiny of his lovers. Today is this world, when all are called upon to live according to God's wishes. Tomorrow is the resurrection and the judgment day, when souls will testify against themselves and be held to account, and God's mercy will be displayed.

Alongside these cosmological themes, mystical psychology in Sufism also takes its origin from the Qur'anic text. Qur'anic Arabic uses a supple range of terms for different aspects of the inner self. The lowest of these is the animal soul (*nafs*), sometimes equated with the New Testament notion of "the flesh." This is the living breath that is created and shared by both humans and animals. This soul at its worst is "the soul that commands evil" (*al-nafs al-ammara bil-su'*, 12:53), but when it is aroused as a conscience, it becomes "the blaming soul" (*al-nafs al-lawwama*, 75:2). Once it has become pacified, however, it is the means to salvation: "Soul at peace (*al-nafs al-mutma'inna*), return to your lord, both pleased and pleasing [me]; enter among my servants, and enter my paradise!" (89:27–30). That inner sensorium known as the heart has multiple levels too. Its outermost part is the breast (*sadr*), seat of the emotions. Within this is the fleshly heart (*qalb*), the pericardium (*fu'ad*), and the inner heart (*lubb*). Further subtle distinctions in psychology have been introduced by later authors. The most important faculty, however, is the spirit (*ruh*), which God has breathed into the human frame; this relatively immortal part of the inner self is the link to the world of eternity. Numerous other technical terms from Sufi practice have been developed out of the Qur'anic vocabulary.[4]

The Prophet Muhammad as Mystical Exemplar and Object of Devotion

The Qur'an as the word of God reverberates throughout the religious consciousness of Muslims. The messenger who brought that revelation is very special too. The fundamental profession of faith for Muslims is to repeat with conviction the formula "There is no god but God, and Muhammad is the messenger of God." The first part enunciates monotheism; the second part declares the truth of Muhammad's prophetic career. As indicated above, the descent of the Qur'anic revelation and the ascent of the Prophet to the divine presence are the twin movements in terms of which Islamic tradition has been articulated.

While the sacred book of the Qur'an has been the subject of special reverence, devotion, and study, the figure of the Prophet Muhammad has also been the focus of the prayers and meditations of countless Muslims. It is scarcely possible to overestimate the importance of the Prophet in Muslim religious life. Anti-Muslim attitudes formed among Christians during the medieval period created a negative portrayal of Muhammad that has proven surprisingly long-lived. Early Christian writers, mostly intent on disproving Muhammad's claim to prophecy, depicted him as a power-hungry charlatan, coached by a renegade monk, who invented a false religion in order to satisfy his lusts. In the colonial period, Orientalist scholars seriously suggested that Muhammad was an epileptic. Muslims, who revere the Israelite prophets and who have the utmost respect for Jesus as a prophet (but not as the son of God), are frequently disturbed at the insults that Jews and Christians still direct, often unthinkingly, at their Prophet.

Many are familiar with the rough outlines of Islamic thought, according to which Muhammad proclaimed himself as a human prophet without any pretension to divinity. The Qur'an insists that to give any creature a share of God's divine authority is idolatry. Yet it is important not to allow modern Protestant notions of religion to eclipse the complexity of the divine-human relationship as it applies to Muhammad. The first European writers (beginning with Edward Gibbon and Thomas Carlyle) who could bring themselves to approve of Muhammad generally did so precisely on the grounds that to them he represented a critique of Catholic superstition. Some modern Muslim reformers and fundamentalists would have it that Muhammad was no different than any other human being; he just happened to be chosen by God to deliver a message, to which his personality was essentially irrelevant. Muhammad certainly lived the life of a family man and political leader in addition to being a prophet, and the Qur'an rejects the unbelievers' demand that he produce miracles as evidence of his prophetic mission. But reducing Muhammad to the status of an influential religious reformer comes at the cost of denying the significance of much of Muslim history. Doubtless there are those who would gladly rid Christian history of all saints, miracles, and monks, but such a narrow sectarian point of view hardly does justice to the richness of Christian spiritual life over the centuries. Stripping the Prophet Muhammad of all extraordinary qualities would be equally shortsighted.

The Qur'an alludes to the special status of Muhammad and his closeness to God in a number of places. "Whoever obeys the messenger obeys God" (4:80). His position as representative of God made any agreement with him equivalent to an agreement with God. "Those who swear allegiance to you swear allegiance to God" (48:10). Later Sufi initiations were modeled on that oath of allegiance to the Prophet. The will and heart of the Prophet were so closely identified with God that they were recognized as being one. Alluding to his action during a military engagement against the pagan rulers of Mecca, the Qur'an states, "You did not throw when you threw; God threw" (8:17). Although in some places the Qur'an declines to make distinctions among the prophets, Muhammad is clearly singled out as "the seal of the prophets" (33:40), the one whose imprint on history is as final as a wax seal on a letter. His personal character, widely admired by contemporaries, is sanctioned by the Qur'an (33:21) as a model for imitation. Beyond that, Muhammad has been recognized as having a universal role that is unique among the prophets. While each of them will have the privilege at the judgment of interceding with God on behalf of his own followers, Muhammad will be able to act as intercessor for all humanity. "We only sent you as a mercy for creation" (21:107).

Muhammad's withdrawal from society in the cave on Mount Hira outside Mecca for the purpose of meditation was seen by later mystics as the basis for the systematic practice of seclusion, particularly in the form of the difficult forty-day retreat. But it was especially the ascension of the Prophet that became a model for the mystical experience of others. The pattern of the Prophet's ascension clearly stamped the interior life of the Persian Sufi Bayazid Bistami (d. 874). Among his many provocative sayings are descriptions of his flight to heaven in the form of a bird, who then settles on the celestial tree in paradise and consumes its fruit; he is then transformed with divine knowledge and engages in intimate conversations with God. The symbolism and rhetoric of ascension became widely diffused. For a mystic such as the Persian Sufi Ruzbihan Baqli, the motif of ascension is a key to the extensive visions recorded in his diary. Powerful visions of ascension were recorded by many other Sufis, such as Ibn 'Arabi (d. 1238) in Andalusia, Muhammad Ghawth Gwaliari (d. 1562) in northern India, and Ibn 'Ajiba (d. 1809) in Morocco. While these ascension narratives undoubtedly build upon the model of Muhammad's ascension, they are amplified in two ways. One tendency is to incorporate cosmology from the widely diffused symbolism of ascension narratives that were already old and widely known in other Near Eastern traditions, such as Jewish chariot mysticism and Hellenistic accounts of the soul's ascent through the planetary spheres. The other emphasis delineates the psychological structures of seeking and attaining union, upon which the very notion of ascension is based. It should be acknowledged that there was something daring and even presumptuous about making the assertion that one had ascended into heaven. Claims to this effect could easily be viewed as heretical attempts to equal or surpass the experience of the Prophet Muhammad. Although the tension between the roles of the prophet and saint was never completely abolished, the "official" explanation put forward to justify a saint's ascension typically described it as purely spiritual, while the Prophet alone had entered the highest heaven in his physical body.

Muhammad's ascension, like most of the details of his life, is known principally from a large series of reports called *hadith* (news, narration) collected by his companions and handed down orally for generations. These were compiled into written form some two centuries after the death of the Prophet in a number of collections that have become canonical; the compilations of al-Bukhari, Muslim, al-Tirmidhi, and Ahmad ibn Hanbal are particularly authoritative. *Hadith* reports form one of the main sources of Islamic ethics and law, which use the model of Muhammad as the standard for morality and action in all spheres of life. Study of *hadith* was a central part of Islamic piety, and for many Sufi teachers *hadith* was a principal touchstone of their teachings. All of the early handbooks on Sufism, beginning with Sarraj and Qushayri, emphasize the role of the Prophet as the model and exemplar of the mystic in all the ordinary details of life and daily ritual as well as in internal experience. According to Sarraj, when Dhu al-Nun was asked how he knew God, he said, "I knew God by God, and I knew everything else by the messenger of God." Sahl al-Tustari said, "All ecstasy is vain if it is not witnessed by the Qur'an and the Prophetic example (*sunna*)." Sarraj concluded, "God most high taught us that God's love for the believers, and the believers' love for God, lies in following his Messenger."[5]

A good example of the Sufi focus on the Prophet Muhammad can be seen today in a sign in English displayed outside the Girls' College in Gulbarga, India, which is supported by the charitable trust maintained by the lineal descendants of a famous Sufi saint, Sayyid Muhammad al-Husayni Gisu Daraz (d. 1422). The sign reads as follows:

The Most Beautiful Conduct

In short, a life which fully represents all aspects of human existence and combines all that is best and noblest in terms of sentiments and behavior is the life of the Prophet Muhammad (peace be upon him)—the highest standard for everybody, in every respect, in all times and places.

Supposing you are a rich man, you have an ideal to follow in the merchant of Mecca and the treasurer of Bahrain.

If you are poor, you must emulate the example of the internee of Shahab bin Abi Talib & (later) the guest of the people of Medina.

If you happen to be a king, you had better acquaint yourself with the biography of the Sultan of Arabia.

If you are a commoner, learn a lesson from the conduct of the subject of the Quraish.

If you are a victor, think of the commander of the battles of Badr and Hunain.

If you belong to the vanquished, seek inspiration from the events of the battle of Uhud.

If you are a teacher, let the guide of Suffah [the Bench] be your ideal.

If you are a student, conceive of the one whose guide was the archangel Gabriel.

If you are a preacher, listen to the sermons of the orator of the mosque of Medina.

If you wish to spread the message of truth, remember the performance of the benefactor when he was lonely and helpless.

If you succeed in establishing the power of Islam and overpowering your enemies, think of the role of the conqueror of Hejaz.

If you want to build up your business and improve your lot, follow the example of management set by the owner of the lands of Bani Nuzair, Khaibar, and Fidaq.

If you are an orphan, do not forget the beloved son of Abdallah and Amenah.

If you are a child, recall the childhood of the ward of Abdallah Saadiyah.

If you are a judge, refer to the life of the arbiter who entered the Kaaba before sunrise and fixed the black stone at its proper place.

Then, wherever you may be and whatever state you are in,

the Prophet Muhammad (peace be upon him) is indeed the light which can illuminate your life.

The sign, and the school to which it is attached, provide a good example of *hadith*-based ethics in a contemporary Sufi-related institution.

It is less widely known that there is a special class of *hadith*, called sacred or divine sayings (*hadith qudsi*), which are in effect extra-Qur'anic revelations. There are a number of standard collections of up to one hundred of these *hadith* sayings, in which God speaks in the first person. A number of these divine sayings are of special importance for Sufism, since they develop mystical themes, particularly the way in which the human soul can become close to God. The most famous of these sayings describes how one proceeds from required religious duties to supererogatory worship to become one with God; it is known as the *hadith* of supererogatory worship (*nawafil*). In it, God says:

> My servant draws near to me through nothing I love more than the religious duty I require of him. And my servant continues to draw near to me by supererogatory worship until I love him. When I love him, I become the ear by which he hears, the eye by which he sees, the hand by which he grasps, and the foot by which he walks. If he asks me for something, I give it to him; if he seeks protection, I provide it to him.[6]

As in the case of some of the Qur'anic passages alluded to above, this famous *hadith* has been viewed as a divine charter for mystical experience. The individual worshiper can become increasingly close to God through continued devotion until they are united by love. A number of other divine sayings emphasize the bonds of love and intimacy between God and humanity. One also finds divine sayings on the world as the vehicle through which God can be known. In one of these, God responds to a question from the prophet David by saying, "I was a hidden treasure, and I longed to be known; so I created the world, in order to be known."[7]

In addition, the standard *hadith* corpus contains some notable statements by the Prophet about his own status and mysticism in general. Several of these allude to Muhammad as the first thing created by God, a luminous spiritual substance through which the world itself was created. Thus, Muhammad said, "The first thing that God created was my light, which originated from his light and derived from the majesty of his greatness."[8] Muhammad is not only the final prophet but the first: "I was a prophet when Adam was between spirit and body."[9] Muhammad's unity with God is explicit in some statements, such as, "Whoever has seen me, has seen the Truth."[10] Muhammad's mystical experiences and visions, so tantalizingly invoked in brief Qur'anic passages, are strongly suggested in other *hadith* sayings: "I saw my lord in the most beautiful of forms."[11] Similarly, other *hadith* point to the divine origin of the human form: "God created man in his own form."[12] The basic objective of the spiritual path was described by Muhammad as imitation of divine qualities: "Qualify yourself with God's character."[13]

The veneration of the Prophet has become a major element in most Muslim societies. The concept of the spiritual essence of the Prophet, known as the Muhammadan reality and the Muhammadan light, was first developed within Sufi circles, but it has had a significant impact as well on popular devotion addressed to the Prophet. Contrary to the "Protestant" image of Muhammad favored by Orientalists and modern reformists, the portrait of Muhammad found in most premodern biographies highlighted his cosmic and miraculous traits. The concept of the Muhammadan light seems to have been fully developed by the eighth century. The Sufi Sahl al-Tustari described a vision of the Prophet as a pillar of light from which God created the world. This kind of metaphysical understanding of the role of Muhammad was combined with a narrative unfolding, which focused lovingly on all the details of his life as known from *hadith*. The result was expressed, through poetry as much as prose, as a deepening of the rituals of blessing the Prophet. Poems such as the famous Ode of the Cloak by the Egyptian al-Busiri (d. 1298), translated from Arabic into many other languages, expressed devotion to the Prophet by descriptions of the enchanting miracles that he wrought. Poetry of this type, composed in many local languages, was integrated in ritual observances on a daily basis as well as in connection with celebration of the Prophet's birthday. The same kind of emphasis on the Prophet's extraordinary qualities was found in a host of prose biographies compiled in Arabic, Persian, Turkish, and other languages. A clear sign of the distance of the modern period from this tradition is the orientation of recent biographies of the Prophet, which largely depict him as a social and political reformer with no miraculous abilities.

It has to be acknowledged that controversy was inevitable in a subject as central as the sayings and deeds of Muhammad. In the first centuries of the Muslim era, it was a fairly common practice for people to invent sayings of the Prophet to justify various legal, theological, and political positions. A rigorous science of *hadith* criticism grew up, which focused primarily on the character of the oral transmitters as a guide to the authenticity of the texts ostensibly quoted from the Prophet. *Hadith* criticism, which was equally central to the religious sciences and to the study of history, has thus turned into a process of textual canonization. Of the *hadith* sayings quoted above, the majority are taken from collections considered to be authoritative in Sunni Muslim scholarship. Others are regarded as questionable or even fraudulent by legal specialists. Sufis in particular have often been accused of being "weak" in *hadith* scholarship. A Sufi-minded scholar like al-Ghazali was certainly much more interested in the content of prophetic sayings than in whether they were fully attested by a chain of pious and respected transmitters. For Sufis, the authority of Muhammad as invoked in *hadith* was more than just the kind of accuracy in quotation sought by newspaper interviewers. Fundamental truths acknowledged by the Muslim community would perhaps inevitably be enunciated in the form of sayings of the Prophet, regardless of whether they could be found as such in the earliest textual authorities.

The debate over the use and interpretation of sacred texts has taken on a new sharpness in the contemporary polemics launched against Sufism by Muslim fundamentalists. Fundamentalists claim to have the authentic texts which they simply quote according to the literal meaning. Thus, to give an example, they are fond of citing a particular saying of the Prophet, in which he commanded people not to pay any reverence to his grave. This is a handy proof text to use against what is regarded as the idolatry inherent in the veneration of the tombs of saints or prophets. As in fundamentalist movements in other religious traditions, however, Muslim fundamentalists maintain their position by selective insistence on a limited portion of the tradition. *Hadith* sayings that conflict with this are either rejected as inauthentic or elided in silence. Those who revere the Prophet and the Sufi saints can quote other reports that justify pilgrimage to tombs, and many polemical treatises have been written in recent years on this very issue. Moreover, Sufis appeal to inner experience as proof of the intimate access to the Prophet that such a physical journey to his tomb in Medina can confer. Many are the tales told of Sufi saints who relate *hadith* directly from the Prophet, whom they have seen in visions or visited in a miraculous fashion. This is a form of textual authority very different from literalism.

Another element that complicates the picture with *hadith* is the transition from oral to written culture. There are many indications that *hadith* were initially transmitted orally, and there was at first considerable resistance to writing them down. There are still many examples of reliance on oral transmission in ritual practices connected with the Qur'an; when the standard edition of the Arabic text was first printed in Egypt, it was certified as correct on the basis of oral transmission by recognized Qur'an reciters. There is a personal element in oral culture that does not resolve into the preservation of a fixed text, and it is this irreducible personal element that is invoked by the miraculous transmission of *hadith* claimed by many Sufis. The literalism facilitated by modern print culture is also different from that which prevails in manuscript literary production. One of Muhammad's followers, Abu Hurayra, preserved more *hadith* sayings than any other companion, despite his having been in the company of Muhammad for only three years. He recognized his remarkable ability to absorb and memorize whatever the Prophet said, describing it as a method of concentration by which he collected the Prophet's words as if they were roses he was gathering in the skirt of his robe. This example has been used as a precedent by Sufi disciples who collected the oral sayings of their masters. It is ironic that some modern Muslim scholars, influenced by European-style models of the literary text, have become so alienated from the oral aspects of *hadith* transmission that they have thrown doubt on the reliability of companions such as Abu Hurayra.

It must be emphasized, regarding the contested legacy of the Prophet, that there is no reason why outsiders should automatically regard the fundamentalist rhetoric of "literal" interpretation as privileged. The dominance of this modern form of authoritarianism is an artifact of contemporary politics and the inability of Western reporters to do more than parrot the claims of media-savvy Islamists. The centrality of the Prophet is such that he has been viewed in every field of Muslim culture as the standard against which others are measured. Political theorists regard him as the ideal ruler. Legal scholars view him as the source of authentic law. Philosophers see him as a Platonic philosopher-king, whose wisdom derives from his contact with the Active Intellect. Sufis, in contrast, see the Prophet as the beloved of God, the merciful one who will intercede with God for all humanity, the inner mystical guide who is available to all. It should not be surprising to see that there are so many claimants to Muhammad's legacy. As Rumi said in the opening of the *Masnavi*, "Everyone became my friend from his own opinion, and failed to seek my secrets within me."[14]

A further aspect of the centrality of the Prophet is the reverence paid to his offspring. One of the key figures in early Islamic history is 'Ali, Muhammad's cousin, who as a boy was one of the very first to accept the prophetic message. 'Ali, who eventually became the fourth caliph or successor to Muhammad, also married the Prophet's daughter Fatima. Since Muhammad had no surviving sons, his two grandsons Hasan and Husayn (the sons of 'Ali and Fatima) understandably were viewed as special. The political and religious movement that later became known as Shi'ism regarded 'Ali and his sons as the only legitimate heirs to the authority of the Prophet. The Imams, as they were known, became the focus of hope for many who felt disenfranchised by the political and religious order that emerged in the generation after Muhammad. Without going into the complicated debates that surround the early schisms in the Muslim community, it is important to point out that while the Imams have certainly played the pivotal role for Shi'i piety, they were also greatly respected by most Sunni Muslims. For the largest segment of Shi'is, the twelve Imams are considered authorities second only to the Prophet, and their prayers and sayings form an ancillary *hadith* collection alongside the principal *hadith* collections based on Muhammad. While most Sufis could not be considered sectarian Shi'is in terms of law and ritual, there are some Sufi orders (especially in Iran) that clearly participate in the full range of distinctively Shi'i practices. Nonetheless, all of the Sunni orders include at least one of the Shi'i imams in their lineages, and most Sufi genealogies reach Muhammad through 'Ali (the notable exception is the Naqshbandiyya, which goes through Abu Bakr instead). Aside from this special group of the chosen Imams, many other descendants of Muhammad (known as *sayyids* or *sharifs*) continue to hold a position of respect in most Muslim societies, and many Sufi masters include a *sayyid* genealogy alongside the initiatic list of masters and disciples to which they belong.

3
Saints and Sainthood

The friends of God—for them there is no fear,
neither do they grieve.

—QUR'AN 10:63

ONE OF THE CENTRAL categories in the development of Islamic thought has been that of the "friends of God" (*awliya' allah*), probably best translated in English as "saints." Here, perhaps more than in any other subject, the tensions within European Christianity have been projected onto the language that is used to describe the Islamic tradition. The notion of sainthood, which was one of the pillars of Catholicism, was utterly rejected by the Protestant Reformers. When British Protestants traveling in the Middle East or India saw religious phenomena that reminded them of Catholic saint-veneration, they applied to it the same contemptuous language previously reserved for what they thought of as the superstitious practices of Catholicism. Curiously, Muslim fundamentalists use a similar language of outrage when describing the idolatry of saint-worship. *Sainthood* is thus, like *Sufism*, a contested term in modern Islamic thought, despite the considerable importance of saints in Muslim religious life over most of the previous millenium.

The Arabic term *wali* (plural *awliya'*) commonly means a friend, a client, or one who is protected by a kin relationship. It is a name applied to God in the Qur'an, where he is referred to as "the friend of the faithful" (3:68), and frequently the Muslim is called upon to realize that God is the only real friend and helper. Those who are regarded as the friends of God would therefore be people with a very special status. This relational or functional meaning contrasts with the term *saint*, which implies intrinsic holiness or sanctity as a personal quality. The Islamic tradition has no formal equivalent of the Catholic process of canonization of saints, a quasi-legal procedure that is only undertaken after the death of a saintly person. While Muslims place a comparable stress on the saintly dead, they also acknowledge "saints" who are very much alive, who deal directly with the problems of social and political life. The historian of Christianity Peter Brown has described several important characteristics of saints in Latin Christianity, which can also be seen in Islamic contexts. According to Brown, Christian saints enjoy the special protection of God, replace angels as the intermediaries between God and humanity, and have a relationship with God that reduplicates the patronage network of society; this raises the possibility that they can intervene with God on behalf of the believer.[1] From a structural point of view, these same features can be found in the Muslim *awliya'*. So, leaving aside the juridical aspect of canonization, the term *saint* can usefully describe holy persons in Islamic societies.

Early Sufi writers insisted that sainthood (*walaya*) was the essential principle of Sufism. The handbook of Qushayri gives us a fairly typical summation of the Sufi doctrine of sainthood.[2] Qushayri defined the *wali* in two ways: first, as one of the pious for whom God takes responsibility; second, as one who takes responsibility for devotion to God and obedience to him, with uninterrupted devotion. These definitions of sainthood stress a mutual and close relationship between God and the human soul, expressed on the divine side by protection and responsibility and on the human side by worship and obedience. It is worth noting that in Shi'ism, the Imams are the true "friends of God," and 'Ali is first of that company; to the standard

Muslim profession of faith—"There is no god but God, and Muhammad is the messenger of God." Shi'is add an additional phrase: " 'Ali is the friend of God." Many of the qualities ascribed to Sufi saints are also used by Shi'is to depict the Imams.

From the fundamental relationship of intimacy with God, Qushayri derives other conclusions regarding the experiences and impact of the saints in Sufism. He goes on to say that, just as the Prophet is immaculate, so the saint is protected from sin. He then quotes various early Sufi authorities on the nature of Sufi sainthood. Bistami (d. 874) spoke of saints as the brides of God, known to no other. Saints may not be aware of their own status, and most people will be unable to recognize one. Abu 'Ali al-Juzjani (d. ca. 964) described the saint by using the language of mystical annihilation (*fana'*) of the ego and God's becoming present (*baqa'*), saying, "The saint is the one who is annihilated in his state, while God is present in his witnessing of the Real; God takes responsibility for his governing, and the lights of authority come upon him continually. He has no information about himself, nor reliance on any other than God." This mystical experience could nonetheless have a subtle and beneficial effect on others. Yahya ibn Mu'adh (d. 872) said, "The saint is the perfume of God on earth. The sincere ones scent him, and his fragrance reaches their hearts, so that by it they are roused to longing for their lord, and they increase in devotion according to the diversity of their character."

Traditions going back to *hadith* reports from Muhammad affirm that there is a special class of servants of God, often numbered as 356, upon whom the maintenance of the world rests, though they remain unknown to the world. As mentioned above, this invisible hierarchy includes various categories, such as the seven substitutes (*abdal*) and the supreme figure of the hierarchy, known as the savior (*ghawth*) or the pole or axis of the world (*qutb*). Although the most comprehensive formulation of this hierarchy was given by Ibn 'Arabi, the basic idea is archaic. A typical variation on this theme is Ruzbihan's lengthy description of the different saints through whom God governs the different regions of the world. He salutes the twelve thousand saints of India, Turkestan, Zanzibar, and Ethiopia; the four hundred elite in Anatolia, Khurasan, and Iran; the four hundred on the seacoast; the three hundred in lodges on the coasts of Egypt and the Maghrib; the seventy in different parts of Arabia; the forty in Iraq and Syria; the ten in Mecca, Medina, and the Ka'ba; the seven who travel the world; the three of whom one is in Persia, one in Anatolia, and one among the Arabs; and the *ghawth* or *qutb* who is the world-axis.[3] The spiritual hierarchy was an invisible parallel to the external political order. After the death of the fourth caliph, 'Ali, the Islamic empire had lost its spiritual substance, falling into the hands of worldly dynasties. The saints came to be regarded by many as the real rulers of the world.

Nonetheless, there was a certain reticence among Sufi authors when it came to clarifying the nature of sainthood in relation to the overarching authority of the Prophet Muhammad. Most Sufi theorists came down clearly in affirmation of the supreme position of the prophets over that of the saints. Typical of this opinion was Sulami, who said, "The end of the saints is the beginning of the prophets"; this clearly placed the Sufi saint beneath the prophet, for whom the saint was a devoted follower.[4] The distinction between prophetic and saintly authority was also articulated as a standard Muslim theological doctrine. An important creed of the Hanafi school of law in the early tenth century recognized but distinguished between the wonders (*mu'jizat*) of the prophets and the miracles (*karamat*) of the saints.[5] Apart from this doctrinal position, however, there was a certain tension between the fixed traditional position of the prophet and the ongoing divine inspiration that was always available in sainthood. As a parallel to the final authority of Muhammad as seal of the prophets arose the tantalizing symbol of the seal of the saints, a status first outlined by al-Hakim al-Tirmidhi (ninth century) and claimed in a special sense by Ibn 'Arabi.[6] Ruzbihan, confronted with

those who doubted the mystical experiences of the saints, affirmed
that they are intimately linked with the revelations of the prophets:
"I fear that the people of Muhammad (God's blessings upon him)
will fall into denial and opposition, and they will be destroyed. One
who does not believe in the unveilings of the sincere ones disbelieves
in the miracles of the prophets and messengers (blessings and peace
upon them). For the oceans of sainthood and prophethood interpen-
etrate each other."[7]

One of the great paradoxes of sainthood arises from its most distinctive quality: self-effacement. A saint's ego has been annihilated.
How can one then recognize a saint? The oldest theoretical treatments of sainthood insist that the saints are known only to God;
they are not recognizable to each other and may not know even that
they are saints. The secrecy of sainthood parallels the esoteric character of Sufism generally. As a tenth-century source states:

> The sciences of Sufism are esoteric knowledge, which is the
> knowledge of inspiration, and an unmediated secret between
> God (the mighty and majestic) and his friends [i.e., the
> saints]; it is knowledge from the presence. God the mighty
> and majestic said [that Khidr was one] "whom we taught
> knowledge from our presence" (Qur'an 18:65). That is the
> special knowledge which is the sign of the saints and the
> reality of wisdom. . . . [When asked about this esoteric
> knowledge, the Prophet said,] "It is a knowledge between
> God and his friends, of which neither proximate angel nor
> any one of his creatures is aware." Thus every outer has an
> inner; every inner has a secret; and every secret has a reality.
> This is what God the great and majestic gives to his friends,
> as a secret by a secret. It is one of the signs of sainthood. The
> saints subsist by that, and they live a wonderful life by it.
> They are the most powerful of God's creatures after the
> prophets (God's blessings upon them all), and their sciences
> are the most powerful of sciences.[8]

From this abstract principle it is a big step to the identification of particular individuals as saints. Yet that is what takes place concretely in the collection of hagiographies or biographies of saints, and in the development of institutionalized pilgrimage to the tombs of saints.

The writing of hagiographies has been one of the main forms by which ideas of sainthood have been disseminated in Muslim societies. The first collections of lives of the saints began circulating in the tenth century, at the same time when the first explanatory treatises on Sufism began to appear. The saintly biographies exhibited two basic tendencies. The first tendency was towards viewing the saints as the source of authoritative ethical and spiritual teaching, which resulted in an emphasis on the words of the saints. This stress on teaching was basically an extension of the role of *hadith* sayings of the Prophet as a principal source for ethical and spiritual conduct. This emphasis can be seen in the earliest major hagiography by Sulami, *The Generations of the Sufis*. Sulami organized the work into five generations extending over two centuries, each containing twenty lives of leading Sufis. As far as possible, he represented each Sufi by roughly twenty sayings, and in the majority of cases each Sufi also transmits a *hadith* of the Prophet. These symmetrically cast biographies present the saints as models of piety to be imitated by the reader. This type of biography is less interested in presenting a historical narrative than in providing pieces of wisdom in the form of *hadith*-like sayings. As an example, the life of Sari al-Saqati (d. 865) began as follows:

> One of them was Sari ibn al-Mughallas al-Saqati, whose first name was Abu al-Hasan. It is said that he was the uncle of al-Junayd, and his teacher. He associated with Ma'ruf al-Karkhi, and he was the first in Baghdad to speak in the language of unity, and the realities of spiritual states. He is the imam of the Baghdadians, and their master in his time. Most of the second generation of masters mentioned in this book were affiliated with him.

With the exception of an oral report on the death date of Sari, that is the end of the biographical information about this saint. Then follows a *hadith* narrated by Sari, giving the full chain of transmitters as in standard *hadith* collections:

> We were told by Muhammad ibn 'Abd Allah ibn al-Mutallib
>   al-Shaybani at Kufa,
> that al-'Abbas ibn Yusuf al-Shakli narrated to us,
> that Sari al-Saqati narrated to us,
> that Muhammad ibn Ma'n al-Ghifari narrated to us,
> that Khalid ibn Sa'id narrated to us,
> from Abu Zaynab, the client of Hazim ibn Harmala,
> from Hazim ibn Harmala al-Ghifari, companion of the Messenger
>   of God (God bless him and grant him peace), that he said:
>
> One day I was passing by, and the Messenger of God saw me
> (God bless him and grant him peace), and he said, "Hazim!
> Frequently say, 'There is no protection or might save in
> God,' for it is one of the treasures of paradise."[9]

The gist of this saying, which stresses the value of reciting a pious formula, is perhaps less important than its form, prominently placed at the beginning of the biography. It presents Sari as a transmitter of authoritative prophetic norms. This is followed by some thirty of his own sayings, each of which is prefaced by a chain of transmitters similar to that in the *hadith* report, but shorter because of the smaller interval between Sari and Sulami. An example:

> I heard Ja'far ibn Muammad in Nusayr say, I heard Junayd
> say, I heard Sari say, "I know a short path that leads to para-
> dise." I said, "What is it?" He said, "Ask nothing of anyone,
> take nothing from anyone, and you will have nothing to give
> anyone."

This kind of biography was a source of teaching on how to lead a saintly life.

The second and complementary tendency in saintly biographies was to tell a story. Narrative rather than teaching forms the main emphasis in Sulami's contemporary Abu Nu'aym al-Isfahani, whose *Adornment of the Saints* (currently published in ten volumes) gives a lengthy series of portraits of holy persons beginning with the earliest phase of Islamic history. Abu Nu'aym's stories of the saints found its extension in Farid al-Din 'Attar's extremely popular Persian hagiography, *Memoir of the Saints*. 'Attar tells engaging stories that supply far more in the way of personal details than Sulami gives, but without any attempt to follow the demanding standards of *hadith* transmission. Here, for example, is a story that explains Sari's last name (*Saqati* means "junk seller"; in his early life Sari seems to have bought and sold secondhand goods), while it makes a point at the same time:

> It is related that in buying and selling, Sari sought no more than five percent profit. Once he bought almonds for sixty dinars, and almonds became more expensive. A broker came and said, "Sell to me; how much do you want?" He replied, "Sixty-three dinars." The broker said, "The price for almonds today is ninety dinars." Sari replied, "My rule is to make no more than a half dinar on ten dinars; I will not break this resolution." The broker said, "I don't think it is right for you to sell your goods for less." The broker didn't buy, for Sari didn't think it was right.
>
> At first he used to sell junk. One day the market in Baghdad burned; they told him, "The market has burned!" He said, "I'm finished with it too." Then they went to look, but his shop had not burned. When he saw that, he gave what he had to the dervishes, and took up the path of Sufism.
>
> He was asked, "What was the beginning of your spiritual

state?" He said, "One day, Habib Ra'i passed by my shop. I gave him something, telling him to give it to the dervishes. He said, 'May God reward you.' The day he said this prayer, my heart became tired of the world. The next day, Ma'ruf Karkhi came with an orphan boy. He said, 'Make him some clothes.' I made him some clothes, and Ma'ruf said, 'May God make the world your enemy and give you rest from this business.' At a single stroke, I was finished with the world, from the blessing of Ma'ruf's prayer."[10]

These stories have an intimacy and directness that are not found in the didactic instructions and more abstract principles that are the subject of Sufi sayings. 'Attar's stories certainly have an ethical and spiritual content, but the emphasis here is on portraying the spiritual power of the saint. The stories of conversion are especially important for this purpose. Sari is shown as already having good moral principles in his attitude towards business, and his entry into mysticism in one story is inspired by an internal decision to give up his shop when he thinks it has been burned. In the other story, however, his decision to renounce the world is due entirely to the grace of two Sufi saints who have prayed to God on his behalf. These stories of Sari demonstrate both the importance of correct religious attitudes and the power of the saints to transform people's lives.

Later Sufi biographies contain both instructive sayings and edifying stories. The literature of Muslim hagiography is immense, and only a tiny fraction of this material is available in translation. Studying the lives of the saints was an important activity in itself, because reciting (or writing) the deeds and sayings of deceased saints was also a way of calling their blessings upon oneself. Meditation on the saint as a model for behavior could also be an important element in establishing ethical standards for society. Some stories of the saints dispense with ethical models altogether and simply assert that the saint is a catalogue of spiritual virtues; in narration, these hagiographies concentrate on episodes that demonstrate miraculous power. To this category belong the fabulous stories that are told of the great saint of Baghdad, 'Abd al-Qadir Jilani. An example of this kind of hagiography is found in the life of a woman saint of western India, Bibi Jamal Khatun (d. 1647), written during her lifetime by the Mughal prince Dara Shikuh. While female saints are less numerous than male ones in the annals of Sufism, their presence is quite important, particularly the early woman saint Rabi'a of Basra (d. 801); she is indeed held up as a model in the account of Bibi Jamal Khatun, who was the sister of Dara Shikuh's teacher, the Qadiri Sufi master Miyan Jiv (also called Miyan Mir). Bibi Jamal Khatun is an example of a woman who independently pursues a spiritual path in a way that includes but goes beyond the normal social roles of family life:

> She is the sister of the revered Miyan Jiv (may God sanctify his conscience), and she is the daughter by whose existence the noble mother of the revered Miyan Jiv was ennobled. Today, in the year 1050 [1640–41], she is still living. The revered Bibi Jiv mastered lofty states and stages, austerities, and exertions, and in renunciation and detachment she is unique. She is the Rabi'a of her time, and many miracles and wonders manifested from her and continue to do so.
>
> In the beginning of her spiritual career, she entered into the path of spiritual exercises under the guidance of her illustrious mother and father. After that, the revered Miyan Jiv sent word to her, through the intermediary of his brother Qazi Tahir, to occupy herself with his path. Thereafter, Bibi was occupied in this path.
>
> In accordance with fate conformable to the religious law, she became joined to one of the nobly born and a legal bond was made between them, and for a space of ten years she was his spouse. Altogether six years passed that they were bedfellows. After that, a divine longing and love won the victory

over her in respect to married life, and maintaining complete aloofness, she kept herself separate in her room. She has two maidservants who are at her service in the day, who prepare water for ablutions and other necessities. At night she is alone in that room, occupied with the remembrance of God. In these days absorption prevails over her. And from the time that the revered Miyan Jiv left his homeland, she did not come to see him, nor did the revered Miyan Jiv go to see her, but there was mutual inquiry, and the revered Miyan Jiv frequently praised her.[11]

The biography then recounts a number of miracles performed by her: a fish that becomes luminous after she looks at it when emerging from a trance, a visit by her brother in a dream with a prediction of the time of his death, the feeding of a crowd with a single rooster, a miraculous supply of milk from a small bottle of oil, the answering of a noble's prayer that his wife have male offspring, a remarkable supply of wheat, and consultation with the spirit of a recently deceased saintly person. Bibi Jamal Khatun is both a model of disciplined spirituality and the example of amazing power provided to the saints by God.

As the hagiographies indicate, the saint's closeness to God is demonstrated by extraordinary power (*baraka*), which permits the performance of miracles (*karamat*). This power can include such unusual abilities as thought-reading, healing the sick, reviving the dead, controlling the elements and animals, flying, walking on water, shape-shifting, and bilocation. Sufi theorists often warned that miracles were temptations by which God tested the adept. While it is permissible for saints to produce miracles, according to Qushayri it is not necessary, nor is a lack of miracles an indication of lack of saintly status. Prophets are sent by God to their people, and the miracles performed by prophets (*mu'jizat*) are necessary to establish their credentials. But in contrast to the public mission of the prophets, the status of saints is private and secret; it is not necessary that anyone know who is a saint, so miracles are not necessary for them. Still, in practice, miracles have generally been accepted as a criterion for sainthood.

In European intellectual circles since the Enlightenment, it is no longer fashionable to believe in miracles. The relentless arguments of critics such as David Hume persuaded many that miracles are nothing but superstitious nonsense (despite counterarguments by defenders of miracles such as C. S. Lewis). The study of religion in the modern university is doubtless a descendant of the Enlightenment, and one of its main concerns has been intellectual independence from the domination of any religious orthodoxy. A result of this laudable desire for independence has been the adoption of the mantle of scientific authority even in many humanistic fields. Inevitably, the pragmatic success of scientific method has translated into a new ideology of authority, a scientism that can be just as intolerant as the religious orthodoxies it supplanted. Thus many scholars who study religion have felt obliged to dismiss miracle stories as fictions produced for the credulous. This debate is irrelevant to what is being discussed here. I will simply observe that miracles are a very important part of the religious outlook of hundreds of millions of people in most religious traditions, even today. If we wish to understand their point of view, it is necessary to take miracles seriously. They are experienced as the interventions of divine powers in the lives of ordinary people. While miracles can include spectacular contraventions of natural processes, they also take the form of subtle presences and recognitions that may not even impinge on the awareness of the nonbeliever.

Perhaps more to the point for those who are interested in Sufism, miracle stories can tell a great deal beyond the mere fact of the amazement they convey. Miracles would be meaningless without a witness. A miracle that no one else sees would be pointless. Miracles are demonstrations that require an audience, and later on a narrator, to achieve their effect. Every miracle story presupposes someone who is there to observe and who later tells the story. The witness is crucial to the efficacy of the miracle. Thus there is a sense in which the importance of the miracle lies in the interchange between one person and another, the testimony that spreads the fame of the miraculous person. Recounting the miracle is an experience that is perhaps as important as the miracle itself. Beyond this, the very form and structure of the narrative often conveys something of considerable importance. A classic example is the story of the Sufi martyr Husayn ibn Mansur al-Hallaj, who was executed in Baghdad in 922 on charges of heresy. The master storyteller 'Attar insisted that Hallaj was killed because he had experienced union with God and was unable to restrain himself from crying out "I am the Truth" (*ana al-haqq*). He described the execution of Hallaj as follows:

> They cut out his tongue, and it was the time of evening prayer when they cut off his head. While they were cutting off his head, he smiled, and gave up his soul. Men shouted; Husayn had taken the ball of destiny to the end of the field of satisfaction. From each of his limbs, the cry arose, "I am the Truth!" The next day, they said, "This will cause more trouble than when he was alive." So they burned his limbs. From the ashes came the cry, "I am the Truth!" Just so, at the time he was killed, every drop of his blood that fell spelled out "Allah." They were stunned. They threw the ashes in the Tigris, but on top of the water the [ashes] still said, "I am the Truth!" Now, Husayn had said, "When they throw my ashes in the Tigris, Baghdad will be in danger of the waters flooding it. Spread out my cloak on the water; otherwise it will destroy Baghdad." When his servant saw this, he took the master's cloak to the edge of the Tigris, so that the waters became still again. The ashes became silent. Then they gathered his ashes and buried them. Not one of the people of the path has had such a victory.[12]

The records of the trial of Hallaj preserved by historians indicate that the saying "I am the Truth!" was not the actual issue; he was condemned on a technicality related to ritual.[13] Nevertheless, the story told by 'Attar is a brilliant evocation of the collision between mystical experience and political authority. The emotional reaction of astonishment is explicitly part of the narrative, on the part of both Hallaj's supporters and his opponents. Wonder and amazement are the purpose of the story, and it succeeds admirably in attaining it. It is in such a mood that listeners are most open to the possibility of spiritual influence. In this case, it would be pretentious and pedantic to protest that limbs and ashes cannot speak.

Standard Islamic funerary ritual calls for burial, with an orientation such that the body of the deceased lies on the right side facing Mecca, as a preparation for the resurrection on Judgment Day. While some *hadith* reports record the Prophet condemning visits to tombs, other *hadith* contain the prayers he recited when visiting tombs, such as those of his parents. Although modern fundamentalists vehemently reject the legitimacy of tomb construction, from a descriptive point of view, tombs have been for centuries one of the principal and distinctive developments of Islamic architecture. In the West, the best known examples are royal tombs such as the Taj Mahal in India; large tombs of this kind frequently have a prayer niche in the appropriate wall indicating the direction of Mecca. The tombs of Sufi saints began to take on public importance in the eleventh and twelfth centuries, when rulers started to see the advantages of forming conspicuous relationships with those whom God had entrusted with authority over the world. Thus the Seljuk Turks constructed a tomb for the Persian master Abu Sa'id ibn Abi al-Khayr (d. 1049), and the Mongols erected one for Bayazid Bistami. Paying reverence to saints' tombs also constituted an important ritual practice for the Sufi orders, which began to emerge about the same time (see chapter 5). While from a Western perspective this kind of tomb-shrine may be considered a colorful and exotic form of architecture, the Sufi tomb has now begun to appear in North America. On a farm outside of Philadelphia, one may now visit the tomb of Bawa Muhaiyadeen (d. 1986), a Tamil-speaking Sufi from Sri Lanka who has a significant following in the United States (see figure 3). In Abiquiu, New Mexico, is located the tomb of American Sufi leader Samuel L. Lewis, while the Iranian Sufi teacher Hazrat Shah Maghsoud is buried in Novato, California.

Why are saints' tombs considered to be so special? Ibn 'Arabi offered the view that particular places are affected by the spiritual concentration (*himma*) of the masters who lived and meditated there. He described this in terms of the experience of "finding" (*wujud*), which is closely related to the Arabic term for ecstasy (*wajd*):

> One of the conditions of the witnessing knower, the master of hidden stations and places of witnessing, is that he knows that places have an influence upon subtle hearts. For if the heart finds itself in any place, its finding is more general. But its finding at Mecca is more resplendent and more perfect. . . . The finding of our hearts in some places is greater than in others. . . . The saint knows that this is on account of the one who has lived in that place. Rather, he is in a spiritual state from the noble angels, the sincere jinn, or from the concentration of the person who lived there and is no more, as with the house of Abu Yazid, called the house of the pious, or the retreat of Junayd at Shunayziyya, or the cave of Ibn Adham at Ta'n. At all the places where the pious perished in this world, and in the places where their influences lingered, subtle hearts are affected. Thus we come back to the differing excellence of places of worship in the finding of the heart. . . . It is not because of the earth (*turab*) but because of the sessions of the companions (*atrab*) and their acts of concentration.[14]

FIGURE 3. Tomb of Bawa Muhaiyadeen (d. 1986) near Philadelphia.

The past influence of the saints thus explains the differing sensations that may be felt at their tombs. Similarly, the Kubrani Sufi master 'Ala' al-Dawla Simnani (d. 1336) pointed out that pilgrimage to tombs increases one's spiritual focus (*tawajjuh*) through contact with the earthly remains of a saint. Simnani said further that, along with the subtle body that will appear at the resurrection, the place of bodily entombment is more closely connected with the spirit than is any other material phenomenon. Citing the example of the Prophet Muhammad's tomb in Medina, he argued that while meditation on the Prophet at any time is beneficial, physically visiting the Prophet's tomb is better, since the spirit of the Prophet senses the extra effort and hardship of the journey and assists the pilgrim in attaining the full realization of the inner meaning of the pilgrimage. By analogy, the saint's tomb has similar virtues. The widespread recognition of this principle meant that visiting the tombs of saints was a regular practice among Sufis. Simnani's disciple Ashraf Jahangir Simnani (d. 1425) observed: "Whenever one comes to a town, the first thing one ought to accomplish is to kiss the feet of the saints who are full of life, and after that, the honor of pilgrimage to the tombs of saints found there. If one's master's tomb is in that city, one first carries out the pilgrimage to him; otherwise one visits the tomb of every saint shown him."[15]

For visitors to the tomb, the saint is considered to be still alive, like the martyrs killed for God's sake (Qur'an 2:154, 3:169). Pilgrims come to visit and adore or even pray to the saint—although in theory one should only pray to God. Offering prayers on behalf of the saint is the preferred technique, as it sets up the possibility of a patronage relationship between the pilgrim and the saint. Many people, especially from the ruling class, have chosen to be buried near "their" saint to take advantage of the blessings in the vicinity, which could be enhanced by charitable trusts supporting the constant recitation of the Qur'an and prayers. Pilgrims to saints' tombs typically make offerings in the form of a vow: if the saint grants the supplicant's wish, the supplicant will fulfill the other side of the bargain by presenting something for maintenance of the saint's tomb or its attendants. Healing is another major attraction of saints' shrines. There are certain saints who specialize, as it were, in the curing of specific problems, such as infertility and mental illnesses. As an example, one can take an Urdu book recently published in Bombay, entitled *Living Miracles of the Friends of God*, advertised as follows in a popular almanac aimed at Indian Muslims:

> At forty-one places in India, living miracles have taken place at the tombs of the friends of God [saints], which you can see with your own eyes. These are astonishing events, even more fascinating than the tales of the *Thousand and One Nights*, which even today men of all nations can see with

their own eyes. Read their fascinating contents, and give them to your friends to read; reading the living proof of the truth of the Islamic religion will strengthen your faith and belief. These living miracles will change your life. These are the places where the broken is mended:

1. [At Ajmer,] the miracle of the great food vat at the court of Khwaja Gharib Nawaz [Mu'in al-Din Chishti].
2. At Khuldabad, the childless obtain children at the court of Hazrat Jalal al-Din Ganj-i Ravan.
3. [At Khuldabad,] the recovery of the stutterer at the holy shrine of Hazrat Amir Hasan' 'Ala' Sijzi.
4. The recovery of the injured and the bewitched at the shrine of Hazrat 'Abd al-Rahman Shah of Ceylon.
5. Counteracting the poison of mad dogs at the court of Hazrat Haddan Shah.
6. The cure of elephantiasis sufferers at the forty-day retreat site of Hazrat Baba Farid Shakkar Ganj.
7. The never-extinguished lamp of Hazrat Muhammad Badshah Balkhi.
8. A sword flying from the holy shrine of Hazrat Musa Qadiri and going to the house of the tax collector.
9. The curing of seven blind men, seven lepers, and seven barren women every year at the shrine of Hazrat Ghazi Salar Mas'ud [in Bahraich].

See forty-one amazing living miracles in this book.[16]

While secular modernists would regard this popular approach to saints as embarrassing superstition and fundamentalists would condemn it as idolatrous worship of humans, there is clearly a large constituency of Indian Muslims for whom it is not only meaningful but also directly linked to "the truth of the Islamic religion." A major aspect of popular Muslim piety involves pilgrimage to the tombs of saints, which are depicted in poster art that is widely available throughout South Asia (see figure 4).

FIGURE 4. Poster showing the shrine of 'Abd al-Rahman Baba in Bombay.

Since Islamic law specifies that children are the main inheritors of property, many tombs are supervised by the descendants of saints, who have thus become managers of the annual festivals. While they are often accorded respect based on their birth, these "keepers of the prayer-carpet" may or may not have a predilection for mysticism. In any case, the shrines of saints are often supported by charitable trusts set up originally according to Islamic law. These trusts frequently include support of the descendants of the founder as one of their objectives. Law reforms undertaken by colonial rulers and modernizing independent regimes in some cases have disenfranchised the offspring of Sufi saints. In other instances (as in the large tombs of the Indian Punjab), shrine administrators were recognized as local notables and major landlords, and have continued to play important political roles after independence.

In eastern Muslim countries, on the anniversary of the death of the saint, followers may celebrate the saint's *'urs* (wedding), a metaphor for the union of the saint's soul with God. The *'urs* custom is attested in Anatolia and in South Asia as early as the thirteenth century. Even in Turkey, which has officially proclaimed itself to be a secular state and in 1925 banned all *tekkes* (Sufi lodges), the *'urs* of Jalal al-Din Rumi is celebrated every December at his tomb with official approval, and it has now become a popular tourist attraction. The largest Sufi festival in South Asia is probably the *'urs* of Mu'in al-Din Chishti (d. 1236), held according to the Muslim lunar calendar on 6 Rajab at Ajmer in western India; hundreds of thousands of pilgrims of all backgrounds (including Hindus, Sikhs, and Christians) attend the ceremonies. In Mediterranean countries, the preferred term for a saint's festival is *mawlid* or birth. Among the most significant of these festivals is that of Sayyid Ahmad al-Badawi, held every year at Tanta in the Nile Delta of Egypt, where it is estimated that up to a million pilgrims attend. It would not be an exaggeration to say that every Muslim country has its own patron saints, whose shrines are held in reverence by a large proportion of local residents. For Moroccans, the tomb of Moulay Idris in Fez is a central symbol of their Islamic past. The shrine of Baha' al-Din Naqshband in Bukhara has become revitalized as a center of pilgrimage with the blessing of the post-Soviet government of Uzbekistan. In China and Indonesia, saints are recognized as protectors of the land and mediators of divine power.

In recent years, the chief debates over Sufism have hinged on the nature and authority of Sufi saints. For their followers, the saints continue to provide immediate access and personal contact. More approachable than almighty God, the saints can be consulted concerning the personal details of life. In a way, they reflect the social structures of an earlier age, when access to kings was controlled by notables who acted as intermediaries. Saints still preserve this feudal kind of hierarchy. A taxi driver in India once told me a story involving his brother, who had been subject to a psychological disturbance. He took the case to a local saint's shrine, but in a dream the saint appeared to him and announced that he could not handle the problem personally because of its difficulty; he was instead referring the matter to one of the most famous saints in India. The man accordingly made a trip to the major shrine as demanded in his dream and later found that his difficulty was solved.

It is precisely the intermediary status of saints that is objected to by fundamentalists. They object strongly to the position of authority assumed by the saint. The main theorists upon which modern fundamentalists draw include figures like Ibn al-Jawzi (d. 1200), whose book *The Devil's Delusion* includes many Sufis in a sweeping critique of deviations from Islamic norms. The main source for anti-Sufi polemics, however, is Ibn Taymiyya (d. 1328), who wrote many treatises against Sufi metaphysics and blameworthy Sufi practices; he fervently resisted the powerful Sufi orders who dominated the social and religious scene in Mamluk Egypt and died miserably in prison for his pains. Ironically, most anti-Sufi reformists today are unaware that both Ibn al-Jawzi and Ibn Taymiyya were initiated into the Qadiri Sufi order. While their views on correct religious doctrine and practice were uncompromisingly severe, it would be false to say that they were against Sufi mysticism altogether; instead, they argued for a different interpretation of the role that Sufism should play with respect to normative religious practice as a whole.

In modern times the situation has changed, beginning with the movement of Ibn 'Abd al-Wahhab, founder of the Wahhabi movement upon which the Saudi regime is based. Even nineteenth-century reformist Sufi thinkers, such as Ahmad ibn Idris of Fez, agreed with the Wahhabis in condemning saintly intercession and pilgrimage to their tombs. Founders of twentieth-century fundamentalist movements, such as Hasan al-Banna in Egypt and Mawdudi in Pakistan, were actually raised in social circles where saint-veneration and Sufi orders were the norm. It has been argued that they appropriated the hierarchical social organization of Sufism to develop mass movements, while rejecting the cosmic mediating role ascribed to saints. The violent opposition of fundamentalist movements to Sufism could be described as basically a rivalry between competing authorities. As mentioned before, the Wahhabis demonstrated this hostility in the early nineteenth century by destroying all the tombs of Sufi saints and Shi'i Imams that they could find in Arabia and even in Iraq. While the language of the polemic is theological (saint worship equals idolatry), the form of the struggle is distinctly political. Saints' shrines and Sufi orders controlled large sectors of the sociopolitical order and the economic resources of many premodern Muslim societies, and widespread recognition of saintly authority was very much at the heart of the public role that Sufism played. Because of the massive public presence of Sufism, the secular nationalist regime of Ataturk abolished the Sufi orders and forbade the performance of rituals at saints' tombs. The fundamentalist critique is not so overtly a competition for authority, since fundamentalist rhetoric claims to rely on the literal word of God instead of human reasoning; in their view, the Sufi saints are ostensibly only in conflict with God. The social reality is different, however. When the fundamentalist assumes control of cultural and social capital, the Sufi is banished. This is what has happened in contemporary Saudi Arabia and Iran, with the difference that—while expelling living dervishes—Iranian ayatollahs claim the cultural mantle of safely deceased Sufi saints. So, while Sufi saints today retain the devotion and allegiance of millions of Muslims, it is precisely for that reason that they are the chosen foes of the masters of fundamentalist ideologies.

4

The Names of God, Meditation, and Mystical Experience

By recollecting God, hearts become peaceful.

—QUR'AN 13:28

Internalizing the Word of God

IT IS THE QUR'AN that provides the raw materials of spiritual practice for Sufis, as indicated in chapter 2. In a text that functions as the word of God, everything relating to its divine author is of great importance. In this respect, there is nothing of greater significance than the names used to describe God. There are by traditional account ninety-nine names of God, although more names are mentioned in the Qur'an (see the standard list reproduced in figure 5). Of these the most prominent are the two names in the invocation that prefaces nearly every *sura* of the Qur'an: "In the name of God, the merciful, the compassionate" (*bismillah al-rahman al-rahim*). Many other names occur frequently as the conclusion to particular Qur'anic verses, most often in pairs, such as "He is the lofty and mighty one" (*huwa al-ʿali al-ʿazim*). It must not be forgotten that the Qur'an has an auditory as well as a visual dimension. The sound of the words, recited either aloud or subvocally, is an inextricable part of their meaning and texture. But the visual form of the words

FIGURE 5. The Ninety-nine Names of God.

Name	Meaning
1. Huwa Allah alladhi la ilaha illa hu	He is God, there is no god but He
2. al-Rahman	Merciful
3. al-Rahim	Compassionate
4. al-Malik	King
5. al-Quddus	Holy
6. al-Salam	Peace
7. al-Mu'min	Faithful
8. al-Muhayman	Preserver
9. al-'Aziz	Glorious
10. al-Jabbar	Overpowering
11. al-Mutakabbir	Lofty
12. al-Khaliq	Creator
13. al-Bari	Originator
14. al-Musawwir	Shaper
15. al-Ghaffar	Forgiver
16. al-Qahhar	Wrathful
17. al-Wahhab	Giver
18. al-Razzaq	Nourisher
19. al-Fattah	Conqueror
20. al-'Alim	Knower
21. al-Qabid	Seizer
22. al-Basit	Liberator
23. al-Khafid	Diminisher
24. al-Rafi'	Exalter
25. al-Mu'izz	Strengthener
26. al-Mudhill	Abaser
27. al-Sami'	Hearing
28. al-Basir	Seeing
29. al-Hakam	Judge
30. al-'Adl	Just
31. al-Latif	Gracious
32. al-Khabir	Understanding
33. al-Halim	Gentle
34. al-'Azim	Great

Name	Meaning
35. al-Ghafur	Pardoning
36. al-Shakur	Grateful
37. al-'Ali	Lofty
38. al-Kabir	Mighty
39. al-Hafiz	Preserver
40. al-Muqit	Guardian
41. al-Hasib	Sufficer
42. al-Jalil	Splendid
43. al-Karim	Noble
44. al-Raqib	Watcher
45. al-Mujib	Answering
46. al-Wasi'	Comprehending
47. al-Hakim	Wise
48. al-Wadud	Loving
49. al-Majid	Exalted
50. al-Ba'ith	Source
51. al-Shahid	Witness
52. al-Haqq	Truth
53. al-Wakil	Protector
54. al-Qawi	Powerful
55. al-Matin	Strong
56. al-Wali	Ruler
57. al-Jamil	Beautiful
58. al-Muhsi	Reckoner
59. al-Mubdi'	Maker
60. al-Mu'id	Restorer
61. al-Muhyi	Giver of Life
62. al-Mumit	Giver of Death
63. al-Hayy	Living
64. al-Qayyum	Eternal
65. al-Wajid	Finder
66. al-Majid	Supreme
67. al-Wahid	Single
68. al-Samad	Everlasting
69. al-Qadir	Forceful

FIGURE 5 *(continued)*

Name	Meaning
70. al-Muqtadir	Decreer of Destiny
71. al-Muqaddim	Quickener
72. al-Mu'akhkhir	Delayer
73. al-Awwal	First
74. al-Akhir	Last
75. al-Zahir	Outer
76. al-Batin	Inner
77. al-Wali	Ruler
78. al-Muta'ali	Sublime
79. al-Barr	Good
80. al-Tawwab	Absolver
81. al-Muntaqim	Avenger
82. al-'Afuw	Exonerater
83. al-Ra'uf	Kind
84. Malik al-Mulk	Holder of the Kingdom
85. Dhu al-Jalal wal-Ikram	Majestic and Generous
86. al-Muqsit	Apportioner
87. al-Jami'	Encompasser
88. al-Ghani	Rich
89. al-Mughanni	Enricher
90. al-Mani'	Preventer
91. al-Darr	Damager
92. al-Nafi'	Provider
93. al-Nur	Light
94. al-Hadi	Guide
95. al-Badi'	Renewer
96. al-Baqi	Subsisting
97. al-Warith	Inheritor
98. al-Rashid	Leader
99. al-Subur	Patient

is also an important aspect of the experience of the names of God. The form of the letters is an abstract depiction of the qualities of God. The names of God, Qur'anic passages, and other Arabic prayers and phrases have played an extremely important role in Sufi practice, both as spoken and written.

The Qur'an itself frequently alludes to the pen and writing, generally in contexts that emphasize writing as a medium for conveying the divine message to humanity. The earliest Qur'ans exhibit large letters on parchment in the austere yet graceful Kufic style, so that the relatively small number of words on the page appear more like a visual icon than an ordinary book. Visualization of the actual form of the Arabic script in the Qur'an seems to have played an important role in Muslim religious experience from an early date, centered as it was on recitation from the holy book. The controversies that raged over whether the Qur'an was co-eternal with God are an indication of the extraordinary position that the scripture assumed for the Muslim community. As art historian Anthony Welch observes: "The written form of the Qur'an is the visual equivalent of the eternal Qur'an and is humanity's perceptual glimpse of the divine."[1] Visual concentration on the Qur'an as the word of God was the closest possible approximation on earth to seeing God face to face. Qur'anic passages and the names of God in calligraphic form play a prominent role in public monuments such as mosques, as well as in the more privately accessible arts of the book. According to a well-known *hadith*, "God has ninety-nine names; one who counts them will enter paradise." Thus it is not surprising that calligraphic depictions of the Ninety-nine Names can frequently be found decorating Muslim homes. A suggestive example of the symbolic use of calligraphy is a modern piece by Muhammad Siyam of Syria, depicting the Qur'anic verse (17:1) that invokes the Prophet's ascension ("Praise be to him who brought his slave by night from the holy mosque to the farthest mosque"); in this composition, the text begins at the bottom, and raises the reader's eye to the top in an esthetic reenactment of the ascension (figure 6).

A considerable amount of Sufi practice, like the practices of other religious traditions, rests firmly on the efficacy of prayer. When speaking of prayer, we must be careful to indicate that for Muslims, prayer means a much more fixed body of formulas than the unstructured individual free prayer that many people in the West identify prayer with today. Five daily ritual prayers are prescribed for Muslims, and this requires a structuring of time to permit ablutions if needed, followed by specified sequences of bowing, kneeling, and prostration interspersed with prescribed formulas; one performs two, three, or four complete cycles of prayer depending on which of the five times of prayer it is. Sufi practice begins with these five daily ritual prayers, which can be amplified by reciting additional Qur'anic passages or well-known prayers recommended by the Prophet Muhammad or by famous saints. There are, moreover, particular prayers recommended for different times of day, for different days of the week, and for use when performing all sorts of actions—such as awakening, getting dressed, eating, traveling, answering the call of nature, and grooming oneself. There are special prayers that accompany weddings and funerals. In addition, each special holiday in the Muslim lunar calendar has a series of prayers associated with it that are recommended for Sufis. This kind of ramified prayer ritual is basically a development of ordinary Muslim piety. But it is in the performance of the five additional supererogatory prayer times that Sufi practice distinguishes itself. Among these, the late night prayer after midnight has a special importance. As a fourteenth-century Chishti Sufi of India put it:

> Just as one performs the five obligatory ritual prayer times
> [at dawn, noon, afternoon, sunset, and evening], the dervish
> should also perform the five supererogatory times. They are

FIGURE 6. Calligraphic Representation of the Prophet's Ascension from Qur'an 17:1, reading from the bottom upwards (Muhammad Siyam, 1987).

the morning, the mid-morning, early afternoon, between sunset and evening, and late night. The late night prayer is between two sleeps. At first one sleeps, then rises [after midnight] and performs twelve cycles of prayer with six peace salutations. He recites whatever he knows of the Qur'an. But if the hopeful devotee in every cycle says the Throne Verse once after the Opening, and recites the *sura* of Sincerity [Qur'an 112] three times in every late night double cycle, everything that he asks of God will come to pass. Then he sleeps a while, and gets up at the end of the night.[2]

Although this prescription of prayer sequences might seem dry or even a chore, those who seriously engaged in this routine looked forward to it enthusiastically.

A famous saint of North Africa, Abu Madyan (d. 1198), has described the deep emotion with which the true lovers of God look forward to night worship:

They call for darkness during the day, just as the compassionate shepherd calls his flock, and they yearn for sunset, just as a bird yearns for its nest at sunset. When night falls, when darkness overcomes [the light], when the bedcovers are spread out, when the family is at rest, and when every lover is left [alone] with his beloved—then they arise, pointing their feet towards Me, turning their faces to Me, and speak intimate words, adoring Me by virtue of My grace. They [find themselves witless], between crying and weeping, between moaning and complaining, between standing and sitting, and between bowing and prostrating themselves in My sight. [All of this] they bear for My sake and reveal what they suffer for the sake of My love.[3]

The enthusiasm that could accompany this kind of spiritual regimen made prayer nearly a full-time occupation. It would be difficult to follow any other profession while adhering to a daily schedule that

includes ten lengthy prayer sessions plus extensive periods of meditation and chanting. From this point of view it is understandable
that Sufi lodges eventually developed as residential centers where
one could pursue this kind of intense prayer routine without in-
terruption.

It is obvious from Sufi meditation manuals that every phase of
ritual prayer has special qualities and that the effects of prayer may
be felt at every level from the spiritual and the psychological to the
physical and material. To give another example, one may cite the
properties of the first *sura* of the Qur'an, the Opening, according to
the Indian Chishti master Burhan al-Din Gharib (d. 1338):

> The virtue of the Opening is for finding guidance. Whoever
> recites daily the Opening forty-one times with the formula
> "In the name of God" will be shown the right path by God.
> If someone does not know how to recite it, let him say one
> hundred times, "Guide us to the straight path," and the
> same result is obtained. Whoever recites the Opening thirty
> times with the formula "In the name of God" on the first
> night of the new month will have his purity protected by
> God most high during that month, and all afflictions and
> disasters will be averted.[4]

Here the search for spiritual guidance is combined with protection
from disasters. Sufi masters have composed countless collections of
prayers in Arabic, with instructions regarding which may be employed to increase one's love of God, to speak with Khidr, to be
forgiven for sins, to banish evil thoughts, to ease a woman's birth-
pangs, to heal sickness, to lengthen life, and to solve financial diffi-
culties. For Christian missionaries and Orientalists, the fixed character of Muslim ritual prayer combined with the belief in its efficacy
made it "simply a superstitious . . . mechanical act."[5] It may be
remarked in passing that such an objection would not have occurred
to medieval Christians, who were very much concerned with the

practical results of prayer and other acts of worship. As with the
modern suspicion of miracles, in the case of prayer a certain critique
almost inevitably arises nowadays. To use prayer for spiritual guidance, and even as a means of establishing supernatural communication with the Prophet or attaining visions of angels, may seem to be
an appropriate enough goal for prayer. But to pray for someone to
be cured of fever, for instance, seems not only unscientific but also
somehow unspiritual. The modern concept of religion has yielded its
authority to science in the sphere of nature, and the secular nation-
state claims control of the political realm; religion has now been
banished to "spiritual" realms that secular intellectuals no longer
wish to contest. This was not the case in the premodern Muslim
societies where Sufism arose. The power of the word of God—in the
Arabic chants dictated in the Qur'an, by the Prophet, and by the
Sufi saints—was more powerful than anything else in the universe.

Prayer manuals such as those quoted above were designed for initiates who could spend most of their time in devotional exercises,
although lay disciples of a Sufi master would certainly receive instructions for performing certain prayers. A subsidiary practical aspect of the power of prayer was available to ordinary people who
respected Sufi masters but did not engage in the full practice of Sufi
discipline. In times of difficulty, in many Muslim societies people
would approach reputed Sufis and request them to undertake protective actions based on prayer; the prayer of a saint, after all, was
more likely to be heard by God. These prayers for protection
(*ta'widh*) take their name from the last two *suras* of the Qur'an (113
and 114), which are supplications for refuge and protection from the
evils of the world. Sometimes referred to disparagingly as "charms"or
"talismans," the protection formulas typically took the form of Arabic prayers written out by the Sufi master on paper, which could
then be rinsed with water; drinking the rinsed ink solution was often
a prescription for curing disease. Thus, we find that when one of the
disciples of Rumi got a fever, the master wrote out an Arabic formula

banishing the fever and ordering it to transfer to an unbeliever; it was rinsed off and given to the sick man to drink, and he was soon cured.[6] This practice of employing the names of God and Arabic prayers for protective purposes has been widely applied, so that in most large cities in Muslim countries today one can easily obtain inexpensive printed collections of these formulas intended for mass consumption. Those who wish to define Sufism as a rarefied philosophy may frown on this kind of activity as a kind of superstitious magic, but as the example of Rumi shows (and numerous similar instances could be cited), it is not so easy to separate the "popular" practices associated with Sufism from the "elite" circles of Sufi masters.

Within the broad range of Sufi practices one can find indications of esoteric teachings regarding the properties of the Arabic alphabet, based upon the numerical values of the letters. This kind of numerological analysis of Arabic formulas, which has a strong resemblance to the Kabbalistic practices of Jewish mysticism, goes back to the enigmatic isolated letters that preface a number of *suras* of the Qur'an. So many rival explanations have been advanced regarding these mysterious letters that they may be said to remain truly baffling to the uninitiated. Certain esoteric schools of Islamic thought, such as the Isma'ili Shi'is, developed teachings about letters into a remarkable esthetic phenomenon, which used letters of the alphabet to represent the human form and face. Entire portraits were created using only the names Allah, Muhammad, and 'Ali. Sufi-influenced groups—such as the Bektashi order in Ottoman lands, the Hurufi ("letter") sect, and the Nuqtawi ("dot") school—employed letter-symbolism and diagrams to convey their teachings; their elaborate metaphysical speculations on the cosmic significance of the letters were frequently combined with messianic activism. Quasi-magical treatments of the Arabic alphabet, associated with the circle of the sixth Shi'i Imam, Ja'far al-Sadiq, were elaborated in connection with the occult sciences. Intricate formulas based on the properties of the divine names, with instructions regarding how many hundreds (or thousands) of repetitions were required to obtain the desired results, appear in such popular handbooks as *The Sun of the Greatest Knowledge* by the Egyptian scholar al-Buni. While in themselves these texts may appear marginal to the aims of Sufism, it has to be recognized that similar practices can be found in some of the most important Sufi teachings, such as the complex meditations of Ibn 'Arabi, and the elaborate calculus of divine formulas employed by the Shattari Sufi order.

In terms of discipline, the most important class of Sufi practices involving the word was the recitation of divine names as a kind of meditation. While the intensive prayer routines described above could be considered merely as extensions and intensifications of standard Muslim piety, the development of meditation techniques employing the divine names may be called a specialty of the Sufis. The term for this recitation is *dhikr*, meaning recollection. *Dhikr* (pronounced *zikr* by non-Arabs) is mentioned very frequently in the Qur'an, since humanity is often called upon in the sacred text to remember God and his commands. The movement towards interiorization of the Qur'an that was so decisive for the development of Sufism lent itself especially to the practice of meditation in which the names of God are chanted over and over again, either in solitude or in company, aloud or silently. The practice of *dhikr* seems to have become well established by the eleventh century, though there are indications of it among earlier Sufis. In the description of *dhikr* by al-Ghazali, it has assumed a great importance as the single technique best adapted to concentrate the heart on nothing other than God. Reading the Qur'an, studying *hadith*, and reciting prayers are doubtless beneficial activities, but in themselves these activities will not make it possible for the heart to be filled with God and nothing else.[7]

A prominent Egyptian Sufi, Ibn 'Ata' Allah of Alexandria (d. 1309), writing in what seems to be the first treatise devoted to *dhikr*, *The Key to Salvation and the Lamp for Spirits*, defines *dhikr* as "purification from heedlessness and forgetfulness by the constant presence of the heart with God."[8] He conceives of *dhikr* as a multileveled process, in which all of the faculties are employed, beginning with the tongue as the outermost, then engaging the heart, the soul, the spirit, the intellect, and the innermost conscience called the secret. *Dhikr* must be undertaken in a state of absolute sincerity as the psychological precondition for remembering God without distraction. It also requires scrupulous religious behavior regarding proper and clean clothing, as well as strict adherence to the laws of diet and purity. He describes how in preparation one should sit in a place that is sweetly perfumed to welcome the angels and jinn, sitting cross-legged facing the direction of Mecca even if alone, with palms on thighs and eyes closed. Even if in sight of one's master, one should visualize him between the eyes, as the companion and guide, whose power of assistance ultimately derives from that of the Prophet. One raises up the formula "There is no god but God" from the navel, using "There is no god" to erase everything except God from the heart, and using the "but God" to reach the heart itself so nothing else remains.[9]

The formula "There is no god but God" is in effect the second part of the first of the Ninety-nine Names of God, that is, Allah (the God). This formula is, next to the name Allah itself, probably the most frequently used *dhikr*. The many other names of God have more particular meanings and correspondingly particular effects, some of which are appropriate for beginners and devotees and some of which can be used by advanced adepts. Ibn 'Ata' Allah's description is so interesting that it is worth quoting at some length:

> Recollection of the Most Beautiful Names of God comprises remedies for the diseases of hearts and tools for wayfarers to the presence of the teacher of hidden things. Remedies are not to be used except for the diseases which that name cures. When, for example, the name "the Giver" (*al-Mu'ti*) is help-

ful for a particular disease of the heart, then the name "the Provider" (*al-Nafi'*) is not desirable in this case, and so forth. The principle is that the heart of one who recollects a *dhikr* which has an intelligible meaning will be influenced by that meaning. Its corollary effects continue until the reciter is qualified by these meanings, except if it is one of the names of vengeance, in which case the reciter's heart is affected by fear. If a [divine] manifestation reaches him, it is from the world of majesty.

The recollection of the divine name "the Sincere" (*al-Sadiq*) bestows upon the veiled one a sincere tongue, upon the Sufi a sincere heart, and upon the gnostic realization.

The divine name "the Guide" (*al-Hadi*) is useful in seclusion. It is useful when there is scattering and distraction, which it removes. One who seeks God's help but does not see the external form of the helper should know that his persistence in seeking help is what he asked for.

The divine name "the Source" (*al-Ba'ith*) is recited by the heedless, but it is not recited by those who seek annihilation (*fana'*).

The divine name "the Exonerater" (*al-'Afuw*) is an appropriate *dhikr* for ordinary people, since it suits them. Reciting it is not worthy of the [advanced] traveler towards God, since it mentions sin, but the *dhikr* of the Sufis does not mention sin, or even virtue. But if the ordinary people recite it, it improves their spiritual state.

The divine name "the Master" (*al-Mawla*), or the helper and friend, is only recited by the [beginning] devotees, because that is their special concern. If someone on a higher level recites it, it is with a different meaning.

The divine name "the Beneficent" (*al-Muhsin*) is right for the ordinary person who wishes to attain the station of trust in God. This *dhikr* brings about intimacy and hastens illumination and is a remedy for the aspirant who is fearful of the world of majesty.

The divine name "the Knower" (*al-'Allam*) when recited awakens from heedlessness and makes the heart present with the Lord. It teaches the people of beauty manners in meditation and the attainment of intimacy, and the people of the world of majesty are renewed in fear and awe.

The divine name "the Forgiver" (*al-Ghafir*) is taught to ordinary students, who fear the outcome of sin. But for those who are fit for the presence, the recollection of sins produces gloom. Likewise the recollection of virtue produces the happiness of renewal for the soul, as with the plea to God most high to serve him in obedience, while recollection of evil is harmful.

The divine name "the Strong" (*al-Matin*) is hard; this name is harmful to the masters of seclusion, but it is useful to those who mock religion, for their extended recitation of it brings them to humility and submission.

The divine name "the Rich" (*al-Ghani*) when recited is useful to those who desire isolation and are not capable of it.

The divine name "the Sufficer" (*al-Hasib*): if the reciter is enamored of possessions, he leaves them behind for isolation, in contentment with the Sufficer or the Sufficient.

The divine name "the Guardian" (*al-Muqit*) when recited provides isolation from possessions and gives trust in God.

The divine name "Majestic" (*Dhu al-Jalal*) is appropriate in seclusion for those who are heedless.

The divine name "the Creator" (*al-Khaliq*) is one of the *dhikr*s for those in the station of devotion, necessitating the useful knowledge suitable for practical piety. It is not appropriate to teach it to those who are capable of unity, for it distances them from gnosis, and brings them near the bond of learning.

The divine name "the Shaper" (*al-Musawwir*) is one of the *dhikr*s of devotees.

The divine name "the Knower (*al-'Alim*) is one of the *dhikr*s of devotees, and it is appropriate for beginners among the wayfarers. It contains wakefulness for meditation, and by it fear and hope are attained.

The divine name "the Reckoner" (*al-Muhsi*) is one of the *dhikrs* or devotees.[10]

It will be observed that this list presupposes the use of divine names beyond the standard list of ninety-nine. In this respect Ibn 'Ata' Allah joins other Sufis such as al-Ghazali and Ibn 'Arabi in expanding the possibilities of the divine names. There are many other specific instructions in this manual, but it should also be recalled that these instructions were meant to be used and interpreted by qualified masters whose oral teaching would supply much additional information appropriate to each individual student. One other stipulation of the author is worth quoting: "Remember, remember not to omit the recollection of the Prophet (may God bless him and give him peace), for he is the key to every door, by the permission of the Noble, the Giver."[11]

Since much has been written on Sufi metaphysics, I do not propose to spend much time expounding this complex theme.[12] This is a difficult and specialized subject that lies beyond the scope of an introductory survey such as this book, in which the practical aspect of Sufism is the main consideration. In relation to the topic under discussion, however, it is important to point out that Muslim theology works largely from the names of God as the primary givens from which extrapolations may be made. God's Essence is forever unknowable and transcendent. But his names designate his attributes, which are the intelligible aspects that constitute the world. Calling upon the widely accepted theological formulation of al-Ash'ari, Ruzbihan Baqli described the primary attributes of God as follows:

He is knowing, powerful, hearing, seeing, speaking, living, willing. These attributes are eternal without beginning or end in his essence. It is likewise with all the names and qualities by which he has described himself [in scripture]. He speaks by his speech, knows by his knowledge, wills by his volition, lives by his life. These attributes are an augmentation to the essence, though not in the sense of division, joining, or separation.[13]

The divine names can be divided into two classes reflecting God's majesty (*jalal*) and beauty (*jamal*). The names of majesty are the names of power, wrath, authority, and justice; as Ibn 'Ata' Allah indicated, these names can be so overpowering that they only produce fear in the beginner, so they are generally not advised for use in meditation by novices. The names of beauty are the names of grace, generosity, compassion, and mercy. Both the names of majesty and the names of beauty are necessary for the existence of the world. Underlying this division is the assumption that everything comes from God, both life and death, hardship and success. Meditation on God by the practice of *dhikr*, expelling from consciousness everything but God, would reinforce the conviction that God is responsible for everything in creation.

When Sufism emerged from its early, relatively private role to the more public manifestation of the Sufi orders (see chapter 5), one of the noticeable effects was the practice of *dhikr* in public contexts. Ibn 'Ata' Allah's *dhikr* manual had been designed more for the practitioners of solitary retreat:

> When you go into seclusion from the people, beware of their seeking you out or your receiving them. The purpose of going into seclusion from people is to avoid associating with them, not just to avoid their forms. Your heart and ear will not be able to contain this purpose when they come to you saying foolish things, nor will your heart be purified from the idiocy of the world. So close your door to people, and the door of your house to your family, and practice the recollection (*dhikr*) of the lord of the people. One who goes into seclusion

> but opens the door is sought out by people. That one seeks
> power and glory, but is rejected at the door of God.[14]

But the spoken *dhikr* could be recited by a group in a way that inten-
sified religious feeling. It was also subject to fewer restrictions than
standard ritual prayer, which has to be performed in a state of purity.
Marshall Hodgson has argued that this vocal *dhikr* was one of the
means by which Sufi practice was popularized across many strata of
Muslim society.

While many Sufi groups have continued to practice vocal *dhikr*
in groups, there was a strong countertradition that insisted on the
superiority of silent *dhikr*, which lends itself to solitary repetition in
seclusion. This was the preference of 'Ala' al-Dawla Simnani and the
masters of the Kubrawi order, who developed and perfected elaborate regimes for meditative practice in forty-day retreats (see the
section below). Likewise, many of the Naqshbandi Sufi masters insisted on exclusively following the silent *dhikr*. This was a controversial point, however. Sufi circles in western China that had adopted
vocal *dhikr* practices were caught up in conflict in the seventeenth
century, when travelers returning from Yemen and Arabia reported
that only the silent *dhikr* was to be approved. Factions developed in
Chinese Sufi circles that struggled for years in the dispute over which
was the correct method. While it may be supposed that other political differences were at work in this conflict, still it is remarkable that
such a passionate disagreement could be formed over the issue of
this practice.

Advanced Spiritual Stations, Practices, and Experiences

The meditative procedures outlined above were available at least
partially to many who were only peripherally involved with Sufism;
while full-time practice was considered necessary to obtain the full
benefit of *dhikr* recitation, even a little bit was beneficial to the aver-

age person. Likewise, all Muslims are called upon to fast during the day for the entire month of Ramadan. Ascetics and mystics went beyond this ritual requirement, which for many people alternates with nightly feasts during Ramadan. Fasting on alternate days (known as the fast of David), fasting for protracted periods during the year, and generally reducing food intake to a minimum are all practices frequently found among Sufis. The basic psychological reasoning behind this recommendation is clear: a full stomach creates a sense of self-satisfaction and indifference, while hunger is an acute reminder of one's dependency on God. As Abu Madyan put it, "I have examined the writings of the Prophets, the pious, the Companions [of the Prophet and their] Successors, and the scholars of past generations; yet I have not found anything that causes attainment to God Most High without [the addition of] hunger. [This is because] one who is hungry becomes humble, one who is humble begs, and the one who begs attains. So hold fast to hunger, my brother, and practice it constantly, for by means of it you will attain what you desire and will arrive at that for which you hope."[15]

In the current climate of opinion in Islamic thought, some controversy attaches to asceticism, whether in terms of fasting, sexual abstinence, reducing sleep, or any other disciplining of the body. There is, after all, a celebrated *hadith* of the Prophet that states, "There is no monasticism (*rahbaniyya*) in Islam" (although a better translation might read, "Monasticism does not form part of submission [to God]"). Opponents of Sufi asceticism argue that the model of the Prophet Muhammad excludes the monk's life of seclusion and celibacy as religious possibilities. Muhammad was, after all, a husband and father as well as a political and military leader. The defenders of ascetic practice point to Muhammad's own practice of fasting, his self-denying way of life, and the abstemious practices of well-known companions of the Prophet such as 'Ali and Abu Dharr. There have certainly been well-known Sufis who lived celibate lives, such as Ibn 'Abbad of Ronda (Spain) and Nizam al-Din Awliya' of Delhi

(d. 1325). But Sufi manuals of discipline recognize that there is a time and place for ascetic renunciation and another time and place for family life. Some people may be more suited for one practice than the other. Those who defend Sufi asceticism compare seclusion and withdrawal from the world to the retreat of the Prophet when he retired to Mount Hira for meditation. This kind of retreat is a necessary preface to the return to the world for the benefit of others.

Probably the earliest description of spiritual retreat in Sufism is a short manual written by the Persian master Shaqiq al-Balkhi (d. 810) in eastern Iran. *The Manners of Worship* outlines four way stations (*manzila*) on the path to God: asceticism, fear, longing, and love. The structure of this treatise indicates that the notion of progression of the soul towards God was recognized as a basic principle of mysticism. As with the concept of esotericism, which is based on the difference between those who know and those who do not, spiritual progression assumes that there are lower and higher stages that can be attained. Manuals such as Shaqiq's are the fruit of individual experience, reformulated in terms meant to be of use to others who wish to attain the same goal.

Shaqiq began by describing the importance of fasting for the initial station of asceticism: "The beginning of entry into asceticism is training the soul by cutting off the desires for food and drink beyond minimum sustenance, and to prevent it from being satiated either by day or by night, so that hunger becomes its distinction and food becomes superfluous." It is recommended that the belly only be one-third full of food, and that the rest be supplied by prayer and Qur'an recitation. "If one passes a day thus, it is known that God has made one's intention sincere, banishing from one's heart a host of worldly desires and filling their place with the light of asceticism and hunger." The object is to complete a forty-day regime, which will empty the heart of its darkness and fill it with light. One may reside in this state for the rest of one's life or advance to the next stage.

The second stage is fear, which is closely related to the self-denial of asceticism. Fear begins with the recollection of death, imposing on the soul the dread that comes from contemplating the warning of God's judgment. Continuing for more than a day brings the intensification of awesomeness: "Light will grow in his heart, and awe will be in his face. If he completes the full forty days, God will perfect him in awesomeness, so his wife and child will be in awe of him. . . . He is constantly weeping, much in prayer, sleeping little, fearing much." This state may be permanent or may yield to the next one.

The third way station is longing for paradise, in which one thinks constantly of the blessings God has reserved for the inhabitants of paradise. Completion of forty days in this meditation utterly overwhelms the heart with longing, and it makes one forget completely the fear that characterized the previous stage. One grows to be utterly indifferent to things of the world: "He is truthful of speech and noble of deed. You will never meet him when he is not laughing, rejoicing at what he has, and devoid of envy and wants." One may continue in this state until death or else move on.

The fourth and last of these stations is the love of God, which not everyone attains; it is the highest and noblest of these stations. It is attained by those whose hearts are strengthened by sincere conviction and by behavior purified of sin. Being filled with the light of divine love, the heart forgets the preceding stages of fear and longing for paradise: "The beginning stage of the love of God is that God inspires his heart with the love of what God loves and displeasure with what displeases God, so that nothing is more lovable to him than God and those with whom God is satisfied." On completing forty days, his heart is so filled with love that it overflows so that the angels and the devotees love him: "On that day he becomes the beloved, the noble one, the near one, the pure one, the sweet one. . . . You will never meet him when he is not smiling, sweetly and nobly, pure in morals, never frowning, good in company, full of good news, avoiding sins, contradicting liars, never hearing anything except what God loves. One who hears or sees him loves him, because of the love of God the Mighty and Majestic for him."[16] In this final stage as articulated by Shaqiq we can recognize the famous formulation of disinterested love proposed by his contemporary Rabi'a of Basra (d. 801). When asked about the reality of her faith, she replied, "I have not worshiped him from fear of his fire, nor for love of his garden, so that I should be like a lowly hireling; rather, I have worshiped him for love of him and longing for him."[17]

Centuries of refinement of these techniques for meditative retreats resulted in two major developments. One was the elaboration of a mystical psychology that charted out with great subtlety the possibilities of mystical experience. It is easy to see how a model such as Shaqiq's four way stations could serve as a basis for more elaborate maps of a path to be traversed by spiritual travelers. The metaphor of a path, as we have seen, is implicit in the designation of Sufism as a way (*tariqa*). At the same time it was quite clear that a way was also a spiritual method; the territory to be traversed was within the soul. In the case of mystical psychology, it is possible to see the growth of a tradition over a remarkably wide geographic and temporal extent; individuals contributed from their own experience to a growing repertoire that was embodied in classifications of the states and stations of the soul. The states (*hal*, plural *ahwal*) were generally defined as gifts from God that overtake the wayfarer involuntarily; they were essentially beyond the control of the individual. The stations (*maqam*, plural *maqamat*), on the other hand, form a series of discrete psychological and ethical qualities that the individual must attain and progress through. As in the fourfold sequence of Shaqiq, the more elaborate descriptions presuppose that the seeker must experience each stage to its completion before moving on to the next. The wide variation among descriptions of the stations of the path and the occasional overlap between states and stations can probably best be accounted for by two complementary explanations. First, each list of spiritual stations was to some extent a reflection of the individual experience of the list's author. Second, the presentation of such a list was inevitably tailored to the aptitudes of the specific audience that the Sufi master had in mind. Because the states were essentially regarded as divine grace, they do not figure as prominently in manuals of Sufi practice; the stations, insofar as they are accessible to human effort, are typically described at much greater length.[18]

Among the early Sufi authors who speak of spiritual states and stations one should mention Dhu al-Nun the Egyptian (d. 861), who is credited with lists of eight or nineteen stages, while at the same time in Iran, Yahya ibn Muʿadh (d. 872) spoke of seven or four.[19] The French scholar Paul Nwyia has traced the Sufi concern with the structure of mystical experience to the sixth imam of the Shiʿa, Jaʿfar al-Sadiq (d. 765), whose Qurʾan commentary had formed the basis for the Sufi exegesis of Dhu al-Nun. Jaʿfar al-Sadiq compiled three lists of stages, which analyzed the spiritual itinerary towards the vision of the face of God: the twelve springs of gnosis, the twelve constellations of the heart, and the forty lights deriving from the light of God. As Nwyia pointed out, the order and selection of the terms included in the different lists vary considerably, indicating that the stages of the soul's progress were far from being fixed at this time.[20] Qushayri in his famous handbook on Sufism listed about fifty stations, while Ansari wrote treatises in Arabic and Persian, providing different lists of one hundred stations (see figure 7).[21] Ruzbihan Baqli in one treatise in Arabic described one thousand and one stations through which the soul progresses, from the beginning of creation until the final union with God. These are only a few of the more prominent texts that describe the itinerary of the soul towards God. The lists of spiritual stations differ considerably on the level of detail; Ansari's list of one hundred stations in his *Way Stations of the Travelers* replicates only thirty of the fifty stations given by Qushayri (see figure 7). But in the general outlines and progression of the path there is a recognizable similarity to the archaic pattern outlined by Shaqiq al-Balkhi, in which the soul progresses from ascetic denial

FIGURE 7. Spiritual Stations according to Ansari and Qushayri (Total number of Qushayri's terms used by Ansari: 30)

Qushayri

1. Repentance (*tawba*)
2. Striving (*mujahida*)
3. Solitariness (*khalwa*)
4. Withdrawal (*'uzla*)
5. Fear of God (*taqwa*)
6. Abstinence (*wara'*)
7. Asceticism (*zuhd*)
8. Silence (*samt*)
9. Fear (*khawf*)
10. Hope (*raja'*)
11. Sorrow (*hizn*)
12. Hunger (*ju'*)
13. Abandoning desire (*tark al-shahwa*)
14. Fearfulness (*khushu'*)
15. Humility (*tawadu'*)
16. Opposing the soul (*mukhalafat al-nafs*)
17. Recollecting its vices (*dhikr 'uyubiha*)
18. Contentment (*qana'a*)
19. Trust in God (*tawakkul*)
20. Thankfulness (*shukr*)
21. Certainty (*yaqin*)
22. Patience (*sabr*)
23. Meditation (*muraqaba*)
24. Satisfaction (*rida'*)
25. Servanthood (*'ubudiyya*)
26. Desire (*irada*)
27. Uprightness (*istiqama*)
28. Sincerity (*ikhlas*)
29. Truthfulness (*sidq*)
30. Bashfulness (*haya'*)
31. Magnanimity (*hurriya*)

Qushayri

32. Recollection (*dhikr*)
33. Chivalrousness (*futuwwa*)
34. Insight (*firasa*)
35. Character (*khuluq*)
36. Generosity (*jud*)
37. Bountifulness (*sakha'*)
38. Jealousy (*ghayra*)
39. Sainthood (*wilaya*)
40. Prayer (*du'a'*)
41. Poverty (*faqr*)
42. Purity (*tasawwuf*, Sufism)
43. Manners (*adab*)
44. Travel (*safar*)
45. Companionship (*suhba*)
46. Unity (*tawhid*)
47. States when dying (*ahwal 'inda al-khuruj min al-dunya*)
48. Gnosis (*ma'rifa*)
49. Love (*mahabba*)
50. Yearning (*shawq*)

Ansari

1. Wakefulness (*yaqza*)
2. Repentance (Qushayri, no. 1)
3. Self-examination (*muhasaba*)
4. Penitence (*inaba*)
5. Thought (*tafakkur*)
6. Remembrance (*tadhakkur*)
7. Continence (*i'tisam*)
8. Flight (*firar*)
9. Discipline (*riyada*)
10. Audition (*sama'*)
11. Sorrow (Qushayri, no. 11)
12. Fear (Qushayri, no. 9)

Ansari

13. Compassion (*ishfaq*)
14. Fearfulness (Qushayri, no. 14)
15. Abasement (*ikhbat*)
16. Asceticism (Qushayri, no. 7)
17. Abstinence (Qushayri, no. 6)
18. Renunciation (*tabattul*)
19. Hope (Qushayri, no. 10)
20. Affection (*rughba*)
21. Kindness (*ra'aya*)
22. Meditation (Qushayri, no. 23)
23. Reverence (*hurma*)
24. Sincerity (Qushayri, no. 28)
25. Refinement (*tahdhib*)
26. Uprightness (Qushayri, no. 27)
27. Trust in God (Qushayri, no. 19)
28. Resignation (*tafwid*)
29. Trustworthiness (*thiqa*)
30. Surrender (*taslim*)
31. Patience (Qushayri, no. 22)
32. Satisfaction (Qushayri, no. 24)
33. Thankfulness (Qushayri, no. 20)
34. Bashfulness (Qushayri, no. 30)
35. Truthfulness (Qushayri, no. 29)
36. Preferring others (*ithar*)
37. Character (Qushayri, no. 35)
38. Humility (Qushayri, no. 15)
39. Chivalrousness (Qushayri, no. 33)
40. Joy (*inbisat*)
41. Seeking (*qasd*)

Ansari

42. Resolution (*'azm*)
43. Desire (Qushayri, no. 26)
44. Manners (Qushayri, no. 43)
45. Certainty (Qushayri, no. 21)
46. Intimacy (*uns*)
47. Recollection (Qushayri, no. 32)
48. Poverty (Qushayri, no. 41)
49. Wealth (*ghani*)
50. Desired (*murad*)
51. Beneficence (*ihsan*)
52. Knowledge (*'ilm*)
53. Wisdom (*hikma*)
54. Vision (*basira*)
55. Insight (Qushayri, no. 34)
56. Magnification (*ta'zim*)
57. Inspiration (*ilham*)
58. Tranquillity (*sakina*)
59. Peace (*tama'nina*)
60. Concentration (*himma*)
61. Love (Qushayri, no. 49)
62. Jealousy (Qushayri, no. 38)
63. Yearning (Qushayri, no. 50)
64. Agitation (*qalaq*)
65. Thirst (*'atsh*)
66. Ecstasy (*wajd*)
67. Stupor (*dahsh*)
68. Astonishment (*hayaman*)
69. Lightning (*barq*)
70. Taste (*dhawq*)
71. Gazing (*lahz*)
72. Time (*waqt*)
73. Purity (*safa'*)
74. Happiness (*surur*)

FIGURE 7 *(continued)*

Ansari

75. Secret (*sirr*)
76. Breath (*nafas*)
77. Exile (*ghurba*)
78. Drowning (*gharq*)
79. Hiddenness (*ghayba*)
80. Firmness (*tamakkun*)
81. Unveiling (*mukashafa*)
82. Witnessing (*mushahada*)
83. Contemplating (*mu'ayana*)
84. Life (*hayat*)
85. Constriction (*qabd*)
86. Expansion (*bast*)
87. Intoxication (*sukr*)

Ansari

88. Sobriety (*sahw*)
89. Conjunction (*ittisal*)
90. Separation (*infisal*)
91. Gnosis (Qushayri, no. 48)
92. Annihilation (*fana'*)
93. Subsistence (*baqa'*)
94. Realization (*tahqiq*)
95. Concealment (*talbis*)
96. Finding (*wujud*)
97. Separation (*tajrid*)
98. Isolation (*tafrid*)
99. Joining (*jam'*)
100. Unity (Qushayri, no. 46)

and fear of hellfire to longing for paradise and love of God. The more refined descriptions still usually begin with repentance, proceed through stages of asceticism and fear to contentment and satisfaction in God—eventually culminating in knowledge or love of God, according to the author's emphasis.

The other major development of meditative practice was the working out of countless specific techniques linked with spiritual stations, employing psychophysical means such as breath control, repetition of formulas derived from *dhikr* recitation, and visualization. This is another immense subject that is only beginning to be studied. One of the most extensive systems of meditation was that developed by the Kubrawi Sufi order in Central Asia, under the direction of masters such as Najm al-Din al-Kubra (d. 1220) and 'Ala' al-Dawla Simnani.[22] These teachers combined intensive concentration on *dhikr* recitation as a purification of the heart with the analysis of the layers of the heart based on Qur'anic terminology (see chapter 2). The result was the articulation of a complex psychophysiology of the body's subtle centers (*latifa*, plural *lata'if*). Drawing upon the ancient cosmological symbolism of the seven climes, the Kubrawis favored an account of seven subtle substances associated with the body, each of which was linked with a type of human being and with a particular prophet mentioned in the Qur'an (see figure 8a). Each of the subtle substances is the locus of a mystical experience of light in a particular color. The spiritual substances are also connected to complicated cosmological processes drawn from Qur'anic themes. The system of seven subtle centers developed by Simnani underwent further evolution in India in the Naqshbandi order, from the fif-

FIGURE 8. Subtle Substances (*lata'if*) in Sufi Psychology.

a. The Seven Subtle Substances in the Kubrawi system of 'Ala' al-Dawla Simnani
(Adapted from Jamal Elias, *The Throne Carrier of God*.)

Subtle Substance	Human Type	Prophet	Color
1. body (*qalab*)	barbarian (*afaqi*)	Adam	dark
2. soul (*nafs*)	infidel (*kafir*)	Noah	blue
3. heart (*qalb*)	submitter (*muslim*)	Abraham	red
4. conscience (*sirr*)	faithful (*mu'min*)	Moses	white
5. spirit (*ruh*)	saint (*wali*)	David	yellow
6. mystery (*khafi*)	prophet (*nabi*)	Jesus	black
7. reality (*haqq*)	seal of prophets	Muhammad	green

b. The Six Subtle Substances in a simplified Naqshbandi system
(Adapted from Dhawqi Shah, *Sirr-i dilbaran*)

Subtle Substance	Location	Color
1. heart (*qalb*)	two fingers below left breast	red
2. spirit (*ruh*)	two fingers below right breast	white
3. soul (*nafs*)	beneath navel	yellow
4. conscience (*sirr*)	center of breast	green
5. mystery (*khafi*)	above eyebrows	blue
6. arcanum (*akhfa*)	top of brain	black

teenth through the late nineteenth century, into a new arrangement assigning six subtle centers to particular parts of the body. A typical version of the Naqshbandi subtle centers puts the heart (*qalb*) two fingers below the left breast, the spirit (*ruh*) two fingers below the right breast, the soul (*nafs*) beneath the navel, the conscience (*sirr*) in the middle of the breast, the mystery (*khafi*) above the eyebrows, and the arcanum (*akhfa*) at the top of the brain. The colors associated with the subtle substances differ from those in Simnani's system as well (see figure 8b).[23]

In tandem with this mystical psychology went an elaborate series of *dhikr* meditations that incorporated breathing techniques, visualization, and the localization of particular chants and syllables in the parts of the body associated with the subtle substances. Typical instructions for such meditation are contained in the following three-part example from a fourteenth-century Kubrawi, in an exercise designed to banish unwanted suggestive thoughts:

> *Part one*: Sit cross-legged, placing the right foot over the left foot, the left hand on the right foot, and the right hand on top of the left hand, facing the direction of Mecca. Hold the image of your master in front of you, because his heart is similarly linked with the heart of his master, and is thus connected all the way to the Prophet (God bless him and give him peace) and the presence of the Almighty (whose name is mighty). . . . Also, similarly look upon your earthly body as dead, to loosen the roots of the thoughts that are the tool of the soul and the devil. With a little effort you can pull them out and gather the internal and external senses in order. The veils of thoughts between the *dhikr* and the heart disappear, and the *dhikr* quickly enters the heart. When you hold in view the image of the master and your dead earthly form, with awe and reverence draw out the totality of thought veils from the bottom of the navel with the phrase "There is no god but God" (*la ilaha illa allah*), until it is at the right

breast and neck. Hold it here a little while, but make it an actual halt, not verbal.

Part two: Bring the left shoulder with the head and neck towards the right shoulder, with the power of "There is no god but God" and the power of the master's sainthood, throwing the totality of thoughts and veils, together with your dead earthly body, behind your breast. Up to this point one should keep remembering the master, but afterward, remembering the master gives way to remembering the Truth.

Part three: [From] the right shoulder knock powerfully with the *dhikr* "Allah," with perfect awe and reverence, on top of the heart. The *A* of *Allah*, along with the negation [of the *dhikr* in parts one and two], draws out the thoughts. When thought becomes excessive [again], go to the beginning of the *dhikr*.[24]

This laconic description is evidently shorthand notation that needs to be supplemented by oral instruction from someone trained in the tradition. Still, it is possible to get a sense of the lively concentration that is required of the practitioner. It is noteworthy that this meditation includes in its third phase a visualization of the letters of the word *Allah* along with vigorous movement of the chanted phrase into different parts of the body.

Individual Sufi teachers developed distinctive practices, including such variations as the "two-beat," "three-beat," and "four-beat" *dhikrs*. Since they were developed in a teaching context, special *dhikr* exercises of this type were in fact one of the things that distinguished one Sufi order from another. In the seventeenth and eighteenth centuries, widespread travel by Sufis (in particular the pilgrimage to Mecca) made it possible to obtain initiations in the *dhikr* exercises of many different orders. Some Sufi manuals of that period contain extensive descriptions of the meditation practices of different orders, with their chains of transmission (as in *hadith*) and their expected results. To this class belong such relatively late writings as *The Clear*

Fountain on the Forty Paths, written by the North African scholar Muhammad al-Sanusi al-Idrisi (d. 1859); as its name implies, it contains examples of *dhikr* practices from forty different Sufi orders from many countries (see figure 9, pages 112–13). Similar collections were made in India by the Naqshbandi scholar Shah Wali Allah (d. 1762) and the Chishti master Nizam al-Din Awrangabadi (d. 1729).

Those who are familiar with other ascetic and spiritual traditions may see a certain similarity between some of the Sufi practices described above and the types of meditation associated with Indian yoga. There are a number of reasons for being extremely cautious about any sweeping generalizations regarding connections between Sufism and yoga. First, as indicated above (chapter 1), there is a long-standing bias in European Orientalism that seeks to reduce all Eastern mysticism to a single source. The tendency to seek an Indian origin for Sufism exists independent of any historical evidence that might support such a thesis; it is, in other words, ideological, and one should be suspicious of any unsubstantiated claim of this type. Second, there is historical evidence regarding knowledge of yoga among Sufis, but it indicates that yogic practices had a limited impact, and that their use was decisively shaped by Islamizing tendencies and interpreted in terms of standard Islamicate philosophical and cosmological categories. In a separate unpublished study, I have translated and analyzed the only known text on hatha yoga practice that circulated in Muslim cultures (Patanjali's *Yoga Sutras* was translated into Arabic by the scholar al-Biruni [d. 1048], but he omitted practical aspects of the text, and his translation was largely unknown). This text, originally entitled *Amrtakunda* (The Pool of Nectar) or *Kamrubijaksa* (The Kamarupa Seed Syllables), was translated into Arabic during the fourteenth or fifteenth century, and subsequently into Persian, Turkish, and Urdu; it was eventually known and used in a number of Sufi circles from India to Turkey and Morocco. It did not, however, play any important role in the development of Sufi meditation techniques. Third, the Sufi techniques are conceptually and historically unrelated to the psychophysiology of yoga. Superficially, the spiritual substances of Sufi meditation might look similar to the seven yogic chakras, or subtle nerve centers located along the region of the spine, although some of the Sufi centers are clearly unconnected with the spine. But Sufi sources lack any reference to the characteristic yogic descriptions of subtle nerves (*nadis*), the breaths, the sun and moon symbolism, or the kundalini serpent coiled at the base of the spine. While breath control is employed in Sufi meditation, its function is different from yogic breathing techniques. In addition, Sufi meditations contain a multileveled prophetology and mystical Qur'anic exegesis tied to each of the seven subtle centers, with visualizations based on the Arabic letters of the names of God, so that distinctive Islamic symbolisms are embedded in the system. Finally, the whole notion of "influence" is based on the dubious concept of pure religious essences that become debased or polluted by foreign intrusions. In short, the argument for yogic "influence" on Sufism is not based on anything that Sufis were aware of.[25]

Meditation in solitary retreat was the crucible of mystical experience for Sufis. The topics of cosmology and metaphysics, which for philosophers are proved by logic and demonstration, are for Sufis the subject of direct unveiling. So it is with the manual for retreat composed by Ibn 'Arabi:

> If you want to enter the presence of the Truth and receive from Him without intermediary, and you desire intimacy with Him, this will not be appropriate as long as your heart acknowledges any lordship other than His. For you belong to that which exercises its authority over you. Of this there is no doubt. And seclusion from people will become inevitable for you, and preference for retreat (*khalwa*) over human associations, for the extent of your distance from creation is the extent of your closeness to God—outwardly and inwardly.[26]

FIGURE 9. List of Forty Sufi Orders according to al-Sanusi (d. 1859).

Order	*Founder*	*Region*
1. Muhammadiyya	Muhammad the Prophet (d. 632)	(theoretical)
2. Siddiqiyya	Abu Bakr al-Siddiq (d. 634)	(theoretical)
3. Uwaysiyya	Uways al-Qarani (7th century)	(theoretical)
4. Junaydiyya	Junayd al-Baghdadi (d. 910)	(theoretical)
5. Hallajiyya	al-Hallaj (d. 922)	(theoretical)
6. Qadiriyya	'Abd al-Qadir al-Jilani (d. 1166)	all regions
7. Madyaniyya	Abu Madyan (d. 1197)	North Africa
8. Rifa'iyya	Ahmad al-Rifa'i (d. 1182)	Turkey, Egypt
9. 'Urabiyya	'Umar ibn Muhammad al-'Urabi (16th century)	Yemen
10. Hatimiyya	Muhyi al-Din ibn 'Arabi (d. 1238)	(theoretical)
11. Suhrawardiyya	Abu Hafs al-Suhrawardi (d. 1234)	Iran, India
12. Ahmadiyya	Ahmad al-Badawi (d. 1276)	Egypt
13. Shadhiliyya	Abu al-Hasan al-Shadhili (d. 1258)	North Africa
14. Wafa'iyya	Muhammad Wafa' (d. 1358)	Egypt, Syria
15. Zarruqiyya	Ahmad al-Zarruq (d. 1494)	North Africa
16. Jazuliyya	Muhammad al-Jazuli (d. 1465)	North Africa
17. Bakriyya	Abu Bakr al-Wafa'i (d. 1496)	Egypt, Syria
18. Malamatiyya	Abu Yazid al-Bistami (d. 874)	(theoretical)
19. Khalwatiyya	'Umar al-Khalwati (d. 1397)	Egypt, Turkey
20. Kubrawiyya	Najm al-Din Kubra (d. 1221)	Central Asia, Iran
21. Hamadaniyya	'Ali Hamadani (d. 1384)	Kashmir
22. Rukniyya	'Ala' al-Dawla Simanani (d. 1336)	Central Asia
23. Nuriyya	Nur al-Din Isfara'ini (d. 1317)	Iran
24. Naqshbandiyya	Baha' al-Din Naqshbandi (d. 1389)	Central Asia, India, Turkey
25. Shattariyya	'Abd Allah Shattari (d. 1438)	India, Indonesia
26. Ghawthiyya	Muhammad Ghawth Gwaliyari (d. 1563)	India
27. 'Ishqiyya	Abu Yazid al-'Ishqi (14th century)	Turkey, Iran
28. Mawlawiyya	Jalal al-Din Rumi (d. 1273)	Turkey, Syria
29. Jahriyya	Ahmad al-Yasawi (d. 1167)	(theoretical)
30. Burhaniyya	Ibrahim al-Dasuqi (d. 1288)	Egypt, Arabia
31. Hafifiyya	Ibn al-Khafif (d. 982)	(theoretical)

Order	Founder	Region
32. Khawatiriyya	'Ali ibn Maymun al-Idrisi (d. 1511)	North Africa
33. 'Aydarusiyya	Abu Bakr al-'Aydarus (d. 1509)	Yemen, India, Indonesia
34. Mushari'iyya	Sufyan al-Thawri (d. 778)	(theoretical)
35. Qushayriyya	Abu al-Qasim al-Qushayri (d. 1074)	(theoretical)
36. Kharraziyya	Abu Sa'id al-Kharraz (d. 890)	(theoretical)
37. Chishtiyya	Mu'in al-Din Chishti (d. 1236)	India
38. Madariyya	Badi' al-Din Shah Madar (d. 1437)	India
39. Qalandariyya	Jamal al-Din Savi (d. 1233)	(theoretical)
40. Suhayliyya	Muhammad al-Suhayli (16th century)	Arabia

The manual consists mainly of a description of the experiences that will befall one who undertakes a meditative retreat. Recitation of the *dhikr* "Allah" is combined with the need to see every vision, no matter how exalted, as something less than God. The higher spiritual faculties reveal to the seeker a series of visions that recapitulate the hierarchical structure of the universe, from the lowest minerals to the divine presence and the cosmic realms beyond time. Each of these is a temptation, for if the seeker is satisfied and stops at any level, the result will be something less than God. While Ibn 'Arabi's retreat manual is thus a reenactment of the primal spiritual achievement—the ascension of the Prophet—it also spells out the difference between the roles of the Prophet and the saint.

In a more exuberant fashion, the visionary diary of Ruzbihan Baqli is filled with astonishing encounters with God, the prophets, the angels, and the Sufi saints. For him these encounters with God were the product of unmediated divine grace. He himself had practiced Sufi meditation techniques from an early age, but writing in his late fifties, he acknowledged that the "discipline and striving" of his youth had been replaced by the mystical experiences that he calls unveilings:

> I recalled the days of discipleship, and the requirements of striving that had overwhelmed me, and their falling away from my heart over a space of twenty years. I remained without discipline or striving, and the chants of the masters and their many preceding disciplinary exercises fell away from my heart, as though I no longer approved of them in the court of gnosis. For gnosis with me makes use of grace and other things besides them [that is, discipline and striving], [otherwise] it is the gnosis of the common people. But I rejected my thought in that and was concerned whenever a thought occurred to my heart. A visitation of the hidden befell me and the Truth (glory be to him) was unveiled to me twice, once in the form of beauty and once in the form of greatness. I looked at the beauty of his transcendent face with the eye of the heart, and he said to me, "How can they reach me by strivings and disciplines, if my noble face remains veiled to them? This is reserved for my lovers and the near ones among the gnostics; there is no way to me except through me, and by the unveiling of my beauty." After the ecstasies, the spiritual states, and the visitation, I returned to the creed of unity and the election of his favor through what he wishes, to whom he wishes, as he wishes: "Grace is in the hands of God; he gives it to whom he wills" (Qur'an 57:29). And the sweetness of that remained until I slept.[27]

For Ruzbihan, the exercises of Sufi discipline were necessary, but not sufficient, preparations for spiritual experience. Still, his visions are clearly modeled on the ascension of the Prophet.

The private processes of meditation are perhaps the least visible, though perhaps the most important, aspect of Sufism. It is difficult to have access to this inner dimension of experience. Spiritual states, by their very nature, are not publicly accessible. Controversy over Sufism in Muslim societies typically broke out in reference to unusual behavior or statements caused by experiences that the average person would rarely meet with. While the manuals of Sufi discipline presuppose a disciplined teaching situation where progress could be regulated, the Sufi terminology for mystical experience clearly indicates that there were whole ranges of spiritual states that were far beyond the control of the individual. Ruzbihan indicated these states by descriptions like the following:

> This is the station of the lovers who have drunk the oceans of unity in primordial gnosis and the rest of it, who are upon the ocean of greatness, whose clashing bequeaths the unknowings of realities to the people of gnosis and love. They are in the station of annihilation; they have no eye that is not obliterated, no heart that is not dismayed, no intellect that is not annihilated, no conscience that is not vanishing.[28]

This is the language of drunkenness, which has served as a potent symbol for the transformations of consciousness found in mystical states. In this passage, Ruzbihan links the drunkard's lack of conscious control with the annihilation (*fana'*) of the individual self. The outrageous statements and claims that burst forth from someone in such a state could certainly cause an uproar.

Islamic culture has a long tradition concerning the "wise fools," madmen who have an intimate relationship with God but who flout the conventions of society. Collections of Sufi biographies sometimes contain appendices giving the lives of intoxicated saints, who have been attracted (*majdhub*) to God with such force that their intellects have been overpowered. How can people like this be assimilated to any kind of social standard? While this category of unconventional behavior overlaps somewhat with the "self-blaming" Sufi who deliberately incurs the criticism of others, the holy fool was excused from ritual duties, by analogy with insanity. This is how Sufis understood the Qur'anic verse "Do not approach prayer when you are drunk" (4:43), though it is commonly taken just as a prohibition of alcohol. Here is a description of a God-intoxicated person as told by a thirteenth-century Persian Sufi:

> Once someone told me that there was a strange Luri tribesman who had come to the city, named Jamal al-Din. He was overpowered by a strong divine attraction (*jadhb*) and was staying in the congregational mosque. I went to the congregational mosque and saw that he had a powerful divine attraction and was totally absorbed; from the intensity of his state, his eyes were like two cups filled with blood. I went up to him and greeted him, and he replied. Then he said, "I have nothing to do with the black-and-white makers," meaning that he had nothing to do with legal scholars, learned people, and writers. Someone present said, "This person is one of the Sufis." I sat in front of him and asked about his spiritual states. He said, "I am an illiterate Luri tribesman, and I don't know anything. I used to be happy taking care of the horses, and taking care of horses was my job. One day I was sitting at the stable in front of the horses. Suddenly a spiritual state was unveiled to me, and a divine attraction occurred. The veil of ego was taken away from me, and I became unconscious. I fell and rolled under the horses' hooves. When I regained consciousness, the whole divine unity was revealed to me"[29]

As this account shows, a *majdhub* did not need to have followed the discipline of Sufism, since a spiritual state could overtake an ordinary person as a gift of divine grace. This phenomenon is by no means limited to medieval times. A British physician, William Donkin, has provided a lengthy account of hundreds of contacts with intoxicated souls (Persian *mast*) made by the Indian spiritual master

Meher Baba all over South Asia during a period of ten years (1939–1949). This remarkable document, which is unparalleled in the history of religion, also contains a detailed analysis of the different types of spiritual intoxication and madness, in a classification drawn from the categories of Sufism. The fact that both Hindus and Muslims are included in the ranks of the *masts* makes it all the more noteworthy as a kind of pragmatic description of uncontrolled mystical experiences.[30]

Besides unusual behavior, the other way in which spiritual states could become visible was through speech, particularly the ecstatic utterances (*shathiyyat*) that resulted from overpowering states. These could easily become controversial by passing beyond the limits of the conventional understanding of God. Many ecstatic sayings express states of experiencing union with God. As a result, the form that they take appears to be an outrageous boast, which appears to be the claim that the speaker is God. The most famous ecstatic sayings are Bayazid Bistami's "Glory be to me, how great is my majesty" and Hallaj's "I am the Truth." The standard explanation of these sayings offered by Sufis was that the ego of the individual is annihilated during an ecstatic state, and so it is really God speaking, not the human being. 'Attar explained Hallaj's saying by analogy with the burning bush seen by Moses; while Moses heard the words, "I am I, God," coming from the bush, it was really God who was speaking. In the same way, when Hallaj said, "I am the Truth," it was really God who spoke, since Hallaj was not really there. Here is an example of one of the remarkable outbursts of Bayazid, with a detailed commentary by Ruzbihan:

> Bayazid said, "You will not see anyone like me in heaven and earth."
>
> *Commentary*: These are the words of the drunkards of gnosis in intoxication. From jealousy in love, he sees no one but himself with the beloved. Don't you see that Solomon's

bird from extreme intoxication with his beloved said, "Bring your head near, or else I will seize Solomon's kingdom with my beak and cast it into the infinite ocean"? This is the rule for lovers. . . . It is also right that when you pass beyond the temple of earth and the pass of water, and you fly beyond the station of the world of fate, you will hear the voice of the self of Truth from the tongue of every atom. He is speaking, describing himself, with the tongue of every gnostic. [When] Bayazid said, "Glory be to me," I say that was the Truth who described himself with his tongue.[31]

Nevertheless, the shock value of such sayings was such that most Sufis expressed some ambivalence about them. It is common to find defensive explanations that attempt to defuse criticism of ecstatic sayings, sometimes by explaining them away as misquotations or interpreting them as the result of uncontrollable intoxication. In the case of the *majdhub* Jamal al-Din, mentioned above, he was accused by some religious scholars of heresy and infidelity and was brought before the ruler of Shiraz. When the ruler sought the opinion of two leading Sufis, they delivered written verdicts stating that it was not permissible to kill anyone overpowered by divine attractions, regardless of what he said. Despite the famous execution of Hallaj, heresy trials of Sufis have been rare, and when they have occurred they inevitably have reflected underlying political conflicts.

Not everyone among the Sufis agreed that this kind of ecstatic saying was wise or even that it represented the ultimate spiritual experience. The basic esotericism of Sufism rested on the principle that only certain qualified people would be able to understand and experience the highest spiritual truths. Therefore, to blurt out something revealing one's intimate experience with God was rash, to say the least; it could also create among foolish people the mistaken impression that everyone is actually God and that law and morality are no longer binding. From this point of view, Sufis like al-Ghazali could say that Hallaj's statement "I am the Truth" was authentic but that its public expression required his execution for having revealed the secret to the unworthy. Another criticism of ecstatic sayings was that they reveal immaturity and lack of control. The highest goal, from this perspective, is to experience union with God without losing control of one's words and actions. Hallaj's outburst was in this case the result of his limited capacity; he was a shallow vessel who quickly overflowed. Ibn 'Arabi was particularly critical of unrestrained ecstatic utterances on the grounds that they consist of boasting and claims to spiritual states; this was an insightful comment in that the style and form of ecstatic sayings closely resembles the boasting contest as practiced by ancient Arab tribes. Strikingly, however, Ibn 'Arabi makes a number of astounding statements about his own position, including the assertion that he is the seal of the saints (a status that appears perilously close to that of Muhammad as seal of the prophets). These differ from ecstatic sayings, he explains, in that these are not boasts or claims; since he has been ordered to say these things by God and by the Prophet, these statements are merely a form of obedience. It is in fact common to find in later Sufi literature self-descriptions that outdo in cosmic significance the claims of all earlier masters. It is almost as if an overpowering experience of union with God makes all previous descriptions seem inadequate. In a rhetoric of transcendental hyperbole, later Sufi masters like Ahmad Sirhindi and Shah Wali Allah describe themselves as having reached stations that make the achievements of Bayazid and Ibn 'Arabi seem insignificant—the currency of spiritual states has become devalued. But still the word of God permeates Sufi practice and experience, even at the levels where it is no longer easy to distinguish who is speaking it.

5

The Sufi Orders

Mastery, Discipleship, and Initiation

One who has no master has Satan for a leader.

—Bayazid Bistami

WHAT WAS AT FIRST a fairly private movement of like-minded people in the early Islamic centuries eventually grew into a major social force that permeated most Muslim societies. The self-articulation of Sufism in the theoretical manuals of the tenth century was followed by the growth of many circles of teaching, initially in the central areas of the old caliphate in Iraq and Persia, but soon reaching to the frontiers of Spain, East Africa, Central Asia, and India. Residential institutions were founded by eminent Sufi teachers, and they rapidly attracted the support of local rulers. Through the orders, Sufism became much more widely known and practiced throughout different levels of society. Distinctive rituals of initiation and special practices were adopted among the many lineages that proliferated in Muslim lands. As Marshall Hodgson observed regarding the growth of medieval Sufi orders, "a tradition of intensive interiorization re-exteriorized its results and was finally able to provide an important basis for social order."[1]

The expression "Sufi orders" adapts a term originally used for the great Christian monastic orders such as the Franciscans and the Benedictines. To the extent that order implies a group of people living together under a common discipline, this term can be usefully employed to describe the various teaching ways (*tariqas*) or chains (*silsilas*) of masters and disciples typical of later Sufism. The analogy cannot be pressed too far, however. While Sufi orders employ ritual initiations and often follow rules that have been codified by founder figures, they do not take the vows of celibacy typical of Christian monks and nuns, nor are they legally authorized by a central authority such as the pope. The authority of Sufi teachers is based on that of the Prophet Muhammad, who is viewed as the source of all Sufi lineages. Although many Sufi lineages have maintained lodges where members could reside under the instruction of a master, there were various levels and degrees of involvement with Sufi orders by merchants, rulers, and ordinary people on a less than full-time basis. While entering a Christian monastic order established an exclusive loyalty to a single order, it has been common for many Sufis to obtain multiple initiations into the practices of several Sufi orders, though the primary orientation would remain in a single order.

When one attempts to describe the Sufi orders, it is necessary to observe once again the difference between the sociological approach of Western Orientalists and the practical engagement of Sufis with particular teachings. That is, Orientalists have tended to see the Sufi orders as social phenomena with clear historical and geographical boundaries. The colorful parades of officially recognized Sufi orders in Cairo, for example, provide the opportunity to identify a particular group of people who are attached to specific lineages and masters. In this sense one could speak of adherents of a particular branch of the Shadhili order in Cairo as a body of people whom one could presumably describe and quantify on the basis of interviews and other research. No doubt part of the description would be a historical account of the lineage of masters and the branching that took place over the years as particular Sufis established distinctive suborders.

Furthermore, the strong sociological and political interests of Western scholars have led to a fascination with Sufi orders as authoritarian structures, and there has been an automatic tendency to view the orders as something like political parties with distinctive ideological characteristics. While this social and historical reality is not ignored by Sufi theorists, they tend to take a different approach when describing the orders. Each chain is of course embodied by the linkage of master to disciple going back through the years all the way to the Prophet. This is seen, however, not as a social institution but as a mystical transmission that makes possible the entry of the individual into the spiritual life. The different ways are not regarded as strictly corporate entities but as spiritual methods or techniques that are maintained and passed on by the community that participates in them.

To reiterate a distinction made at the beginning of this study, the difference between scholarly and personal approaches to the Sufi orders could also be phrased in terms of descriptive and prescriptive viewpoints. When colonial French officials in North Africa wanted to produce a description of Sufi orders with a view to predicting their political behavior, the results were embodied in works like Depont and Coppolani's comprehensive work on "Musulman confraternities," which appeared just a century ago.[2] The account of Sufi orders included in that book was an attempt to articulate the relationships between corporate groups that played powerful roles in society. The descriptive technique of Orientalist scholarship could have practical implications, however. The underlying attitude of colonial officials towards their subject was similar to that of current Western political analysts who attempt to predict the behavior of "fundamentalists" in order to safeguard international policy goals. While most modern scholars of Islamic studies are not involved directly with policy, they also hold the outsider's descriptive position, and the highly politicized character of any discussion of Islam today makes their studies potentially political.

In contrast, if one looks at a compilation such as *The Clear Fountain on the Forty Paths*, written by the North African scholar Muhammad al-Sanusi al-Idrisi (d. 1859), one sees a highly personalized account of the Sufi orders. The book provides examples of *dhikr* practices from forty different Sufi orders from different regions, but they are not selected at random, nor do they claim to describe every existing order. The principle of selection is based on the fact that the author happened to be initiated into all of these practices. He also evidently adjusted the number in order to reach the desirable round figure of forty, since the notion of describing one's forty initiations was already an established literary genre. As a list of the forty orders described in his book indicates (see figure 9, page 112), Sanusi included twelve methods of *dhikr* that were not embodied in actual Sufi orders; these "theoretical" orders are essentially separate meditative practices and psychological emphases, which could be loosely linked to known Sufi masters but which were preserved for transmission by masters who sought multiple initiations. Sanusi's work also served the purpose of showing how his own teaching subsumed and comprehended all the available spiritual methods. As he put it, "The ways to God most high are many—the Shadhiliyya, the Suhrawardiyya, the Qadiriyya, and so forth—so that some say that they are as numerous as the souls of human beings. Nevertheless, although they have many branches, they are in reality one, since the goal of all is one."[3] Similar collections of *dhikr* methods from different orders made by Naqshbandi and Chishti masters in eighteenth-century India likewise worked to establish authoritative personalized teachings based on multiple sources; they were in no way intended as sociological descriptions of the observable activities of large social groups.

The experiential origin of the social institutions of Sufism was the master-disciple relationship. While the Protestant image of Islam visualized a religion without priests, for much of Muslim society the role of intermediaries was of great importance, whether this role was assumed by the Prophet, the Shi'i imams, or the Sufi saints. The Sufi master was known by the Arabic word for an elder (*shaykh*; Persian *pir*), a title also assumed by religious scholars, but the master assumed an extraordinary role as intermediary linked to the Prophet and God. Abu Hafs al-Suhrawardi (d. 1234) described the effect of the master on the disciple as follows:

> When the sincere disciple enters under obedience of the master, keeping his company and learning his manners, a spiritual state flows from within the master to within the disciple, like one lamp lighting another. The speech of the master inspires the interior of the disciple, so that the master's words become the treasury of spiritual states. The state is transferred from the master to the disciple by keeping company and by hearing speech. This only applies to the disciple who restricts himself to the master, who sheds the desire of his soul, and who is annihilated in the master by giving up his own will.[4]

In the most extreme formulation, the disciple was to be to the master like a corpse in the hands of a corpse-washer. It is hard to overestimate the importance of the master-disciple relation in Sufism. Manuals of practice and discipline contain extensive discussions of how the disciple is to behave with respect to the master. Obedience to a master was understood psychologically as renouncing the lower self and replacing it with a purified self made possible by the annihilation of the master's ego. The relationship between the two was indicated by the term *irada*, meaning longing or desire. The disciple is called the *murid*, or one who desires, while the master is the *murad*, or the one who is desired.

From a historical point of view, the first nuclei from which Sufi social institutions began to emerge were the lodges or hospices that were created as residential centers for Sufis, mostly beginning in the eleventh century. It may be that other residential communities were looked to as models by the founders of early Sufi lodges; possible examples of earlier spiritual communities include the Christian monasteries of the Near East and the hospices of the Muslim ascetic movement of the Karramis in tenth-century Central Asia. Sufi writings instead look to the early model of Muslim community as exemplified by groups such as the People of the Bench. As early as the eighth century, a religious community was founded on the island of Bahrein by the ascetic 'Abd al-Wahid ibn Zayd. But the first enduring residential institutions for Sufis emerged in Iran, Syria, and Egypt during the eleventh century and later. These lodges would later be known by a variety of names (Arabic *ribat, zawiya*; Persian *khanqah, jama'at-khana*; Turkish *tekke*), and they could assume several forms, ranging from a large structure for several hundred residents to a simple dwelling connected to the private home of a master. Some of the most important of these early centers were those established by Abu Sa'id (d. 1049) in eastern Iran and the Sa'id al-Su'ada' hospice founded in Cairo by Saladin in 1174.

The social extensions of Sufism did not occur in a vacuum, indeed they may be said to have emerged in order to fill one. Many commentators have observed that the earliest Sufi circles came into existence at the time when the early Arab empire of the caliphate was at the peak of its wealth and power; the asceticism and condemnation of the world expressed by Hasan al-Basri was to some extent a response to the luxury and corruption that went with political power. Yet by the tenth century the caliphate had run its course as a viable political entity, as the caliphs were effectively stripped of power by ambitious soldiers and rebellious governors. This upheaval created a crisis of political legitimacy. Despite the religious shortcomings of the caliphate, which was widely criticized as a worldly royal dynasty, it was the only successful political institution that claimed to perpetuate the sociopolitical order established by Muhammad. But when the Persian armies of the Buyid princes took Baghdad in 945 and made the caliphs into puppets, the ground rules for political legitimacy changed. By the following century, large areas of the eastern former provinces of the empire were under the control of the nomadic Turkish troops of the Seljuks, whose religious credentials were dubious to say the least. The new rulers of Persia and Central Asia quickly adapted to the new situation, taking on both the court culture and the Muslim faith. They soon became patrons of religion by establishing two parallel kinds of institutions to demonstrate their legitimacy: academies for training Muslim scholars, and residential hospices for Sufi devotees. The legitimating role of Sufis became even more pronounced after the destruction of the caliphate by the Mongols in 1258. From that time until European conquest began five centuries later, support of Sufism was an integral part of any regime that invoked the Islamic heritage.

From the start, the relationship between Sufis and rulers created ambiguities. Sufi theorists warned against accepting funds acquired by methods contrary to Islamic law. Critics pointed out contradictions between the ideal of Sufi poverty and the comfortable or even luxurious way of life possible to a "faqir" living in a sumptuously maintained lodge. These contrasts sharpened the traditional distinction between real and imitation Sufis as found in prescriptive Sufi literature. But if Sufis were not to be isolated hermits, they had to interact with the affairs of society; adopting poverty became an internal attitude of detachment rather than a purely external deprivation of possessions. Some Sufi leaders saw the advantages of having the ear of rulers, who could thus be influenced to make decisions based on ethical and religious considerations. They could in this way intercede on behalf of the pious, the poor, and the rejected members of society. Rulers in turn respected Sufi saints as individuals who were connected to an even higher level of authority. After overthrowing the Shi'i Fatimid dynasty, Saladin endowed a number of Sufi lodges in Cairo in the twelfth century, and from that time onward Sufis played leading roles in Egyptian society. One of the first leaders of what became the Suhrawardi Sufi order, Abu Hafs al-Suhrawardi established a close relationship with the contemporary caliph al-Nasir and even acted as an ambassador to Egyptian, Turkish, and Persian kings. His disciple Baha' al-Din Zakariyya (d. 1267), after moving to northwest India, set up a Sufi lodge where he and his successors lived more like kings than dervishes, supported by considerable land revenue. Naqshbandi masters, such as Khwaja Ahrar (d. 1490), owned vast stretches of land and played pivotal roles in the politics of the day. The sometimes uneasy but necessary relationship between kings and dervishes was nicely summarized by the poet Sa'di in his picaresque *Rose Garden*, written in 1258:

> One of the pious saw in a dream a king in heaven and an ascetic in hell. He asked, "What is the cause of the elevation of the one and the debasement of the other, contrary to the people's expectations?"
>
> A voice came saying, "This king is in heaven from following dervishes, and this ascetic is in hell from being near to kings."[5]

The paradoxical ideal was thus to be inwardly a dervish even if wearing the crown of a king.

The organization of the Sufi orders as societies based on teaching lineages seems to have been largely the work of the twelfth and thirteenth centuries. Most Sufi orders are named after a famous figure, who is viewed in effect as the founder (see figure 9, page 112). In this way the Suhrawardiyya order is named after Abu Hafs al-Suhrawardi, the Ahmadiyya after Ahmad al-Badawi, and the Shadhiliyya after Abu al-Hasan al-Shadhili.[6] The founders are generally those masters who have codified and institutionalized the distinctive teachings and practices of the orders, although in many cases their reputations as saints go far beyond the circle of initiates. Most orders were localized to particular regions, though a few such as the Qadiriyya and the Naqshbandiyya are found widely distributed across many Muslim countries. The orders expanded as teaching networks based on initiatic genealogy; each master's authority derived from that of his predecessor in a chain going back to the Prophet Muhammad. Within each main order there are frequently suborders, sometimes designated by composite names with two, three, or more elements to indicate how many levels of branching have occurred. In this way one sees the Ma'rufi-Rifa'i order, the Jarrahi-Khalvati (or Cerrahi-Halveti) order, and the Sulaymani-Nizami-Chishti order. Some of the main sub-branches were formed in the fifteenth and sixteenth centuries or even later.

The institutional support of Sufism inevitably linked teaching circles to centers of political power. The means by which this was carried out established the basis for future relations with the court. Some groups, such as the Chishtiyya, recommended avoiding formal ties through endowments, although accepting donations in cash or kind was permissible with the stipulation that they be spent quickly for appropriate purposes such as food, living expenses, and ritual necessities. When Burhan al-Din Gharib was authorized as a Sufi master, his master Nizam al-Din told him, "Take worthy people as disciples, and on the subject of donations, 'no rejecting, no asking, no saving.' If anyone brings you something, do not reject it, and do not ask for anything, but if they bring a little of something good, do not reject it to get it increased, and do not accept by specifying everything [that you need]."[7] As might be imagined, visitors to Sufi lodges were from all classes, and ordinary people and merchants would make pious donations according to their means. The lodge of Ruzbihan Baqli was constructed by followers belonging to the stone-masons' guild, without support from the ruler of Shiraz.

Despite the desire to remain outside royal control, the significant resources that medieval rulers directed towards the support of Sufi establishments created a constant pressure to accept patronage. When Burhan al-Din Gharib's lodge ceased to have active direction after the death of his successor, the trustees and attendants sought donations and eventually land endowments from the sultans of the Deccan. Ultimately, by the eighteenth century, the shrines of Burhan al-Din and his disciples became extensions of the authority of the court, with royal music balconies built into the shrines themselves for the performance of court ceremonies. This is just one example of the way in which Sufi institutions became integrated into the economic structure of society. The pagan Mongols soon grasped the benefits of associating with Sufis, and they accelerated the pace of patronage of Sufi shrines; the first land revenue for the shrine of Ruzbihan was awarded by a Mongol governor in 1282, at the same time that he converted to Islam. By the sixteenth century, the Ottoman and Mughal empires had established elaborate bureaucratic hierarchies that dispensed royal funds and land revenue to Sufi shrines, often appointing the trustees and regulating the internal affairs of the shrines as well. Shrines were exempted from ordinary taxes on the condition that the attendants pray for the welfare of the ruling dynasty. Descendants of Sufis frequently had opportunities to enter the ranks of the nobility. Probably the bulk of royal support of Sufism was nevertheless directed at the shrines of deceased masters rather than the circles of living teachers. There were fewer opportunities for conflict and controversy with dead saints.

Another, much more radical interpretation of dervish poverty unleashed a very different form of Sufism in the Qalandar movements.[8] With a certain amount of scorn for the comfortable Sufi establishments that had official support, these deliberately deviant wanderers adopted lifestyles that challenged society as directly as the Cynics of the ancient world. The modes of rejection espoused by these ascetics were so varied that they are known in different regions by many different names: Haydaris, Qalandars, Torlaks, Babas, Abdals, Jamis, Madaris, Malangs, and Jalalis. Begging while rejecting property, these wanderers were celibate and practiced severe bodily mortification. They were careless at best about the fulfillment of Islamic ritual duties, and they frequently went naked or wore rough dark wool, with a bizarre assortment of hats and other paraphernalia, including iron chains. In rejection of standard grooming codes, they shaved the hair, eyebrows, mustache, and beard, and many of the groups were renowned for use of hallucinogens and intoxicants. As a symbol, the Qalandar still stands for utter detachment from the world, and the name has been adopted by more conventional Sufi groups such as the Indian Qalandari order at Kakori near Lucknow. But the radical and literal enactment of this idea led to sometimes severe social conflicts, including attacks on more established Sufis, and even full-scale peasant revolts in the Ottoman empire. The legacy of this aggressive kind of renunciation has partly survived in some of the practices of formal orders such as the Bektashis (shaving) and the Rifa'is (unusual mortifications). One can still observe what one scholar dismisses as "spiritual delinquents"[9] at traditional Sufi festivals in different parts of the world today, such as the tomb of La'l Shahbaz Qalandar in Sind, most recently made popular in song by the Pakistani *qawwali* singer Nusrat Fateh 'Ali Khan. Here we have a category that strains any fixed prescriptive definition of Sufism.

The historical development of the Sufi orders is still imperfectly understood, since so many sources remain unstudied. This has not prevented some scholars from attempting to describe a historical pattern to the Sufi orders taken as a whole. The most ambitious attempt to provide a historiographical interpretation was provided by J. Spencer Trimingham, a specialist in the history of Islam in Africa, in his book *The Sufi Orders in Islam*. Trimingham enunciated a three-fold theory of the development of Sufism, which has more than a passing resemblance to the tripartite schemes that litter the landscape of Western historiography (ancient-medieval-modern, and so on). The valuable information collected in this sympathetic and learned compendium is marred by a theory of classicism and decline, divided into three periods. Trimingham called the first period of early Sufism "a natural expression of personal religion . . . over against institutionalized religion based on authority." This stage was succeeded by a second period, of the formation of *tariqas*, or ways, in groups based on chains of masters and disciples, around the twelfth century. The full institutionalization of Sufism into *ta'ifas*, or organizations, was the third and final period, beginning about the fifteenth century. While the association of the orders with saints' tombs as state-sponsored centers of devotion ensured their popular success, Trimingham argues, this institutionalization led to a decline of Sufism from its original pure mysticism. After this point he sees no originality, but sterile repetition of the past, and an unfortunate tendency to hereditary succession of authority. The result of this "deeper spiritual malaise" was the transformation of the orders into hierarchical structures that, to him, were uncomfortably similar to the Christian church and its clergy.[10]

Trimingham's observations contain a modern and strongly Protestant attitude that champions personal religion over institutionalized religion, and his theory of decline logically derives from his assumption that mysticism must be a personal and individual phenomenon. The notion of historical decline is basically a rhetorical strategy for evaluating and classifying history, according to what one considers to be of real value and what constitutes a departure from that. Most theories of the rise and fall of civilizations (from Gibbon to Toynbee) are very selective in the time frames used for comparison, and their assumptions about the relationship between moral status and the success of political power are basically unprovable. The "classicism and decline" model has long exercised a fascination over students of Islamic culture. It is especially odd to notice that the "decline" of Islamic civilization has been unquestioned axiom, accepted until recently by most Orientalists and still maintained by fundamentalists but for different reasons. In both these cases, the colonization of much of the Muslim world and the consequent loss of political power by Muslims were interpreted moralistically as the judgment of either history or God upon a civilization that had become inadequate. The notion of the decline of Muslim nations was especially attractive to the self-image of Europeans in the colonial period, since it provided a noble justification for conquest and empire on the basis of the "civilizing mission" of the West (also known as "the white man's burden"). If we do not intend to support, however, the agendas of either colonialism or fundamentalism, then the notion of classicism and decline is distinctly unhelpful in the study of a tradition such as Sufism.[11] I would like to suggest instead that we need to enlarge our concept of mysticism to include wider social and institutional contexts, if we are to use this word usefully to describe Sufism. Unlike the individualistic notion of originality found in romantic modernism, the expression of mysticism in a vast cumulative tradition such as Sufism rests upon multiple contributions to a common idiom deployed over generations.

Within the Sufi tradition, after the formation of the orders, their articulation in the form of an initiatic lineage was to some extent a retrospective reconstruction. There are few examples of complete lineages going back to the Prophet prior to the eleventh century, and critics were suspicious of their historical authenticity.[12] Yet the symbolic importance of these lineages was immense; they provided a channel to divine authority through the horizontal medium of tradition. Regardless of their verifiability in external historical terms, the chains of masters and disciples were necessary for the transmission of spiritual power and blessings. In a case that I have analyzed separately, Ruzbihan Baqli in his own writings makes no reference to any standard Sufi lineage, nor does he even mention as a teacher any contemporary figure known from other sources. His two great-grandsons, writing a century after his death in 1209, went ahead and supplied him with fully detailed genealogies in the Kazaruni Sufi order. It is as if his mystical experiences in the vertical dimension of spiritual ascension could not be effectively translated into the institutional mode without the guarantees offered by a historical genealogy of previous Sufi masters.[13]

In another respect, the transhistorical character of Sufi initiation seriously undermines the conventional understanding of tradition. The model for this kind of relationship was Uways al-Qarani, a contemporary of the Prophet Muhammad who never met him, but was nevertheless an adept saint, deeply devoted to the Prophet. This kind of internal relationship, called Uwaysi initiation, shows up in a number of well-known Sufi lineages. In this way Abu al-Hasan Kharaqani (d. 1034) was initiated by the spirit of Bayazid Bistami, and this is accepted as a standard link in the Naqshbandi chain of masters. There are in addition a number of famous Sufis who have been initiated by the deathless prophet Khidr. The power of this kind of transhistorical transmission was so great that at certain periods, one finds mention of an Uwaysi (or Uveysi) order as if it were another standard lineage. What is remarkable about this formulation is that it preserves the historical form of the initiatic genealogy while completely somersaulting over the need for external physical contact. The Sufi order, then, as a historical construction has greatest meaning for the person who is being initiated. It creates the line of spiritual transmission and authority to the initiated individual through the central figures of Sufism. It should also be emphasized that the formal orders by no means include all the important figures of Sufism. The names of a number of early Sufi authorities simply do not occur in the principal genealogies. On a more practical level, a rough check of the Department of Charitable Trusts in Pakistan has revealed that about half the shrines of Sufi saints in the Punjab province do not clearly belong to any major Sufi lineage.[14]

So important was the symbolism of the lineage that it was embodied in a ritual of writing out the names of the masters of the order, to construct what was called a tree (*shajara*; see figure 10). A nineteenth-century Indian Sufi author explains how memorizing the chain of masters formed an essential part of the process of meditation, precisely because it made direct access to the Prophet possible:

FIGURE 10. Initiatic Genealogy or "Tree" (*shajara*) of the Indian Naqshbandi Order.

It is necessary for the disciple, after receiving from his own
master the names of the [preceding] masters, that he memorize them up to the revered exemplar of prophecy (blessings
and peace be upon him). This is one of the requirements of
the seeker on this path. For the one practicing spiritual exercises it is necessary to bring the master to mind during *dhikr*
and meditation. If he is not successfully present [in the meditation,] at first he thinks of the master. If he still does not
attain presence, [he thinks of] the master of the master. If
he still does not attain presence, [he thinks of] the master of
the master of the master. If he still does not attain presence,
[he thinks of] the master of the master of the master of the
master, all the way up to the Prophet (God bless him and his
family and give them peace). While recalling each of these
saints to whom the revered [Prophet] has given the hand [of
initiation,] he begins the *dhikr* with that one [that is, the
Prophet], and visualizes him in the form of the master. Then
he asks for assistance and practices the *dhikr*.[15]

Knowing the names of previous masters has a virtue comparable
to the recitation of the names of God; the spiritual qualities of those
saints will communicate themselves to those who write or recite their
names. Writing out a genealogical tree is said to have become necessary in later times, when the number of intermediaries multiplied.
This distance in time from the Prophet is not necessarily a diminu-
tion of spiritual power. Since the chains are attested by trustworthy
masters, those with more links have greater merit—just as additional
lamps contribute more light. Authorities differ on the question of
where to start writing the tree. Some prefer to begin with the
Prophet, but others start with their own names and ascend up
through the masters, to fulfill the manners of respect to each in
order.

While the genealogical tree is probably the most elemental representation of a Sufi order, there are much more detailed constructions

of the historical relations of masters and disciples. Some tree documents contain brief biographical notes, and they represent not only the principal masters but also the circles of minor disciples that surrounded them. While a simple tree document can be contained on one page, there are shrines in India where genealogical scrolls hundreds of feet long are preserved. The precise meaning of these more complicated diagrams is elusive in the absence of oral commentary. Eminent masters of other orders are juxtaposed alongside the chief representatives of a chain in a relationship that is suggestive but enigmatic. It is clear that each document represents a principal line of transmission that eventually reaches the disciple whose name is inscribed at the bottom.

The apparently simple statement of authority contained in these graphic representations conceals significant differences of opinion about legitimate succession. As was the case with the Shi'i imams, Sufi shaykhs did not always leave a single successor whose authority was unambiguously recognized by all. The branching off of sublineages is an implicit acknowledgement of multiple authority in a Sufi order. Each individual representation of the order will, however, consider itself as a single uncontested chain of mastery. A case in point is the Indian Chishtiyya, among whom an archaic formulation referred to "the twenty-two masters" as forming the ancient cycle of authority in the order. Members of the order in northern India, who begin by counting the angel Gabriel as first in the sequence, still regard the last figure in this chain of twenty-two to be the principal disciple of Nizam al-Din Awliya in Delhi, Nasir al-Din Mahmud Chiragh-i Dihli (d. 1356). The branch of the Chishtiyya that settled in southern India thinks differently; starting with the Prophet as first, they count Nizam al-Din Awliya's disciple Burhan al-Din Gharib (d. 1337) as twenty-first and his successor Zayn al-Din Shirazi (d. 1369) as twenty-second.[16] The same structure can in this way support conflicting identifications of the standard-bearers of the tradition.

The structures of authority revealed in tree documents took on much more complicated dimensions in biographical dictionaries of Sufi saints. While the early hagiographies broke down their subject into generations, following the model of biographies of *hadith* scholars, the proliferation of Sufi orders as distinct lineages encouraged the production of collections of lives of Sufis belonging to particular orders. A Sufi order thus tended to be locally defined in biography, through narrative texts that stood midway between the simple genealogy and the comprehensive hagiographies that strove for inclusiveness rather than definition. It is surprising how widely two accounts of a single Sufi order could differ; as Bruce Lawrence has shown, the Indian scholar 'Abd al-Haqq Muhaddith (d. 1642) and the Mughal prince Dara Shikuh (d. 1659) both produced histories of the Qadiri order during the early seventeenth century, but their visions of the nature of the order and its leading figures were quite dissimilar.[17] It was also not uncommon for hagiographies of particular orders to include significant reference to local political authorities who supported (or resisted) the authority of the order; this political tendency even included dedications to royal patrons, placing these hagiographies at least partly in the courtly and dynastic tradition.

The larger biographical dictionaries made some attempt to describe relations between the different Sufi orders. Some relied on the classification of twelve Sufi schools proposed by Hujwiri in the eleventh century, despite the fact that these were theoretical tendencies that Hujwiri admitted were not for the most part preserved by living traditions. He designated these twelve schools by the names of famous early Sufis, but they do not correspond to any of the well-known Sufi orders of later times. Still, many later authors writing in Persian employed the same technique of using leading early Sufis as the basis for their own classifications, frequently in a classification system of "the fourteen families." Much work remains to be done in order to get a clear picture of the way Sufi orders were represented in such texts.

Another variable in Sufi orders has been the adoption of Shi'ism.

While most Sufis revere the family of the Prophet and in particular the twelve Imams beginning with 'Ali, some Sufi groups carried this farther than others. Among the Kubrawis reverence for the house of the Prophet was particularly strong. Other groups—such as the Nurbakhshis, the Dhahabis, the Khaksar, and the Ni'matallahis (Nimatullahis)—have explicitly adopted the norms of Twelver Shi'i Islam, the form of Shi'ism prevalent in Iran. The overall relationship between Sufism and Shi'ism is difficult to formulate, because neither term has hard-and-fast boundaries. Some historians argue that the Sufi orders filled the void left by the defeat of Isma'ili Shi'ism, in the form of the Fatimid empire in Egypt and the Assassins in Syria and Iran (in Isma'ili Shi'ism, a continuous series of Imams descended from the Prophet is recognized as holding supreme authority; today many Isma'ilis regard the Aga Khan as the present Imam). Both Sufism and Isma'ilism are forms of spiritual esotericism made available to the people through charismatic leaders. Others point to the remarkably similar descriptions of the spiritual qualities possessed by the Sufi master and the Shi'i Imam. The very notion of sainthood is conceptually and historically related to the authority of the Imams. Some Sufi genealogies explicitly include the first six or eight Imams, and 'Ali figures as the first transmitter of Sufism from the Prophet in nearly all genealogies, with the notable exception of the Naqshbandis, for whom Abu Bakr plays this role.

An assertion that is often met with is that Sufism, especially through the Sufi orders, was one of the principal channels for the diffusion of Islam. The notion that one gets is that Sufis acted as missionaries, bringing people around the world into the fold of Islam through example, sermon, and persuasion. It is also frequently maintained that the remarkable literary production of Sufis in local languages (see chapter 6) was part of a deliberate effort of conversion. There are a number of problems with this idea. First of all, the concept of Sufis spreading Islam contains a number of unexamined assumptions about the relationship between the terms *Sufism* and

Islam and also about the nature of conversion. What does it mean to become a Muslim? From the viewpoint of Islamic law, the simple assertion of the profession of faith (in the unity of God and the prophecy of Muhammad) constitutes the minimum form of submission to God. Making this simple transition constitutes a juridical change of status, but it does not in itself indicate anything further about the degree to which an individual follows Islamic law and ritual. In other words, one could become a Muslim but be religiously indifferent or even act reprehensibly; to use internal religious language, one who has submitted to God (*muslim*) may not be dedicated enough to be considered faithful (*mu'min*), and may even through disobedience to God become an infidel (*kafir*). To the external sociological observer, however, the question of religious practice and devotion is entirely subordinated to the issue of group identity. In other words, the outsider only wants to know whether an individual can be classified as a member of the Muslim community or some other religious group. The term *conversion* also has strongly Christian implications, linked to the very strong Christian missionary programs of the modern era.

From what we know of the Sufis, it is difficult to make a case for them as self-conscious missionaries. Sufi manuals do not contain any instructions for converting nonbelievers to Islam. Travel to foreign lands is recommended for Sufis, to be sure, but as a difficult penance for the lower self rather than as a missionary tour. Sufism was self-consciously esoteric; if the ordinary Muslim could not understand it, how should one expect Sufis to seek a following among those who had never even heard of the Prophet? Because of the modern preoccupation with ideology in politics, it is customary to look at the medieval societies ruled by Arabs, Turks, and Persians as Muslim societies. Certainly the rulers of these societies acknowledged the authority of the Prophet and Islamic law through certain legal institutions, but the degree of application of Islamic law varied widely, as did the amount of local custom and ancient political tradition. It is important to remember, too, that Muslims were minorities for long periods of time in many lands where they are now majorities and that their political structures were composites of different systems; to call these Muslim societies is a simplification. Certainly the Arabs had an amazingly successful period of conquest in the period immediately following the Prophet, but contrary to the standard stereotype, conversion of nonbelievers to Islam was not an objective of that military program. Nor was the Turkish conquest of northern India a campaign by religious fanatics to turn heathen Hindus into Muslims. Still, it is clearly through the political support of expansive imperial regimes that Islamic legal and religious institutions have been maintained. The accretion of Islamic norms among subject populations must have been a centuries-long gradual process—in which different groups and individuals took on particular customs and practices for a variety of reasons, while still preserving differences of ethnicity, language, class, and wealth. That kind of explanation has not satisfied European Christians, who have for centuries been intent upon a program of missionary conversion. They at first concocted ferocious images of Islam as "the religion of the sword." In the nineteenth century, Christian missionaries and colonial officials then imagined that there must also have been some Muslim counterparts to themselves, who brought about a change of heart that caused non-Muslims to convert. This imagined Muslim missionary they identified as the Sufi.

While there are premodern texts that describe early Sufis as instrumental in the Islamization of whole tribes and regions, there are strong reasons for interpreting these accounts as political and economic claims that invoke the Sufis as authorities for legitimation. Some late political histories portray Sufis as the peaceful or militant agents of Islam, but neither of these images can be found in early Sufi literature. One suspects that later princes and royal chroniclers found it very useful to portray ancient saints as forerunners of their own claims to domination. Oral traditions collected by colonial administrators in the nineteenth century have frequently portrayed Sufi saints performing miracles that caused whole tribes to become Muslims. This kind of story was frequently linked, however, with issues of patronage and control of saints' shrines administered by large landowners. Today the Islamic regime of Pakistan identifies famous early Sufis as missionaries of Islam, and by extension, as predecessors of the modern state; India, in contrast, invokes some of the same saints as examples of its own official secularist tolerance (both countries are sensitive, in different ways, to the powerful implications of joining or separating the terms *Sufism* and *Islam*). But if we momentarily decouple the Sufis from political issues of this type, it is still possible to construct an estimate of the effect of Sufi institutions on non-Muslim populations, especially since Sufi shrines to this day are widely frequented by Hindus, Sikhs, Christians, and others. In other words, while there was no overt missionary policy among Sufi orders, the impact of the shrines established to commemorate famous saints probably played a significant role in popularizing certain Islamic norms and practices among non-Muslims.[18]

How did one join a Sufi order? Sufis trace the customs of initiation to the Prophet Muhammad and to the way in which he was said to have formalized his relationship with his disciples. The term used for initiation, *bay'a*, is taken from the oath of allegiance that Muhammad's followers swore to him. The basic elements of the initiation were shaking hands and the presentation of garments, usually a cloak but frequently also a hat or other apparel. Often men's heads were shaved, again in imitation of the action of the Prophet. Muhammad remarked, "My companions are like the stars; whichever of them you follow will guide you." This is understood by extension as an allusion to the Sufi masters. How masters judged whether someone should be taken on as a disciple was another question. Frequently it was said that the master gazed upon the tablets of destiny to see if the disciple's connection was decreed from pre-eternity; in other words, not everyone had the proper affinity. The exact procedures of initiation differed from one order to another. Here is an interesting and detailed account of the ritual from a master of the Shattari and Qadiri orders who lived in Lahore at the end of the seventeenth century.[19] First the prospective disciple should bring fruit and flowers and sweets, if he can afford it, to present to the dervishes; if the disciple is poor, some flowers will do. "For there is no reliance on the life of this world; there is no telling what will happen from one hour to the next." The procedure that follows is complex and dramatic:

> When he intends to become a disciple, he does not suddenly go to the lodge, nor does he tell anyone. First he goes to kiss the feet of the master's attendant, saying, "I long for the revered master; cast me at the feet of the revered master, and have me be accepted." Then the attendant takes him by the hand to the presence of the revered master. When he gets near the room, he kisses the room. When he sees the master, he kisses the ground. Then when he is taken to the feet of the master, he quickly places his head at the feet of the master and kisses them, with much crying and emotion, saying, "I long to be a disciple; accept me and make me one of your slaves." Then the master should excuse himself and say, "I am not worthy to be a master. There are others greater than I; go, be a disciple of them." But he should seize the feet of the master and say, "I am very certain about you. Without you, I have no belief in any other, nor will I be a disciple of anyone else." When the master sees a pure intention, he tells the attendant to make this person perform ablutions and then bring him back. After having him perform ablutions, the attendant has him face the master, with the master's back towards Mecca, so the disciple is facing Mecca, standing before the master and taking his hand. The master should first have him say three times the formula of seeking forgiveness. . . . Then the master should say, "I am not wor-

thy to be a master. Accept me as a brother." The disciple says, "I accept you as a master." Then the master says, "Have you accepted me as a master?" The disciple says, "Yes, I have accepted you as a master." Then in this way, the master makes him accepted in every order that he intends, from himself up to the Prophet Muhammad (peace be upon him).

Then follow detailed instructions for reciting Qur'anic passages, prayers for forgiveness, abjuration of the devil, obedience to God, vows of upright behavior, prayers of thanksgiving, and general celebration and congratulations from other disciples. The master takes scissors and cuts some hair from the right side of the disciple's forehead and then has the disciple take a vow to perform the five pillars of Islam (profession of faith, ritual prayer, fasting, pilgrimage, and alms). Then he places a hat with four corners on the disciple's head for a regular Shattari initiation, although the hat may differ if it is a Shah Madari or Naqshbandi initiation. He then tells the disciple to write out the tree of the order's genealogy, first writing in himself the name of the disciple. The disciple's offerings are then distributed, with the first portion going to the new disciple. The offerings are divided into three parts: one for the attendants, one for visitors whether rich or poor, and one for the master. If the master has a family, however, the offering is divided into four parts, with the fourth part going to his wife. The manner of initiating women disciples is basically the same as for men, except that they refrain from the physical contact of the handshake and the cutting of hair. Instead, the woman disciple puts her fingers into a cup of water into which the master places his index finger; if she has a scarf, she holds one end while the master holds the other. For men disciples, it concludes with placing the right hand between the hands of the master. This symbolizes reaching the Prophet through the intermediate degrees of the masters who have each performed this ritual in the past.

There were a number of relationships with a Sufi order indicated by rituals in which the presentation of a cloak (*khirqa*) from a master was an important symbol.[20] In this respect Sufi customs paralleled the customs of caliphal and royal courts, where the gifts of rich fabrics and garments were an important part of courtly ritual. Again, Sufis traced this custom to the practice of the Prophet, as for instance when he made a point of giving a special shirt to an Ethiopian woman disciple named Umm Khalid, telling her to wear it out. The symbolism of the shirt also recalls the story of the prophet Joseph. In the Qur'anic account the scent of Joseph carried by his shirt restored the eyesight of his blind father Jacob; it is said that this shirt (the "many-colored coat" of biblical tradition) was the very shirt that Gabriel provided to the prophet Abraham when Nimrod threw him naked into the fire. Some Sufi orders refer in addition to the shirt given to the Prophet by Gabriel and worn by him during his ascension; this is believed to have been handed down by masters to their successors over the generations. In earlier times, the cloak was frequently dark blue, according to some because it was easier to keep clean. Another form it took was that of a patched cloak. In any case, the importance of the garment is a reminder of the original etymology of Sufism from *suf*, or wool. The principal types of cloak used in early Sufi rituals were the cloak of longing or discipleship (*irada*), given to the true disciple, and the cloak of blessing (*tabarruk*). The cloak of discipleship signifies the relationship between master and disciple and is a constant reminder of the master's presence. More than that, as the stories of the shirts of the prophets suggest, the shirt is a sign of the possibility of the presence of God; in the cloak the disciple sees divine mercy and grace. The cloak of blessing is available to those who are not at the point of becoming disciples but who are drawn to Sufism. They obtain the blessing of the garment of the Sufis and will be influenced by them, perhaps to the point of becoming disciples some day. Another type of cloak found in later times was the cloak of succession (*khilafa*), given to a disciple who was judged to be ready to stand in the master's place and initiate others. The term for a successor (*khalifa*) is the same term used for the successors of the Prophet, usually Anglicized as caliph. This indicates once again how important the model of the Prophet was for Sufis, particularly in such a crucial area as the transmission of religious knowledge and authority.

The emphasis on something so apparently external as dress brings us back to something very important about Sufism: namely, external comportment as a necessary part of the mystical tradition. Contrary to the subjective and individual character of mysticism as it is often understood in the modern West, Sufism requires that inner experience be coordinated with correct social interaction. This is why the term *Sufi* was defined at the beginning of this study as a prescriptive ethical concept. This stress on the social dimension found its expression in the formulation of rules of conduct, designed for the use of a community. The form that these rules took was the enumeration of morals or ethical norms (*adab*), an approach that also had been articulated for other areas of Muslim society, such as the court. The earliest collections of such norms predated the establishment of the Sufi orders, and they dealt with general topics, such as relations between master and disciple, relations with fellow disciples, and the control of selfish desires. More detailed rules appeared in the first lodges, such as that of Abu Sa'id in eastern Iran, where a list of ten rules applying to communal life emphasized purity, constant prayer, meditation, and hospitality. Later rules became more elaborate, and they included many dispensations or relaxations of the stricter rules that suggest a wider circle of adherents than previously. Topics such as how to behave during performance of music and poetry were treated in detail, including such items as how to divide Sufi cloaks that had been torn in ecstasy. Other forms of behavior covered in these manuals were things such as how to sit with the master, how to behave while traveling, how to respond to offers of food when fasting, and how to deal with pride in one's literary accomplishments. Disciples are warned to refrain from the company of mad

Qalandars, wine drinkers, and disreputable Sufis. As usual in the case of pointedly detailed rules, one suspects that particular cases of ostentatious, bad behavior lie behind each of these stipulations. The sheer volume and detail of the many manuals of ethical conduct testify to the widespread application of the Sufi path to many different circles of teaching in widely scattered locations, which still shared the basic ethical concern of regulating one's behavior with God, with Sufis, and with other people in general. It is especially in this sense that one can regard the Sufi orders as the organized means for applying the insights of mystical experience in society at large.

6
Sufi Poetry

Listen to the way this reed flute grieves,
telling stories of its separations.

—RUMI, MASNAVI 1:1 (ED. ISTI‘LAMI)

OF ALL THE PRODUCTS of the Sufi tradition, by far the best known and most appreciated is the legacy of Sufi poetry, together with the music and dance that have accompanied it for hundreds of years. When European Orientalists "discovered" Sufism at the end of the eighteenth century, it was primarily Sufi poetry that excited them and convinced them that they had found something wonderful in the culture of the East. To be sure, the discovery of literary Sufism required separating it from a rigidly conceived Islam. Sufi poetry was first interpreted in terms of universal romantic norms and then "derived" from Greek, Christian, and Hindu sources. Goethe and Emerson were enthralled by the translations of Persian Sufi poetry produced by Sir William Jones and Friedrich Ruckert. British colonial officials, required to learn Persian for diplomacy and revenue gathering, were exposed to the standard curriculum of classical Persian literature for their language examinations. Throughout the nineteenth century, scholarly debates continued over the interpretation of great poets like Hafiz and Rumi. Were their references to wine and love to be taken in a literal or in a symbolic sense? Beyond this academic discussion, the public reception of this poetry was to be largely determined by factors having less to do with historical Sufism than with the internal cultural dynamics of Euro-American society.

The great example of the public reception of Persian poetry in the West was the fortuitous success of Edward FitzGerald's translation of the scattered quatrains attributed to a very minor Persian poet (and major scientist), 'Umar Khayyam. In 1859 FitzGerald, who was a better poet than a scholar, stitched together unconnected Persian verses of uncertain authorship into a rambling ode to skepticism and revolt against Victorian morality; his version of the *Ruba'iyat* was incidentally of higher quality than the original.[1] FitzGerald's work remained obscure until discovered in a bookstore sale bin by Dante Gabriel Rossetti and the Pre-Raphaelites, at which point "Omar" became the center of a literary cult. By the turn of the century, Fitz-Gerald's work had been translated into all major languages, and Omar Khayyam clubs had been formed around the world. The *Ruba'iyat* is probably the most widely known piece of English poetry of the nineteenth century. Khayyam was not a Sufi, though the quatrains contain imagery that is familiar in much of Sufi poetry. But there is something remarkable about the apotheosis of a Persian author in foreign lands, when he had been largely discounted as a poet in his own country until his sudden international fame was perceived back home. One might liken the Khayyam phenomenon to the "pizza effect," in which a homely Italian style of leftover preparation took on a new form abroad and became an international favorite, eventually returning to its homeland to receive a new acceptance. This is not to say that Western audiences are incapable of understanding poetry from other cultures. But there is a signal here that the act of translation is a kind of interpretation that can redefine texts in new and unexpected ways. The present international popularity of Sufi poetry, Sufi music, and Sufi dancing needs to be understood partly in terms of the Sufi tradition and partly in terms of what can be called, for lack of a better term, popular culture. The other Islamic artistic traditions that have a mystical aspect—that is, calligraphy and painting—have not been nearly as easy to transport outside connoisseur circles. The remarks that follow in this chapter and the next will provide a framework for understanding the historical background of the role of literature, music, and dance in Sufism, with occasional asides on the reception of these forms in modern popular culture.

The Basics of Islamicate Poetry

Sufi poetry has been composed in a variety of languages. Initially, in the ninth century, Arabic was used as a vehicle for mystical expression in verse, followed closely by Persian beginning in the eleventh century. Sufis began composing verse in other mother tongues such as Turkish and early Hindi in the thirteenth century. One could expand the list to include a variety of African and Asian languages, all of which have continued to be employed by Sufis until the present day. To give a comprehensive overview of this massive literature is beyond the scope of this essay.[2] Still, it is possible to point out some important aspects of the literary traditions of Sufi poetry, including the principal poetic forms, images, and conventions used by Sufis. This poetry was not simply inspired individual utterance; it was also a highly complex and deliberately composed literature, with more or less elaborate rules of rhyme and meter, and complicated codes of symbolic interpretation that presupposed an intimate acquaintance with the subject. The power of Sufi poetry is borne out not only by its devotees in its traditional contexts but also by the deep and emotional debates that have surrounded its interpretation by Western scholars since the discovery of literary Sufism two centuries ago.

For those who are not familiar with the details of these traditions, it may be said that in general, for Arabic and Persian, the principal poetic forms with which we are concerned are four: the ode (*qasida*), the lyric (*ghazal*), the quatrain (*ruba'i*), and the epic (*masnavi*). The ode was the major verse form of pre-Islamic Arabic poetry, and it is commonly thought that the lyric derives from the erotic prelude (*nasib*) with which the odes generally began. With the exception of the epic verse, which derives from Persian, the same basic rhyme scheme is used in all the other forms. Rhythmically, Arabic verse followed a strict system of quantitative meter, based on long and short syllables. The many possible meters, which had from two to four syllables in a foot, were also the theoretical basis for Persian, Turkish, and Urdu poetry in Arabic script, although earlier poetic traditions in those languages may have been nonquantitative; this situation resembles the use of Greek quantitative meters (iambic pentameter, and so forth) to describe the stressed verses of English and other European languages. The basic unit in all these cases is the single verse, which is always divided in two; poetry is generally written with the two halves in parallel columns. In the ode, the *ghazal*, and the quatrain, the two halves of the first line rhyme, and in following verses only the second half of the line preserves the rhyme. The structure is therefore:

a   a
b   a
etc.

From this formal point of view the only difference between these forms is their length. The quatrain consists of only two complete lines or four half-verses. The lyric is customarily from six to twenty lines, and the ode may be from twenty-five to several hundred lines in length. Both Arabic and Persian are far richer in rhymes than English, so that the composition of a long ode with a single rhyme is not so difficult a feat as it might appear. The epic form, which originated in Persian bardic tradition, resembles the couplet (*masnavi* is the Persian pronunciation of *mathnawi*, an Arabic term meaning

"doubled"). Here the two halves of each verse rhyme, but each suc-
ceeding verse takes a different rhyme, as follows:

a   a
b   b
c   c
etc.

The epic form can be extended to truly enormous lengths, since it is
not limited to the resources of a single rhyme. The royal *Book of
Kings*, composed by Firdawsi, is around sixty thousand lines, and the
Masnavi, the large mystical epic poem by Rumi, is about half that
size.

Arabic Sufi Poetry

To appreciate the aesthetics of Sufi poetry, it is important first of
all to acknowledge the role of pre-Islamic Arabic poetry in the formation of Islamic culture. The Qur'an certainly has had a tremendous
impact on the sense of beauty for Muslims, both for its sound and
for its visual appearance. But the Prophet Muhammad was careful
to distinguish the Qur'an from the poetry of the Arab tribes, which
was produced by bards claiming inspiration from the jinn. The
Qur'anic revelation was of divine origin, not a human composition,
and it transformed life in a way that ordinary poetry could not. "The
poets are followed by the misguided. Have you not seen them raving
in every valley, while they are saying what they do not do?" (Qur'an
26:224–26). Yet the Prophet also appreciated poetry, and he was addressed in memorable verse by Hassan ibn Thabit, a well-known poet
who became a Muslim. The moral status of much of pre-Islamic
poetry was from one point of view ambiguous, because of its glorifi-
cation of tribal warfare, wine drinking, profane amours, and pride.
Muhammad's career effected an ethical revolution in Arabia, replac-

ing the boasts of the warrior with submission to God. Still, the long odes (*qasidas*) of the tribal poets endured as literary models, playing a role for the high caliphate similar to the Greek and Latin classics for European culture. The themes of search for the beloved and reflections on nature, along with distinctive Arabian symbols, all became staples in later Arabic literature and related traditions. Appreciation of this heritage has until recently been hampered by the jaundiced attitude with which many Western scholars viewed Arabic poetry; as a consequence, Arabic Sufi poetry has attracted much less attention than Sufi poetry in Persian. Fortunately, members of the "Chicago school" of the study of Arabic poetry—established by Jaroslav Stetkevych, and including scholars such as Michael Sells and Th. Emil Homerin—have produced new and vigorous translations that open up new vistas for perceiving the aesthetic power of Arabic poetry as appropriated by the Sufi tradition.

The conquests of the Arabs had placed in the hands of the caliphs a vast empire stretching from the Atlantic to India. In the eighth century, the Umayyad house ruled very much in the style of the vanquished Persian shahs and Roman caesars. Despite the commitment to Islamic institutions by the empire, the caliphs themselves and their noble entourage often found the life of royal luxury tempting, and the strictures of Islamic law against wine were ignored in favor of the customs of ancient Persia. Following the royal lifestyle, Arab nobles enjoyed the hunt as their prerogative, and often afterwards they might choose to relax in a convivial setting where wine might be obtained. What better place than a Christian monastery in the countryside, where wine was permitted as a requirement of Christian ritual? From such scenes derived a type of secular Arabic poetry, which extolled the delights of wine while praising the beautiful objects found in the monastery. The youthful Christian boy or girl who brought and served the wine would become, as in ancient Greek poetry, the object of affectionate entreaties and passionate declarations produced by intoxication. The result was an aesthetic deliberately intended to shock Islamic religious sensibilities. The poets, including a few from the Umayyad house, spoke of the cross and the monastery, the joy of wine, and their love of the beautiful cupbearer (*saqi*). This profane trend of poetry was mirrored in the cosmopolitan culture of Baghdad, where the archaic poems of the bedouin lost favor as urban folk lost touch with nomadic ways. The brilliant and dissolute Abu Nuwas (d. 815) stands as a monument to how poetry of genius could be celebrated at court despite its unmistakably defiant focus on wine and sex.[3]

Since much of early Arabic Sufi poetry seems to have been lost, it is known for the most part through brief quotations of verses attributed to early masters, as quoted in later handbooks on Sufism.[4] Many of these verses use the same imagery of love and wine found in secular poetry, so the only thing to distinguish them as mystical is their context and interpretation. Probably the best known example is the cerebral and passionate poetry of Hallaj, of which several hundred verses (some of dubious authenticity) were collected by Louis Massignon from various sources.[5] Many of these were well-known and frequently quoted by later authors. Some of his verses stress love as union with God:

> I am he whom I desire, whom I desire is I;
>> we are two spirits dwelling in a single body.
> If you see me, you have seen him,
>> and if you see him, you have seen us.[6]

Others are abstract meditations, densely laden with the vocabulary of Sufi psychology, or riddles based on the Arabic alphabet. Some of the most notable verses attributed to Hallaj are presented as premonitions of his execution, such as the famous poem beginning, "Kill me, my trustworthy friends! for in my killing is my life. . . ."[7] It is hard to know whether these poems were composed by Hallaj or were written in the style of Hallaj by later authors.

The origins of Arabic mystical verse probably lie in the rhythmic qualities of prayer. The powerful poetic reverberations of the Qur'an as recited on a daily basis must have had a deep impact on the verbalization of religious feeling. Arabic mystical prose writings often display the fascination with rhymed and metrical prose (*saj'*) that is one of the most striking aspects of Arabic literature in general. The short prayers and verses of Rabi'a are outstanding instances of this kind of poetry. Probably the best-preserved Arabic mystical poems are those that continue to be recited by Sufi orders in communal sessions, often accompanied by music (see chapter 7). Arabic poems in praise of God and the saints, written by the North African saint Abu Madyan, can still be heard in Morocco, and Arabic Sufi songs of more recent vintage are performed in Egypt, Sudan, and other countries.[8]

The most famous examples of Arabic Sufi poetry partake of the courtly literary tradition, while still preserving conventions of the pre-Islamic ode with its evocation of nomadic society. While much of the poetry that Ibn 'Arabi inserted into his massive mystical treatise, *The Meccan Revelations*, forms part of highly technical discussions, even here he still recites the names of lovers famed in early Arabic verse. But it is particularly in his *Interpreter of Desires* that we see Ibn 'Arabi making full use of the powerful imagery of the desert.[9] Composed in Mecca in 1215, these poems honor the elegant young Persian woman named Nizam, whom Ibn 'Arabi had met there some thirteen years previously while he was studying prophetic *hadith* with her father and aunt. Although he announced in the preface that the true subject of the work was mystical, the poems have all the earmarks of standard erotic verse, so that some readers evidently complained that Ibn 'Arabi was conducting a love affair that was hardly in keeping with his reputation for piety. At the request of two disciples, Ibn 'Arabi then wrote a commentary to explain the mystical interpretation of the verses, in which, he said, "I indicate lordly knowledge, divine illuminations, spiritual secrets, rational truths, and religious admonitions, but I have expressed them in the style of the erotic lyric. This is because of the soul's passionate love of these expressions, so that they have abundant reasons for paying attention to them. This is the language of every cultivated writer and elegant spiritual person."[10] He employed the erotic style, in other words, because that is how poetry is written, and that is what people like. Some of his poems scarcely differ in imagery from standard love poetry in the classical style and are replete with traces of ruined campfires, camels, flash floods in the desert, and Christian monasteries where a beautiful girl is encountered; the commentary makes it clear, however, that these are not to be understood literally. One short illustration will suffice:

> She said, "I wonder at a youth who with his charms
> swaggers through the flowers and the gardens."
> I said, "Do not wonder at what you see;
> you see yourself in the mirror of a man."[11]

Ibn ʿArabi employs what is apparently lovers' repartee to discuss how the divine presence seeks passionate love from humanity; when a human becomes a perfect slave of God, then God becomes the eye and ear of that person, who becomes all light and a perfect reflection of God's qualities.

Even more important for Arabic Sufi poetry is Ibn al-Farid (d. 1235), an Egyptian whose dense verses have attracted enthusiastic audiences and generated numerous commentaries over the centuries. Ibn al-Farid was a master of the poetry of love and wine, containing strong allusions to the classical tradition combined with clear references to Sufi practice. His longer compositions, particularly the famous *Wine Ode* (*Khamriyya*) and the *Poem of the Way*, became mainstays of Sufi interpretation and performance. In the opening of the *Wine Ode* one can see how he combines wine imagery with distinct signals of its mystical interpretation: "We drank to the beloved's memory a wine / with which we were drunk before the vine was created." During his own lifetime, he was known primarily as a poet with Sufi leanings. The growing popularity of his verse after his death led to a larger reputation, however. His poetry was collected by his grandson 'Ali, who added a biography of Ibn al-Farid as an introduction. In this biography the poet appears, for the first time, with the qualities of a Sufi saint. He is described as going into a trance for ten days before producing the *Poem of the Way*, in an account that has more than passing similarity to portrayals of prophecy and divination. 'Ali also relates a number of miracle stories attesting the power of Ibn al-Farid as a saint. Commentators within a couple of generations explained his poetry by saying that he was a mystic who had scaled the heights of inner experience. His verses were systematically interpreted in light of the metaphysics of the school of Ibn 'Arabi.

Partly because of this linkage with a position that some conservative scholars considered dangerous, in later centuries Ibn al-Farid was attacked, and his works were put on trial; his defenders proved more powerful than his detractors, however. His tomb in Cairo continued to be a site of pilgrimage, and the musical sessions held there have featured ecstatic recitation of the odes of Ibn al-Farid, as several travelers have recorded. In the nineteenth century, the combination of the indifference of modernizers and the hostility of reformers led to the decline of the shrine, though the annual festival has been revived in recent years by a Rifa'i Sufi order. Th. Emil Homerin has explored the poetic legacy of Ibn al-Farid and has shown how the two main early tendencies of interpretation—doctrinal interpretation in terms of Ibn 'Arabi, and sanctification of the poet—have drawn attention away from the poetry itself considered as literature; another major interpretation, derived from European scholars like Nicholson, interpreted Ibn al-Farid's poetry mainly as a record of personal mystical experience.[12] We shall return later to the problem of the transformation of poetry into sacred text. The later history of Arabic Sufi poetry has not yet been written. The tendency to view early Arabic literature as a classical golden age has encouraged a tendency to dismiss the Arabic poetry of the Mamluk and Ottoman periods as a decline from the earlier standard, but there is much still to be learned in this field.

Persian Sufi Poetry

Persian Sufi poetry too had its origin in the community of the Sufi lodge. While the ode (*qasida*) and the lyric (*ghazal*) were cultivated at the courts of the former caliphal governors in eastern Iran, it was the quatrain (*ruba'i*) that was preferred for the expression of brief mystical insights. The language was often direct and simple, but paradoxical. When Abu Sa'id quoted these anonymous verses, it was because they were so memorable, and they communicated a point. In the eleventh and twelfth centuries, the Persian quatrain became the standard way to clinch a point in Sufi literature. Thus 'Ayn al-Qudat concludes a discussion of mystical love:

> Last night my idol placed his hand upon my breast,
>   he seized me hard and put a slave-ring in my ear.
> I said, "My beloved, I am crying from your love!"
>   He pressed his lips on mine and silenced me.[13]

The scenes of ecstasy we see recounted in Sufi literature—describing music and poetry where verses like this were shouted extempore or recalled from memory—reveal poetry as a vehicle for the communication of experience in the most powerful terms.

As with Arabic Sufi poetry, a number of the subjects and themes of mystical poetry were taken over wholesale into Persian from the profane literary tradition. Now these same themes were subject to allegorical interpretation, transformed according to rules outside the text of the verses. Wine was no longer the stuff poured by the caliph's servants but now became the intoxication of divine love. The Christian boy or girl who poured wine in the monastery became a symbol for the Sufi master, the Prophet, or even God; in Persia, the difference now was that a local Persian non-Muslim was substituted, and so the winebearer became a Magian (Zoroastrian) and, later on in India, a Hindu. The key point in this use of non-Islamic symbolism was to suggest the transcendence of conventional norms. Sufi poetry was not about wine drinking, but here it used the shock of reference to wine, and to idolatry, to convey an ultimate goal for which respectability and righteousness were to be sacrificed (it is perhaps for similar reasons that celibate monks and nuns in Christian Europe focused on erotic and bridal symbolism). Idolatry in particular was a tantalizing symbolic complex, but here it had to do with worshiping the divine beloved as an idol rather than recommending attendance at pagan temples. It did not matter particularly which variety of idol worship one invoked. Sa'di in describing his famous escapade at the Somnath idol temple in India uses language derived from Zoroastrian, Jewish, and Christian sources to describe a Hindu deity. The point was not accuracy in terms of religion but to suggest a total devotion that cares nothing for the opinion of others.

The catalog of images found in Persian poetry is a complex of pre-Islamic and Islamic referents.[14] The ancient Persian king Jamshid is famous for his cup (*jam-i jamshid* or *jam-i jam*), which is not just a royal goblet but an equivalent of the mystic's heart; gazing into it, one can see all that exists. The inaccessible pearl is the gnostic and biblical symbol of knowledge gained at great price. The Magi or Zoroastrian priests merge into tavern keepers and represent the Sufi masters. Wine, of course, required for the court ritual of Persian kings, symbolizes the intoxication of mystical love. To this range of themes are joined a series of figures known from the Qur'an or Islamic history. The primordial covenant of the Qur'an, which fixed the relationship between God and humanity, is often recalled by a single word from the Qur'anic text; since humanity affirmatively answered God's question, "Am I not your lord?"

(*alastu be-rabbikum*), that time is known in Persian simply as "the day of 'am I not' " (*ruz-i alast*). At times it is simply invoked by the words "last night," since yesterday was the first day of creation; today is the life of the world, and tomorrow is the resurrection. Moses figures prominently, for his miracles (including the transformation of his hand to snowy white) and for his discovery in darkness of the water of immortality. But he also plays a secondary role to the immortal prophet Khidr, whose esoteric knowledge from God makes him Moses' teacher. Moses' opponent, the magician Samiri, is a sinister trickster like Simon Magus, but his repertory of tricks is nonetheless admired. The prophet Jesus is the master physician; his breath restores the dead to life, as his word can reanimate dead birds. In addition to these scriptural figures, Hallaj figures as a constantly recurring theme. His martyrdom and his cry of "I am the Truth" are referred to again and again. Love poetry focuses in particular on the physiognomy of the beloved. Most prominent are the moonlike face and the black tresses, which reflect the twin divine attributes of grace and wrath, Islam and infidelity. The tresses appear with endless variation as the chain that captures lovers' hearts, accompanied by the eyebrow that shoots arrows to deadly effect. Persian gardens, renowned since antiquity, furnished some of the most enduring images used by the poets. The tall cypress echoes the lovely stature of the beloved, which may merge into the figure of the heavenly tree. Here is where the bird of the soul will perch when it flies up to heaven. Whether it be a nightingale singing forlornly to the rose or a falcon returning to the celestial hunter, its home is the heavenly abode where the phoenixlike simurgh dwells. To this list of images one has to add symbols drawn from a whole range of traditional cosmological sciences, including astrology and alchemy, with which any educated reader would have been familiar.

Arabic and Persian Sufi poetry cannot be separated, however, from the tradition of poetry produced in the courts. In terms of their social environments, it might seem that the poetry recited in Sufi lodges, which celebrated divine love and the intense master-disciple relationship, had little in common with the formal odes that professional poets composed to honor and praise their noble patrons. Lengthy and extravagant odes of praise directed at rulers have been dismissed by modern Western critics as fulsome and insincere flattery. A closer look will reveal, however, that much of the poetry produced in court was saturated with the same imagery used in Sufi circles. The same verses could be read in one situation as praise of ordinary wine and earthly passion, while in another context it could be interpreted as mystical intoxication and divine love. Many of the verses recited in Sufi lodges were in fact first composed in a courtly setting. It is equally possible to read these poems as addressed to a royal patron, to a Sufi master, to God, or to a beautiful young boy who pours wine in a tavern. The effortless mastery with which a poet like Hafiz could evoke all these different readings at once makes it almost impossible to translate with any sense of success.

Many of the attributes of the beloved in these poems are based on the ideal of youthful manly beauty that arose in the Turco-Iranian courts of Central Asia: a moonlike face, skill at polo, long locks of hair, the beginnings of a mustache, a tall and slender stature, and cruel indifference to the sufferings of the lover. It was a male homo-erotic model of love, typified by the tales of Sultan Mahmud of Ghazna and his devoted slave Ayaz, that formed the basis for both courtly and mystical love poetry in the Persian tradition. In countless odes and lyrics dedicated to kings and nobles, poets adopted the convention of treating the object of poetic praise (*mamduh*) as the beloved (*ma'shuq*). This could have the incongruous effect of addressing a middle-aged man with compliments describing him as a handsome fifteen-year-old youth, but these were courtly conventions of praise rather than real love affairs. The poems of Sa'di were addressed to the rulers of Shiraz, but their exquisite evocation of love and beauty made them just as prized in Sufi circles. Perhaps the most remarkable example of how the same verse could serve both functions was the Arabic wine verses of Abu Nuwas, composed in a secular context that mocked religion, but so aesthetically entrancing that Persian Sufis took them over and reinterpreted them in a mystical style.[15] In other words, there was nothing intrinsically mystical about the verses themselves; the mystical interpretation was authorized by a context external to the contents of the poetry. One might go so far as to say that one can only define Sufi poetry as poetry that is recited and appreciated by Sufis; the main requirement of Sufi poetry, then, is that it be interpreted according to prescriptive mystical standards.

As indicated above, Arabic and Persian poetry had strict forms of rhyme and meter, and the subject matter too had to follow strict conventions to win acceptance. Some readers may assume that Sufi poems are to be understood mainly as autobiography, as a personal and individual document of inner experience. Such an expectation is actually foreign to the manner in which Sufis understood poetry. Most contemporary literary critics, regardless of what tradition they study, tell their students to avoid this biographical fallacy. The real subject of poetry is the experience that the poem creates in the reader, and it is part of a literary continuum to which both poet and reader continually refer.

Sufi manuals instruct the novice to interpret all poetry, of whatever origin, along fixed lines: the beloved is God; wine is spiritual intoxication. As an historian of Persian literature remarks with reference to a famous Sufi poet, " 'Attar tells us virtually nothing about himself, his poems contain hardly any allusions to contemporary persons or political events and revolve very much in a timeless world of mysticism."[16] Anthologies of Persian literature have frequently filled in the gap through imaginative stories that personalize poetry, supplying likely incidents sparked by the association with words and phrases in a poem. Thus, from some stray references to India in the poetry of Hafiz, later writers imagined elaborate stories of transactions between Hafiz and the kings of the Deccan and Bengal. From the phrase "sugar cane" (*shakh-i nabat*), a conventional epithet for the beloved, readers have extrapolated a romantic story of Hafiz falling in love with a beautiful Persian girl, for whom he underwent the austerities of a forty-day seclusion, which opened him up to mystical experience instead. Though the story is charming, it can cover up an important point when narrowly understood: if Hafiz was a great mystical poet, he was a poet first. Personalizing poetry removes the challenge to the reader to understand the poetry as literature and the need to comprehend the function of symbolic reference as a figure of speech. Against this tendency I would insist on the need to understand poetry through the conventions acknowledged by the poets, in terms of which they understood their own work.

As an example, I would like to examine a Persian poem sometimes ascribed to Hafiz, which most modern editors have excluded from their critical editions of his poems. It is worth noting that this situation reflects a lack of general agreement about what constitutes the most authentic text of Hafiz. Here is a fairly literal version of the poem:

> God most high! What fortune is mine tonight,
>   for my beloved suddenly came tonight.
> When I saw his beautiful face, I bowed down.
>   Praise God, for I am blest tonight.
> From union with him, the plant of my delight has flowered;
>   from my good luck, I became wealthy tonight.
> Blood will spell out on the ground "I am the Truth"
>   if you put me upon the gallows tonight.
> The decree of "the night of power" reached my grasp
>   from my wakeful rising sign tonight.
> I am resolved that if I die,
>   I shall proclaim my secret from heaven.
> You are the wealthy one; I have a claim;
>   give alms, for I have the right tonight.
> I fear that Hafiz will become effaced
>   from the turmoil in my head tonight.[17]

In the oral tradition and in some commentaries, one can find the explanation that this poem was written on the night when Hafiz experienced spiritual illumination (the endrhyme of the poem is the word *tonight* [*imshab*]). This would be partly an autobiographical reading of the poem and partly an interpretation of the poem as reflecting a particular mystical experience. It should be observed in passing that one can also read this as a standard court poem praising the patron and requesting a reward.

Such a personalized reading, if insisted on as the only meaning of the poem, becomes problematic when we consider the poem as part of the literary tradition. Hafiz was far from being an isolated figure. The Persian lyric was already four centuries old when he began to write. The conservative character of the tradition is indicated by the fact that poets like Hafiz were intimately acquainted with the verses of previous authors; their own compositions were frequently responses to earlier poems, cast deliberately into the same rhyme and meter with reflections on the same symbols and themes. None of the symbols used by Hafiz was invented by him. In the poem given above, conventional images include references to Hallaj, the Night of Power from the Qur'an, and images taken from astrology and Islamic law. The formal similarity of any given poem with previous poems can be easily verified by looking at the Persian text, because collected poems are always arranged in alphabetical order according to endrhyme. A recent commentator on Hafiz has assembled fifty pages of examples of extremely close parallels between the verses of Hafiz and thirteen previous poets, from the eleventh century to his own day, and this list is by no means exhaustive.[18] These precedents indicate that Hafiz was in dialogue with many previous poets. By composing verses to match the poems of others, Hafiz proposed to outdo them at their own game (a contest that had a particularly competitive edge for his contemporaries, such as Khwaju of Kirman, whom Hafiz addresses in dozens of verses).

If we glance at the writings of previous poets, we can easily find examples of similar poems that explain the lyric quoted above from a literary perspective. There are two lyrics by 'Attar with the same endrhyme, and Rumi has three with the same endrhyme that are quite close in style and spirit to Hafiz's verse (a series of later Persian poets, including Fayz-i Kashani, Fayzi, 'Urfi, Bedil, and Ghalib, have also responded to this rhyme).[19] The verse by Hafiz has several elements in common with two of Rumi's lyrics, including the phrase "Praise God" and a comparison with Hallaj: "That very fire that dwelled within Hallaj / even now dwells within my soul tonight." It should also be remembered that "tonight" is a symbol that recalls both the darkness of this world and night as the time for prayer and musical sessions. The poem is much better understood as part of the literary tradition than as individualistic mystical autobiography. The only autograph we know of in the hand of Hafiz is a manuscript in Tashkent containing the poems of Amir Khusraw of Delhi (d. 1325), a superb Persian poet renowned for the complexity and difficulty of his lyrics. From this one can conclude not only that Hafiz, like other poets, occasionally augmented his income by working as a copyist but also that he was extremely familiar with the writings of his predecessors.

Was Hafiz a Sufi as well as a poet? This raises again the question of what constitutes mystical poetry. There have doubtless been many mystics who never expressed their experiences at all, and many others have spoken in prose, always complaining of the inadequacy of words. Poetry is an art and a discipline that is not necessarily mystical; it is partly a gift and partly the product of hard work. Poetry is employed for esthetic effects, such as meter and rhyme, and for the emotional effect of its content; for Sufis, properly interpreted poetry in the ritual context of listening to music was particularly powerful. It was also perfectly possible to write poetry in a Sufi style without being a practicing mystic. It is no exaggeration to say that all of the major Persian court poets of the seventeenth century wrote poems that were loaded with Sufi imagery, though few of them had serious connections with Sufi orders. As the great Iranian scholar Qasim

Ghani pointed out, from reading the verses of Hafiz we can only know that he was a poet. Unlike authors who are known primarily as Sufis, he did not write explicitly about mysticism and the topics of Sufism, but he did write with the vocabulary and style of poets. Mystical experience is different from poetry, and it can be argued that ecstasy fits poorly with the strict forms of rhyme and meter.[20] Hafiz was also clearly employed as a court poet, as shown by the more than fifty poems in which he explicitly mentions the names of various rulers and ministers of the Inju and Muzaffarid dynasties that ruled Shiraz in the fourteenth century; it can be assumed that he presented many other poems at court without directly naming his patrons.[21]

Certainly Hafiz has been greatly loved by Sufis too, and a number of commentaries have been written on his poems from a mystical point of view. But there have been many other interpretations of Hafiz, who is celebrated above all for the delicious ambiguity of his verse; among his notable admirers in this century are the leader of the Iranian Communist Party and Ayatollah Khomeini. It is perfectly possible to find serious writers arguing that Hafiz was a spokesman for the proletariat or that he was a forerunner of the Islamic revolution of 1979.[22] There is some evidence to indicate that Hafiz may have been initiated into the Ruzbihaniyya Sufi order, through a certain Shaykh Mahmud or Muhammad 'Attar (not to be confused with the poet Farid al-Din 'Attar).[23] In this respect Hafiz resembled his predecessor Amir Khusraw, who was initiated into the Chishti order by the great master Nizam al-Din Awliya' while serving as court poet to seven successive rulers of Delhi. But it was probably best put by the Sufi biographer Jami, who briefly described Hafiz a century after his death, together with a handful of other great Persian poets at the end of his collection of lives of Sufi saints: "Although it is not known whether he took the hand of discipleship from a master or had a correct relationship in Sufism with a member of this group, still, his verses are so much in accordance with the teachings of this group that no one disputes it."[24] It matters less who Hafiz was than how his verses have been understood. To the extent that his poetry has been recited and appreciated by Sufis, both in solitary reading and in ritual performance, we may call him a Sufi poet; the extent of his reception, indeed, makes him a major Sufi poet.[25]

No discussion of Persian mystical poetry would be complete, however, without a mention of Rumi (1207–1273). This remarkable figure was born Jalal al-Din Muhammad in the city of Balkh (now in Afghanistan) and as a child traveled to Asia Minor, where his father, an eminent theologian and mystic, found refuge at the Seljuk court at Konya just before the Mongol assault on Central Asia. He is known by different names. Afghans call him Balkhi; Persians call him Mawlavi; Turks call him Mevlana (from the Arabic word for our master). His name Rumi comes from the term for the eastern provinces of the former Roman empire (present-day Turkey), known in Arabic as *Rum*. Rumi is the author of the largest corpus of lyrical poetry in Persian literature, the *Divan-i Shams-i Tabriz* (about forty thousand verses), as well as the mystical epic of the *Masnavi* (twenty-five thousand verses). The story of his career as a preacher and theologian, his meeting with the enigmatic dervish Shams-i Tabriz, and his subsequent transformation into a supreme mystic, has been told often before.[26] In some ways this story illustrates how a free-wheeling *qalandar* (Shams) could change forever the life of a respectable Sufi (Rumi). As in the case of Hafiz and Ibn al-Farid, the verses of Rumi have frequently been read in modern times as transparent expressions of his personal experience as a mystic. In earlier times, his poetry was read as an exposition of Sufi doctrine; as with Ibn al-Farid, Rumi's poetry (particularly the *Masnavi*) was often interpreted through the lens of Ibn 'Arabi's metaphysics.[27] These interpretations, which downplay the importance of the poetry itself, were facilitated by certain remarks that Rumi made in his recorded conversations, indicating that he personally found poetry distasteful; he regarded the composition of poetry as similar to cooking tripe to suit the inclination of a guest. Given the unparalleled amount of poetry that he wrote, one should probably take this declaration with a grain of salt. The condemnation of poetry plays a role similar to the frequent impassioned cries for silence that conclude nearly a thousand of his lyrics; if these were meant literally, he certainly failed to follow his own advice. More subtly, Persian literature specialist Fatemeh Keshavarz has recently shown that Rumi suggests by these rhetorical devices the gap between the power of language and the inexpressibility of the encounter with truth.[28] Like any negative theology, since it points to the divine beyond, Rumi's poetry triggers a response of seeking, which finds its best expression in the structured rituals of Sufi music (see chapter 7).

As in the case of Hafiz, it needs to be emphasized that Rumi wrote in terms of literary convention, though Rumi did not serve as a court poet, and indeed he freely played with Persian poetry as no one else has done. While every other poet signs his lyrics with his pen name, Rumi never did; instead, he frequently invoked the name of his mystical guide, so that his collected lyrics are simply called the *Divan-i Shams-i Tabriz*. He plays with nonsense words, with puns, and adorns his verses with the symbolism of music and dance. At the same time, Rumi was immensely learned, and his *Masnavi* truly demands commentary at many points. Like Hafiz, he often echoes famous lines by earlier poets. To take an example at random, one can consider the lyric that begins with the line, "Someone said, 'Master Sana'i has died,' " which certainly invites reflection on the Sufi poet Sana'i as a predecessor of Rumi. It should be pointed out, however, that this poem was not a response to a contemporary event (Sana'i died in 1131) but was modeled on a verse written three centuries earlier on the death of the poet Rudaki. Rumi was of course familiar with a vast story lore that had previously been employed by 'Attar in his mystical epics. But he also shows his familiarity with the classics of Arabic poetry, being particularly fond of the poems of al-Mutanabbi.

A feature of Persian poetry that is very hard to convey in translation is its diglossic (bilingual) quality. Between forty and sixty percent of the vocabulary of Persian is taken from Arabic, and in Rumi's verse whole phrases and even lines in Arabic come in frequently. This is particularly arresting in places like the dense passage at the beginning of the *Masnavi* (1: 128-29), after Rumi's disciple Husam al-Din asks him to talk about Shams-i Tabriz. At this point Rumi suddenly shifts into pure Arabic, the majestic language of God's Qur'an and the language of passionate love: "Don't bother me, for I am annihilated! My thoughts are wiped out, for 'I can't count up your praises.' Whatever the unenlightened say is useless, no matter how they pose or preen." The mere thought of Shams caused Rumi to revert to the state of annihilation of the ego, further emphasized by the quotation from the Prophet Muhammad, when he spoke directly to God and confessed his inability to praise the infinite. This could only be done by shifting to the higher register of Arabic, because of its powerful link both to the Qur'an and to classical Arabic poetry. The audience for whom Rumi wrote such lines was clearly steeped in the literary conventions of Persian and Arabic, the Islamic religious tradition, and the specialized vocabulary of Sufism as developed over centuries.

How can one adequately render in translation the aesthetic effect of breaking from Persian into Arabic? Another example of this effect would be a verse from Hafiz, who is notable for the large amount of Arabic that he employs in his Persian verses (the Arabic is marked here with italic): "That bitter stuff the Sufi calls *mother of evils / is more luscious and sweet to us than a virgin's kiss.*" This is basically praise of wine, with the aesthetic shock of forbidden pleasure considerably enhanced by language of subtle refinement. A hundred years ago, an English translator could have tried for that effect by using Latin to represent the Arabic, with some expectation that many readers would appreciate it: "That bitter stuff the Sufi calls *mater malorum / nobis optabilior et dulcior quam osculum virginis.*"[29] Today, however, this would be wasted effort. Without a comparable bilingual range accessible to most English readers, the translator simply has to abandon any attempt to mirror this effect.

Translations, Versions, and the Scripturalization of Poetry

In any case, Rumi defies any easy categorization. He proclaims that he is not of East or West, neither of Hindustan or Badakhshan. It is therefore all the more remarkable that he (and to a lesser extent Hafiz) has been redefined and canonized in a new way during the twentieth century. Certainly there is a powerful aesthetic effect in reading Rumi's Persian verses, which is greatly enhanced by hearing them in a musical setting that emulates the Sufi *sama'*. Because of Rumi's exaltation of the power of love and the freedom with which he moves over the whole symbolic range of Persian poetry, he is probably more often quoted and admired by speakers of Persian than any other Persian poet. Still, the elevation of Rumi and Hafiz to the position of eminence that they now hold in English translation is unprecedented. It is as if their verses have been transformed from poetry into holy scripture, through a process of cultural appropriation that could only take place in the modern West. This canonization is especially striking since there is no agreement among scholars about what constitutes the "original" Persian text of authors like Hafiz and Rumi. The differences between manuscript copies of their poetry are often considerable. In poetry, the number and order of verses as well as the words in the text can vary dramatically. These differences are the result of a number of factors, including doubtless some scribal errors, but they also reflect serious revision and experimentation by the poets along with variations due to improvisation in oral performance both by the poets and by later reciters. One can see, for instance, in Rumi's collected lyrics what look like three or more parallel versions of the same poem—in the same rhyme and meter, often with a number of overlapping lines. This is poetry in process rather than the finality of scripture.

Nevertheless, the canonization of Rumi and Hafiz had already begun to take place years ago. Jami called Rumi's *Masnavi* "the Qur'an in the Persian tongue." Hafiz, perhaps because of the supreme ambiguity of his verse, became known as "the Interpreter of the Hidden World" not long after his death, and his verses came to be used for divination, to an extent only exceeded by the Qur'an. There is a royal copy of the poems of Hafiz preserved in Patna (India), which formerly was in the library of the Mughal emperors. On the margins are inscribed details about the occasions when these kings consulted Hafiz about the proper conduct of state and warfare. To this day, there are many people who perform elaborate rituals to select at random a lyric from Hafiz, which is then interpreted (as with the *I Ching*) to guide everyday choices in matters as mundane as real-estate transactions. As religious studies scholar Jonathan Z. Smith has argued, a text used for divination is the most elemental form of scripture; it becomes an authoritative structure that can be transferred and applied to any situation.[30] The problem with this approach is that it removes the text from the realm of poetry. When poetry is considered to be divinely inspired, it is no longer the product of human effort. One is forced to assume, in that case, that it has an unvarying original text that emerged full-blown without revision. In the case of texts published in modern printed editions, the appearance of inerrancy is reinforced by the authority of print, which appears much more final than handwriting and which is identical in multiple copies. The popularity of translations of Rumi, who is reputedly the best-selling poet in America today, is beginning to resemble the translations and paraphrases of the Bible in terms of the number of translators and the variety of approaches to a sacred text in a foreign language.

The authority of the translations of Rumi and Hafiz is a peculiar phenomenon, however, because the current sanctification of the text is accompanied by a comparative lack of interest in the actual form of the original text. When Sufism was first discovered by English Orientalists, it was Persian poetry that drew them into the subject. This was then interpreted primarily as an expression of personal mystical experience, and it was made available in scholarly literal translations such as those of Nicholson and Arberry. For the most part, however, the scholarly translations made no pretension to being poetic. The value of these translations was that they focused on meaning, preserving the metaphors and references that Rumi and Hafiz used to make their points. The translators attempted to make the source accessible in a form that was as transparent as possible, "getting it right" so that other experts would recognize the accuracy of their self-effacing achievement. This made it possible for the reader to reconstruct, with some effort, the overall structure of a lyric, or a section from an epic, with some notion of how it worked for readers of the original language.

In recent years, a new tendency has developed for professional poets to take literal versions of Sufi poetry made by scholars and then to put them into a poetic form suitable to English. This practice, which was developed first probably by Ezra Pound, has led established poets such as Robert Bly and particularly Coleman Barks to produce poetic versions of Rumi that are freed from the pedestrian limitations of literal translation (though Barks makes a practice of citing the page numbers of the poems in standard editions of the Persian text). Poets like Bly and Barks have worked with scholars of Persian to ensure access to the original. Given the dry and pedantic style of the early scholarly translations of Persian Sufi poetry, this kind of literary effort is a welcome change of pace.

Alongside this literary trend, however, one increasingly also finds a new kind of production that bears a much less certain relationship to the Persian; these are sometimes called "versions" to distinguish them from translations. Produced by authors with no track record in either poetry or translation, these poems are basically original writings, inspired either by reading translations of Rumi or Hafiz, or by the private meditations of the author. These versions do not generally attempt to correspond closely with the form of the original *ghazal* except in the loosest sense; two or three lines from a lyric will be picked out and reworked to make a new and independent poem. Even when the status and nature of these new poems with relation to any original are unclear, they still claim the authority of the mystical Persian poet. The authority invoked by the versionizers mirrors, in a strange way, one of the standard problems in identifying the "authentic" verses of premodern Middle Eastern authors. In order to get their own Persian or Arabic writings into circulation, unknown scribes and writers would often sign their work with the name of a famous author, on the theory that readers would always welcome a new piece by their favorite literary authority (it is due to this tendency that the oldest manuscripts of 'Umar Khayyam's poems only give a few dozen quatrains, while in some manuscripts of the nineteenth century the number has risen to more than seven hundred). While anonymous figures of the past in this way gained a vicarious immortality for their own pseudonymous writings, today's creators of poetic versions obtain a reflected light for their own verses from the author they wish to represent.

Many questions can be asked about the new versions of Rumi and Hafiz. They generally (unlike Victorian translations) avoid rhyme and meter, and it is not clear what standards are being used to establish their relative worth as poetry. While certain standard symbols found in Persian poetry are retained, others are omitted as too foreign or too obscure. The versions attempt to locate the mystical essence of the poem, while shedding that which is considered irrelevant. Readers of these versions should recognize that the vision of mysticism that is now presented in English verse depends entirely on the individual perspective of the translator. What is lost in some of these versions is the sense of cultural distance that required translation in the first place; it is easy for such versions to fall into the practice of merely recycling the expectations of contemporary New Age readers and surrounding them with the halo of the Persian mystic.

To match the versions phenomenon, one also finds translations by Iranians, Turks, or Indians who are not literary specialists and whose poetic skills in English have not been previously established. These translators sometimes claim a privileged access to the text due simply to native acquaintance with the Persian language, but it should be recalled that not all speakers of English are experts on Shakespeare. The literary quality of these versions differs widely too. We have in all these instances a kind of fetishization of a sacred text— which is increasingly being redefined as a New Age commodity, with little interest in the literary context in which a Hafiz or a Rumi actually wrote or in the performative situation in which their poems were appreciated. Perhaps the best compromise between these different approaches is the multipronged one, in which there is a transcription of the Persian text in the Roman alphabet, a very literal translation with notes to explain strange terms, and a poetic version that may then be appreciated with a sense of its cultural distance, and in much more depth. The standard was set for this type of translation in a book of the Urdu verse of Ghalib, presented in transcriptions, literal translations, and poetic versions by distinguished American poets. Recent examples include a multimedia dimension, with calligraphy and audio tapes adding to the reading experience.

Sufi Poetry in Other Islamicate Languages

This is not the place to attempt more than a brief indication of the wealth of poetic riches to be found in other languages used by Sufis. Since most of the scholarship on Sufi poetry has focused on Arabic and particularly Persian materials, there are far fewer translations and studies available for Sufi poetry in Turkic, Indic, African, and Southeast Asian languages. Although poetry in these languages plays an important role in Sufi practice, it has been neglected as literature because of cultural hierarchies in premodern Islamicate societies, which are reflected even in modern Western scholarship. That is, literary Arabic has always held a place of pride in Islamicate culture, certainly in societies where Arabic is the spoken language, but even more so in non-Arabophone societies. The Qur'an is studied in Arabic, and translations are used mainly as adjuncts to the Arabic text. To repeat a comparison made earlier, Arabic literature has become a classical literature, playing a role for Muslim countries similar to that of the Greek and Latin classics in Europe and America (it is interesting to see that in recent years the word *klasik* has been imported directly into Arabic-script languages with precisely this meaning). Persian is a literary language with a living tradition over a thousand years, with a geographic range stretching from Turkey to Central Asia and India. Like Arabic, Persian literature has been associated with courtly culture from its inception. Despite the different qualities of the two languages, Arabic and, to a lesser extent, Persian have both been languages of prestige and status in many Muslim societies. While many other languages used by Muslims have been written in Arabic script and used for literary expression, they have generally had a more limited circulation and lower status, even when associated with the court. Frequently poetic compositions have been composed and transmitted orally, a feature which also lowers their prestige in comparison with written literature. Muslim writers who have adopted languages such as Bengali, Turkish, or Berber for religious expression have often apologized for using these less celestial tongues (as Dante did with Italian), though one suspects that these formal excuses conceal a genuine enthusiasm for literature in the mother tongue.

European Orientalists too have adopted this cultural hierarchy, regarding Arabic as the central language for Islam, with Persian as a close second, barely conceding some importance to Turkish for literature and history. For the most part, other languages used by Muslims outside the "heartlands" of Islamic civilization have been often dismissed as local and presumably deviant in some way. This hierarchy reflects an essentialist concept of Islam as Arabic, and it gives short shrift to the cultural riches that are enjoyed by the majority of Muslims who are not Arabs. One unfortunate byproduct of this attitude is that it is extremely difficult to find books on Sufi poetry in these languages outside of highly specialized academic circles. The remarks that follow are therefore quite limited. I have tried above to highlight the aspect of performance in the working definition of Sufi poetry as poetry appreciated by Sufis, but we shall have to await much more complete reports on the uses of poetry in these other Islamicate languages before we can generalize about the state of Sufi poetry in all these instances.

There have been two related trends, however, that have worked to retrieve popular literature of a Sufi bent for public consumption in the twentieth century. One is the study of folk literature, which drew attention to popular and oral poetry and narrative as a valuable part of culture. Local antiquarians and literary enthusiasts in many Muslim countries have helped preserve and publish poetry and other kinds of literature in local languages. Since many popular authors in these languages have been Sufis, the preservation of folklore has been a means to locate and make available to the public this kind of literature. The other trend is nationalist ideology, which promotes the mass publication and canonization of literature in the national language. An example would be the case of Yunus Emre (d. ca. 1320), who wrote simple Turkish verses in the style of the Bektashi dervishes.[31] When Kamal Ataturk secularized Turkey in the 1920s, Sufi institutions such as the dervish orders were abolished. But the Turkish poetry of Yunus Emre, which had little of the high Arabic and Persian vocabulary of Ottoman court Turkish, became a favored subject in the official educational curriculum of the Turkish Republic in the newly adopted Latin script. As a result, practically anyone educated in Turkey can quote Yunus Emre from memory. The fact that Yunus Emre's poetry has a strongly Sufi flavor was of decidedly secondary importance in comparison to its usefulness for national language policy, as far as Turkish educational authorities were concerned.

In speaking of other Islamicate languages, I mean other languages besides Arabic and Persian, which have been used by Muslims (and by non-Muslims) for literary expression. But as the example of Yunus Emre shows, the very way we approach language today is inevitably affected by nationalist politics. The formulation of "one people—one nation—one language" has been politically useful, despite the many cases where the model fits poorly. Thus, "pure" Turkish becomes something to be claimed by the present-day Republic of Turkey, while Arabic-script Ottoman Turkish and the Arabic and Persian literature composed and studied in the former Ottoman Empire are rejected as foreign.[32] Likewise, out of the many languages and dialects spoken in northern India, one (Devanagari-script Hindi) has become the official language of India and is primarily associated with Hinduism, while another closely related one (Arabic-script Urdu) is the official language of Pakistan and is identified as Islamic. Ironically, more Sufi poets used Hindi than Urdu, which they regarded as mainly a secular court idiom. Similar nationalistic problems can be found in what used to be called Serbo-Croatian, which is now divided into Serbian, Croatian, and Bosnian (like Hindi and Urdu) by script, religion, and nationality. A lot of Sufi poetry is not only (as in the cases of Rumi and Hafiz cited above) multilingual but also multicultural. In performance recordings available today one can hear a singer like North Indian *qawwali* master Ja'far Budauni recite songs that mix Arabic verses about 'Ali, Persian poems about the Prophet Muhammad, and Awadhi Hindi couplets about the infant Krishna, all of which are interpreted symbolically from a Sufi perspective. Thus, for the study of Sufi poetry, it does not make sense to break it down according to language. It is, however, useful to look at the subject regionally.

In this sense one can speak of, for instance, a tradition of *tekke* poetry cultivated in the Sufi lodges of the Ottoman empire. The Bektashi dervishes had their poetry and liturgies in Turkish, including the work of figures such as Kaygusuz Abdal and the martyr Nesimi. Although these poems may have been in wider circulation, their performance in the *tekke* was generally aimed at a restricted audience and not meant for public consumption.[33] Included in their repertory were the verses of Shah Isma'il, founder of the Safavid dynasty of Iran, known by the pen name Hata'i; these poems, which have a strong Shi'i flavor and unmistakable hints of divinization, were politically suspect because of their association with an empire frequently at war with the Ottomans. This *tekke* poetry is commonly distinguished from court or *divani* poetry, but as with Arabic and Persian poetry, in practice it is difficult to find any firm boundary between the themes and forms of mystical and court poetry in Turkish. One of the last great monuments of Ottoman Turkish poetry, Shaykh Ghalib's romance *Beauty and Love* (written in 1783), though written in the courtly style, draws heavily upon Rumi's Persian *Masnavi*, and its author became a master in the Mevlevi Sufi order.[34] In a similar way, one can point to the existence of regional traditions in Southeast Asia, where important Sufi figures of the seventeenth century such as Hamza Fansuri composed poetry in Malay alongside metaphysical treatises in the same language (with frequent quotations from Arabic and Persian).[35] Other literary traditions exist in North Africa (in Berber), East Africa (Somali and Swahili), and West Africa (Hausa) that have been employed by Sufis, but in all these cases the amount of material available to nonspecialists is minimal. The same could be said about Sufi poetry in Inner Asia, in the former Soviet Republics and Chinese Turkestan.

Because of the greater amount of Orientalist studies of Indian culture, we have somewhat better access to Sufi poetry in South Asian languages, though here too much remains to be done.[36] Following the arc from Pakistan through northern India to Bangladesh, one encounters such languages as Sindhi, Punjabi, Pashto, different forms of Hindi/Urdu, and Bengali, all of which are Indo-European languages that often share a common stock of Indic literary themes. Sufis such as Shah 'Abd al-Latif employed the languages of the Indus valley to explore mystical themes through popular romances, in which the feminine voice was used to articulate the themes of mystical love.[37] In northern and eastern India, romantic themes from Rajput epics formed the basis for lengthy compositions by Sufis of the Chishti and Shattari orders. In these cases, it is striking to see that Middle Eastern characters such as the lovers Majnun and Layla have been replaced by Indian ones such as Sassi and Punnun, or Padmavati and Ratan Sen. The Bengali bards known as Bauls represent an adaptation of Sufi vocabulary to Tantric practice, and their songs contain all the elaborate symbolism of yoga. In southern India, there is a separate literary tradition linked to Tamil, a language of the Dravidian family, which invokes the models of Tamil court poetry addressed to Rama or the goddess to express mystical insights. This use of local themes gives a strongly multicultural flavor to this kind of Sufi poetry, which extends to the appropriation of themes and characters that are conventionally associated with Hinduism. It needs to be recalled, however, that the religious boundaries of the twentieth century are far more neat and tidy than the multiple overlapping religious and cultural patterns of premodern times.

7
Sufi Music and Dance

Come, let's scatter roses and pour wine in the glass;
  we'll shatter heaven's roof and lay a new foundation.
If sorrow raises armies to shed the blood of lovers,
  I'll join with the wine bearer so we can overthrow them.
With a sweet string at hand, play a sweet song, my friend,
  so we can clap and sing a song, and lose our heads in dancing.

—HAFIZ (GHANI-QAZVINI, NO. 374)

PERHAPS NO OTHER ASPECT of Sufism has been more contentious, and at the same time more popular, than the practice of music
and dance.[1] Music and dance are by no means universally found
among Sufis, for orders such as the Naqshbandis and the Qadiris
typically frown upon music and dance (though there have been notable exceptions in both groups). Still, the chanted recitation of poetry
in Sufi circles has frequently been accompanied by musical instruments, while at the same time physical motions ranging from spontaneous trance movement to measured ritual gestures have also taken
place at these gatherings. Popular appreciation of Sufism today frequently focuses on music and dance, which in our public culture are
much more familiar categories than prayer or metaphysics. Today
Sufi practice in the form of music and dance is being redefined in
terms of contemporary Western aesthetic standards. The Mevlevi

179

sema ritual, developed in Turkey in close proximity to the Ottoman court, is now performed on concert stages as the dance of the Whirling Dervishes. A Pakistani singer trained in Chishti *qawwali* ritual, Nusrat Fateh Ali Khan, records in the world music genre and collaborates with American musicians on movie sound tracks. How are these contemporary manifestations to be understood in terms of the role of music and dance in earlier Sufi tradition?

The term that Sufis used was *sama'* (literally, listening), which referred to listening to chanted or recited poetry that might or might not be accompanied by musical instruments. The accent was therefore on the experience of listening rather than on the performance of music; performance was generally the job of service professionals of relatively low social status, much like actors or dancers in nineteenth-century Europe. The place to begin the consideration of Sufi music is therefore with the voice. Early Sufi theorists are fully aware of the power of the human voice to bring out powerful emotion. Many stories are told to illustrate the power of the voice, starting with the effect of the recitation of the Qur'an, the divine names, and religious poetry. Numerous *hadith* relate that the prophets have all been endowed with beautiful voices of remarkable intensity; it is said that when David recited the Psalms, the coffins of four hundred Israelites who expired during the recitation had to be carried out of the assembly. In contrast, ugly voices are to be avoided. After all, in the Qur'an God said, "The most objectionable of voices is the voice of the ass" (31:19). One of the common examples of the powerful voice in Sufi literature is the cry of the camel driver, which when thoughtlessly employed can cause weary animals to exert themselves to such an extent that they die from exhaustion. A similar theme is the influence of the cries of birds and beasts, in which the sensitive listener can perceive the praise of God:

> I remember one night when I traveled all night in a caravan,
> and slept at dawn at the edge of a wood. A madman who was

our companion on the journey cried out and headed into the desert, but he did not find a moment's peace. When day came I said to him, "What state were you in?" He said, "I saw the nightingales begin to sing in the tree, the partridges on the hill, the frogs in the water, and the beasts in the wood. I thought to myself, 'It is a disgrace that all are praising God, and I am heedlessly asleep.' "

Last night a bird cried out till dawn, ravishing my mind and patience, my strength and thoughts.
The sound of my voice must have reached the ear of a sincere friend.
He said, "I can't believe that a bird's call could drive you so crazy."
I said, "It is contrary to human nature that a bird sings God's praises while I remain silent!"[2]

In all discussions of Sufi music, it is the sensitivity of the listener that is the critical issue.

It is commonly stated in Sufi texts that music is never permissible for all, and in this way it is acknowledged that music is to be approached in terms of Islamic law; it must be evaluated like anything else for its ethical content:

Sama' is of four types. One is the lawful, in which the listener is totally longing for God and not at all longing for the created. The second is the permitted, in which the listener is mostly longing for God and only a little for the created. The third is the disapproved, in which there is much longing for the created and a little for God. The fourth is the forbidden, in which there is no longing for God and all is for the created. . . . But the listener should know the difference between doing the lawful, the forbidden, the permitted, and the disapproved. And this is a secret between God and the listener.[3]

In a famous and simple Arabic phrase, listening to music must be judged according to who, when, and where (*makan zaman ikhwan,* literally, the place, the time, the brethren). It should not be performed as a regular habit; it should not be accessible to the spiritually immature; and it should not be done in uncontrolled public locations. As one early Sufi said, "*Sama'* is forbidden for the masses, so they may preserve their souls; it is permitted for ascetics, so they may attain the goal of their efforts; and it is recommended for our companions [the Sufis], so they may enliven their hearts."[4] Listening to music was therefore treated with the utmost seriousness. One needed to perform ablutions beforehand as if for prayer and dress soberly in clean clothes. Since the verses recited in these sessions can easily be interpreted in a worldly fashion, novices are instructed to focus their attention on understanding them spiritually. It is also important not to be distracted by the singer's voice or personal appearance, because this physical beauty can easily overpower the search for divine beauty. The basic distinction is whether one listens to music out of sensual desire or out of longing for God. Music cannot be spiritually effective without moral purification.

The effect of *sama'* if properly performed is ecstasy (*wajd*). Many discussions have taken place on the problem of distinguishing real ecstasy from imitation. Since the criterion for participation in the musical session is purity of intention, hypocrisy is the greatest danger. Here more than anywhere else one can see the usefulness of the concept of the pseudo-Sufi. In circles where prestige is based on spiritual attainments, it must be tempting for those who lack ecstasy to pretend to have it. Sufi manuals are full of dire warnings against this kind of false claim, as in this catalogue of prohibitions from a fourteenth-century Sufi manual:

> If it is known that the musical gathering contains certain forbidden and unlawful things, such as food provided by the unjust, the proximity of women, and the presence of young

men, with objectionable things [for example, wine], or such
as the presence of anyone unrelated to the Sufis, such as the
would-be ascetic who does not enjoy music but does not dare
to reject it, or the powerful man from the nobility who has
to be treated with insincere respect, or the presence of the
insincere person who falsely manifests ecstasy and with men-
dacious pseudo-ecstasy disturbs the mood of those present,
then the sincere seekers must avoid being present in such an
assembly.[5]

If listening to music ceases to be a session for listening to the
chanted recitation of the beloved's attributes, it becomes a merely
aesthetic occasion, musical self-indulgence. Ibn 'Arabi was highly
critical of those who thought that mysticism was nothing but enjoy-
ment of music:

God does not talk of desire; he has blamed people who take
their religion in fun and jest, who nowadays are the lovers of
music, the people of drum and flute—let us flee to God from
abandonment!
There is no religion in drum, flute, and games;
    religion is in the Qur'an and manners.
When I heard the book of God, it moved me;
    that is listening [*sama'*], and it brought me near the veils
So that I witnessed him whom no eye can perceive
    but one who witnesses the lights in the Book.[6]

Those who focus on the exterior manifestation of music to the
exclusion of its inner form are deluded; for Ibn 'Arabi, the highest
form of spiritual audition in *sama'* is the concentration on the manifestation of beauty in the divine revelation itself, in the Qur'an. In
most Sufi manuals, self-control in both mind and body is demanded
of the novice. Each participant is instructed to avoid being distracted
by what others are doing. Despite these recommendations, other

rules for listening to music indicate that musical assemblies could generate considerable emotional energy, which had to be channeled through ritual. The most notable of these rules are those that deal with the proper method of ripping one's garment when in ecstasy and the correct manner of distributing the torn pieces of cloth, which still retained a fragrance of that ecstasy.[7]

Dance is only peripherally discussed in accounts of listening to music in Sufi literature—except in the Mevlevi tradition, to which we shall return.[8] Although spontaneous dance is acknowledged as a possible result of ecstasy, it is just as possible (and according to some, preferable) to sit unmoving and impassive as the ecstasy pours through. Miniature paintings often depict Sufis dancing in gardens with musicians present, but they do not appear to follow any uniform choreography. While the manuals often urge those who are present to rise and conform to the state of one who enters ecstasy, it is difficult to see how following the spontaneous motions of a person in trance could have any regular dance form, but our information is very sketchy on this subject. Among the Chishtis, for example, the followers of Burhan al-Din Gharib were said to have a particular style of dancing, but there is no indication of what exactly this might be. The miniatures also show long sleeves hanging down over the hand, as the conventional sign of ecstasy (calling to mind the loosened hose of deranged Shakespearean lovers). Texts also refer to stamping the feet, probably in time to the music, clapping the hands, and turning. Since it is constantly emphasized that everyone experiences the music on a different level, it is quite likely that in many of these sessions every dervish danced to a private measure, without any movements in unison.

The rituals of Sufi music took place in an atmosphere saturated with cosmic symbolism, which enables participants to return to the beginning of time. Ever since the time of Junayd (d. 910), it has been common for Sufis to link *sama'* with the Qur'anic theme of the primordial covenant between God and the unborn souls of humanity, when God demanded, "Am I not your Lord?" (Qur'an 7:172). This moment, for the Sufis, was not only the perfect statement of the divine unity but also the forging of the link of love between God and the soul. Moreover, the music of *sama'* is nothing but the reverberation of that primal word of God: "*Sama'* is the recollection of the speech of the covenant, and the burning of the fire of longing." The Sufis describe God as having placed a secret into the human heart that day, which is concealed like a spark in stone but which blazes forth when struck with the steel of *sama'*. Junayd is quoted as saying, "When to the essence of the children of Adam on the day of the covenant there came the words 'Am I not your Lord?' all the spirits became absorbed by its delight. Thus those who came into this world, whenever they hear a beautiful voice, their spirits tremble and are disturbed by the memory of that speech, because the influence of that speech is in the beautiful voice." In other terms, the source of *sama'* is said to be the rapture or attraction (*jadhb*) of God, a kind of energy that irresistibly draws one towards him. The Egyptian Sufi Dhu al-Nun said, "*Sama'* is the rapture of God that incites hearts towards God."[9]

Regional Traditions of Music and Dance

Sufi music is found in all Muslim regions where Sufi poetry is recited, while dance is really a specialty of just one Sufi order, the Mevlevis. The local musical traditions employed in Sufi music vary considerably, and they have long and complex histories that are in many cases hardly known to outsiders. Specialists in ethnomusicology have discussed the technical aspects of these different musical traditions in terms of musical theory and performance. Rather than attempting a detailed historical survey, here I will briefly describe a few representative varieties of Sufi music from the viewpoint of religion and ritual, with attention to those traditions that have been recently popularized in the West and which can be heard in recordings.

One of the best-known traditions of Sufi music is practiced by the Chishti order in India and Pakistan.[10] Because of its wide popularity in contemporary circles far beyond those interested in traditional Sufi rituals, it is a good example to begin with, to raise the issue of the redefinition of Sufi music in the West. Although Persian and Urdu texts written by Chishti authors use the term *sama‘*, nowadays this type of music is known primarily by the term *qawwali*, an Arabic word meaning recited; this name preserves an old terminology, since Arabic Sufi texts from nine centuries ago refer to the reciter (*qawwal*) of poetry as a central figure in musical rituals. The oldest Chishti texts, from the early thirteenth century, testify to the outstanding importance of listening to music in this order. Court historians also indicate that jurists opposed to music challenged its legitimacy at this time, but the sultans of Delhi in every instance found the Sufi arguments in favor of music convincing. The single most striking piece of evidence concerning music among the Chishtis is the death of Qutb al-Din Bakhtiyar Kaki at the end of a musical session held in Delhi in 1235 (his tomb is near the Qutb Minar south of Delhi). He went into ecstasy when the singers recited a Persian verse by Ahmad-i Jam: "Those slain by submission's knife / ever from beyond find life." Convention requires that when someone enters ecstasy during such a session, it is necessary to repeat the same line of verse until the person returns to his senses. An oral tradition has it that each time the singers sang the first half of the verse, Qutb al-Din would be reduced to near unconsciousness ("slain by submission's knife"). But when the second half of the verse was recited ("ever from beyond find life"), he would revive. As the story goes, Qutb al-Din's disciples finally called a stop to the music after this repetition had gone on for three days. Unfortunately, the singers stopped in the middle of the verse, and the saint expired. This is by no means an isolated instance of death during *sama'*. Biographical collections are full of similar incidents, the most recent of which took place less than a century ago when a Chishti Sufi named Muhammad Husayn Ilahabadi died at Ajmer during a recitation of verses about the ascension of the Prophet.

Typically the Chishti *qawwali* performance is a highly structured ritual that is performed at Sufi shrines on the death anniversaries of famous saints and on other religious holidays. The major locations for Chishti festivals in India are shrines at Ajmer, Delhi (Nizamuddin), Gulbarga, Kalyar, and Khuldabad, while in Pakistan the largest Chishti shrine is at Pakpattan. Thursday afternoon (the day before the Friday communal prayer) is also generally a good day to visit Chishti shrines if one wishes to see *qawwali* performed. The musicians, who are service professionals, perform these days on modern instruments, including the harmonium, a bellows-driven keyboard instrument of European origin, and occasionally the clarinet; for percussion they employ north Indian drums and hand clapping. An austere form of *qawwali* called *band sama'*, accompanied only by the drum, is performed on special occasions at Gulbarga. Many Chishti *qawwali* songs are in Indian languages, such as Hindi, Punjabi, and Siraiki, plus some Urdu poetry especially in concert performance; classical Persian poems and a few Arabic pieces also play a part in the repertory. While some *qawwali* singers are trained in the classical Indian musical styles formerly associated with the princely courts, others employ local and regional styles developed at Sufi shrines.

The audience is arranged in a hierarchical fashion with the senior Sufi acting as the master of the assembly. Some Chishti groups call for a planned sequence of songs designed to bring out particular kinds of experiences. One such sequence is to begin with songs addressed to the Prophet, followed by songs of love to excite powerful emotion; then come songs of mystical annihilation, followed by songs of divine presence. Many songs are also dedicated to particular saints, especially of the Chishti order. Ritual today involves the use of paper money (at major festivals, money changers are available to provide bills of small denominations for participants). Those who are especially moved by a song addressed to a favorite saint approach the master of the assembly and present cash donations, which are later distributed to the musicians. If a listener notices that someone else is attuned to a song, he may first approach that person and press the money into the other person's hand, so that together they may deliver the offering to the master of the assembly. Unsuspecting foreign scholars, who believe that they are merely observing the proceedings, may be drawn into the ritual by this device. It is only in secular public performances that the audience gives money directly to the musicians.

Like a number of other Sufi practices, the *qawwali* music of the Chishtis has come under attack by Muslim reformers. The influential theological school at Deoband, though it was founded by conservative scholars trained in the Chishti tradition, has been over the past century a center of *hadith*-based criticism of *sama‘* as an innovation. It has accordingly become necessary for modern Chishti spokesmen to defend the legitimacy of listening to music in terms of Islamic law. Because of the controversies over music, one frequently hears in India and Pakistan a kind of apologetic defense of *qawwali* music based on its alleged role in the preaching of Islam. Because the Sufis were great missionaries, so the argument goes, they would use whatever technique seemed most practical to get their message across. Seeing how fond Indians are of music, the Sufis therefore decided to use music to attract them to Islam, despite their recognition that music is illegitimate. This is a very weak argument for the use of music, since it basically authorizes listening to music only for non-Muslims who are likely converts to Islam. This position ignores the established role of music in early Sufism, and it wrongly views Sufis as dedicated to mass conversion, despite the lack of any early evidence for such a program. It also runs against the grain of Sufi texts, which only permitted music for those mystical elites who are capable of understanding spiritually the powerful emotional message of love poetry put to music. This paradoxical view of Chishti music is another testimony to the intensity of the debate over Sufi practice today.

On the level of popular culture, Chishti *qawwali* music has found a much enlarged audience in the twentieth century through the recording industry, initially in colonial India and now on a broader international basis. For a number of years, the wildly successful Bombay film industry has relied on *filmi* music explicitly based on the Urdu *ghazal* tradition, which in terms of theme, rhyme, and meter is closely linked to the poetry of *qawwali*. The difference lies primarily in the secular and commercial context of film music. More than one observer has commented, however, on the spillover of Bombay musical style into performances at Chishti shrines. The market for *qawwali* as a widely accepted devotional music has been vigorous in India and Pakistan for decades, and it has a popularity extending far beyond the circles of South Asian Muslims; many Hindus and Sikhs enjoy this music as an artistic performance, in the same way that many Hindus and Sikhs visit Sufi tombs on pilgrimage. The initial dissemination of *qawwali* music beyond India and Pakistan has been through specialized niche marketing at Indian and Pakistani shops in Britain and America by subsidiaries of the same British firms (principally EMI) that control the music industry in South Asia.[11]

The reception of this music in the West was initially limited to the specialist ethnomusicology category of international folk music. *Qawwali* performers could be seen in the same concert series as folkloric ballet ensembles and ethnic choral groups. Famous performers such as the Sabri Brothers and Nusrat Fateh Ali Khan have for some years performed in concert tours and music festivals in theaters in Europe, Japan, and America. Some of the best recordings of *qawwali* music (as well as other types of Sufi music noted below) are available from European institutes, such as the Maison des Cultures du Monde run by the French Ministry of Culture or the Ocora label produced by Radio France. UNESCO has included a considerable amount of *qawwali* and other Sufi music in its recording series. This was basically a "highbrow" way of presenting Sufi music, as an aesthetic performance that could be appreciated by the sophisticated and cosmopolitan listener. In the notes to a 1989 recording of Nusrat Fateh Ali Khan made by Radio France, Pierre Toureille cites his meteoric rise to popularity (ten compact disks produced in four different countries), and calls him "one of the greatest voices of this century . . . for centuries to come" (today one can find about one hundred recordings by this artist). These European recordings, in acknowledgment of the distance that separates the Parisian concert stage from the Sufi shrine in Pakistan, often provide scholarly translations of the texts of the songs in the recordings, with notes on the technical aspects of the music as well.

In more recent years, *qawwali* music has taken on a new identity through the popular world music category. This new trend has made singers, percussionists, and instrumental performers from the Middle East, Africa, and Asia much more familiar to Western audiences, not only in recordings but also in motion picture sound tracks (*The Last Temptation of Christ*). The world music recordings are bolder than the European ethnomusicology recordings in treating Sufi music as a universal property that speaks to everyone; it is music that people can dance to. While the notes to world music recordings recognize that lyrics are an important part of the *qawwali* tradition, they generally provide only a minimal annotation and rarely translate the words. This is a major shift from the earlier contexts of Chishti musical performance, where the words were the crucial and essential factor (in a similar fashion, polyphonic harmony was introduced into European church music on the grounds that it improved understanding of the words of hymns).

Nusrat Fateh Ali Khan has now collaborated to produce movie sound tracks with American musicians such as Eddie Vedder of the alternative band Pearl Jam (in *Dead Man Walking*) and Trent Reznor of the mainstream industrial group Nine Inch Nails (in *Natural Born Killers*).[12] Here he performs as a pure vocalist without a recognizable text. His rendition of a song honoring a Pakistani Sufi saint, "Mustt Mustt," was remixed by the British trip-hop group Massive Attack, in 1990 and became an international dance hit. One reviewer recently remarked after a 1996 concert, "As far as Western audiences are concerned, Khan might as well be belting out entries from the Yellow Pages."[13] In an interview, Khan has commented on the way he performs for Western audiences: "The people of the West do not understand the language, but they understand the rhythm, and they enjoy it. As music has no language, it is international in itself. I've met many Westerners who know our language as well. In Pakistan, I tend to sing more poetry along with the rhythm because they know the language."[14] While Khan feels the tension between traditional *qawwali* and new musical experimentation, as a musician he is open to new ideas. His ability to move between secular concert performance and spiritual shrine ritual is not new, however, but continues the role of the musician or poet who could be heard differently by courtly and mystical audiences. It is clear, nonetheless, that the international popularity of *qawwali* involves a radical redefinition of Sufi music. No longer a lower class professional performing for spiritually elite listeners, the singer has become a star performer for mass audiences.

The other example of Sufi music that has captured the imagination of the West has been that of the Mevlevi Sufi order, in the ritual of *sama'* that has given them the name of Whirling Dervishes.[15] This practice has been known for much longer through the reports of travelers, and it is of course the dance aspect of the ritual that has caught the attention of observers. Still, the turning dervish dance of the Mevlevis is inseparable from its musical context, and it is known by the same word for listening to music: *sema* in Turkish pronunciation. The Mevlevi Sufi order was founded by Jalal al-Din Rumi's son Sultan Walad in the late thirteenth century. The complex liturgical performance of today's Mevlevis was introduced at a later period, and attained its present form by the seventeenth century. Certainly Rumi was intimately involved with *sama'* on a regular basis, and his poetry abounds with references to music and dance. In his time, however, these gatherings were less structured events, with food and drink served along with the music, and the musicians were professionals rather than dervishes. As the order developed, a formal performance structure developed, in which the Persian poetry of Rumi was put to music along with poems in praise of the Prophet and Qur'anic recitations. The novices during their 1001-day training studied this poetry as they were trained in the dance, learning to whirl in place by spinning around a large nail placed between the big toe of the left foot and the toe next to it. Musical accompaniment came from the plucked *tambur*, the bowed *rebab*, and above all the reed flute, or *ney*, which has such a prominent symbolic role in Rumi's poetry.

Most of the known Mevlevi musical repertoire was composed from the late eighteenth to the early twentieth century, and the music overlapped in style with that which was composed for the Ottoman court. Indeed, an Ottoman sultan, Selim III (1761–1808) was a Mevlevi and composed a ceremonial musical piece that became accepted in the order. In the nineteenth century, the Mevlevis were one of about twenty Sufi orders active in Istanbul, while there were thirty-seven orders to be found in the Ottoman empire as a whole. Out of some three hundred dervish lodges in Istanbul, four belonged to the Mevlevis.[16] Yet for Western observers both then and now, the Whirling Dervishes became emblematic of Sufism as a whole. This may be partly explained by the remarkable setting of the Galata Mevlevihane in Istanbul, which had been the site of a Mevlevi lodge for centuries. By the nineteenth century, however, the hill of Galata on the Golden Horn had become a well-established colony for foreign merchants and visitors, and the Mevlevi lodge and the twice weekly performances of *sema* became well-known tourist attractions by mid-century. Access to the lodge was made easier by the construction in 1875 of the funicular railroad, or Tunel, leading to the top of the hill, and a French restaurant flourished right next door.[17] It is remarkable how many European books of the time feature pictures of dervishes, with the Mevlevi whirling dance forming the most dramatic and prominent of all the portraits.[18] These portraits, particularly those by artists such as Preziosi, show the Mevlevi dervishes as truly exotic creatures, with feminine-looking skirts and trancelike expressions.

All this would change after the revolution that established Turkey as a secular republic in 1922. Increasingly impatient with the remnants of medieval religious authority, Kemal Ataturk in 1925 promulgated a law banning the dervish orders and the public performance of their rituals. Sufi lodges were seized by the state. The Mevlevi dance was thus declared illegal. The tomb of Rumi in Konya was converted into a state-run museum in 1927, and it has functioned so ever since, though many visitors covertly pay it the reverence due to a saintly shrine. Late in 1953, by agreement with the municipal authorities of Konya, the Mevlevi dance was revived on the condition that it be done only as an artistic performance for tourists. Since then, it has been performed on the anniversary of Rumi's death every December 17, to increasingly large audiences. International concert tours have been undertaken in subsequent years (the use of the Gregorian solar calendar for the festival's date signals its secular origins, in contrast with the Muslim lunar calendar used for most saint's festivals). Although the public climate in Turkey has become somewhat more friendly for religion recently, Sufism is still essentially illegal, and Sufi groups have suffered persecution over the years.

The structure and organization of the Mevlevi liturgy is complex. It is divided into a first part containing a poem in praise of the Prophet, musical improvisations, and a whirling dance cycle, followed by a second part divided into four music and dance sections, called *selams*, followed by an instrumental finale and Qur'an recitation with prayers. The dervishes enter wearing long conical felt hats of Central Asian origin, with black cloaks that are cast off during the dance to reveal white garments. Symbolic explanations are offered of the clothing, in terms of death and resurrection. While turning, the dervish holds the arms out with the right hand turned up to heaven and the left turned down to earth. The movements are slow and stately to begin with, increasing to a fast pace with the music but never out of control.

As in the case of Chishti *qawwali*, the transplantation of the Mevlevi *sema* to the concert stage offers several conundrums about the relationship between music and spirituality. The 1994 concert tour exemplified the tension between symbolic performance and mystical ritual. The first part of the performance at Duke University, preceded by recitation of English versions of Rumi's poems, was essentially classical Ottoman court music, played by musicians wearing distinctive European-style formal wear. This was a high-culture phenomenon as one would see it in a secular Istanbul concert hall. After the intermission, dervishes came onto the stage and, under the direction of two Mevlevi leaders, performed the sequence of the *sema* with instrumental and vocal accompaniment. But who is the performance intended for? As one reviewer noted, "The 10 dervishes and 12 musicians who make up the Mevlevi Ensemble fall somewhere between performers and worshipers."[19] For the audience as a whole, the Mevlevi dance can be an entrancing art form that contrasts interestingly with European ballet. For the dervish dancers, the *sema* can be a meditation. But to what extent does the observation of this ritual become a spiritual event?

Other Turkish Sufi groups have also made the transition to the concert stage. The Qadiri (or Kadiri) *dhikr* ritual can be heard on a compact disk recorded by a European ethnographic center. The ceremony begins with prayers in Arabic chanted in unison. This is followed by poems in Turkish recited in a beautiful tenor solo, overlaid upon a deep bass line of male voices chanting the profession of faith (*la ilaha illa allah*, "There is no god but God."). I had the opportunity to observe this group in Istanbul in 1990, in a lovely wooden lodge attached to a seventeenth-century tomb. The main room for the *dhikr* (and the meal that followed) was decorated with striking dervish paraphernalia, amidst which was set a poster advertising the order's European tour of the previous year. That evening a recording crew from an ethnomusicology program on Belgian radio was present with recording gear and intrusive bright lights. The chief recording engineer was repeatedly heard to make disparaging remarks; to him the music was interesting, but the "superstition" of the dervishes was ridiculous. Yet this necessarily private ritual, performed with considerable energy after the end of Ramadan, was clearly an act of worship for those who participated. The late Shaykh Muzaffer led a group of Cerrahi-Halveti dervishes from Istanbul on an international tour in 1980, and at the climax of a stately dervish dance with musical accompaniment, he invited spiritual seekers in the audience to join him on the stage. There is an ambiguous line between performance and participation in these situations, which ends up being defined differently according to one's perspective. Turkish music that falls more neatly into the ethnographic or classical categories, such as recordings of the folk music of Chinese Turkestan, or the classical *mugam* (*maqam*) of Azerbaijan, lacks this ambiguity even when it retains some of the characteristics of Sufi music.

Outside the Sunni Sufi orders, such as the Qadiris, Mevlevis, and Halvetis, there is an important tradition of Shi'i-oriented Turkish Sufi music and dance related to the Bektashi order that is still practiced in certain communities. The Turkish Alevis (related to the Syrian 'Alawis) are a Shi'i group of about fifteen million people who regard 'Ali as a divine manifestation superior even to the Prophet. They have historically been regarded as heretical by Sunni authorities and have suffered serious persecution. Their sober and devout musical rituals, always held in private, have also been regarded with suspicion by outsiders because both men and women take part. It is clear that Alevi music has a strong leaning towards the rituals of the Bektashi order, since their repertory of songs includes many written by Bektashi-related poets such as Yunus Emre, Nesimi, Pir Sultan Abdal, Hata'i, and others. In recent years Alevi music has become widely available on recordings and on Turkish national radio, as part of the official sponsorship of culture in the national language. In the musical rituals of highly esoteric groups like the Alevis, or the Kurdish Ahl-i Haqq, the musical performer is the audience, and there is no question of professional musicians performing for elite listeners.[20]

Another Sufi-related group that has found popularity in the West is the Moroccan society known as the Master Musicians of Jajouka (or Jahjouka).[21] This group was initially discovered by several expatriate American writers, including Brion Gysin, Paul Bowles, and William S. Burroughs. Gysin hired the group to play in his Tangier restaurant The 1001 Nights in the late 1950s. Later on Brian Jones of the Rolling Stones visited the musicians in 1967, producing a recording of their music in 1971. What seemed to interest these visitors was the theory, first promulgated a century ago by the Orientalist Westermarck, that the wild Moroccan music produced on double-reed pipes was somehow connected to ancient Greek Dionysian mysteries (Jones's recording was called *The Pipes of Pan at Jajouka*). This theory seemed to be verified by ritual dances of animal representation (the goat-man Bu Jlud) and spirit possession (the demoness Aisha Qandisha) which occur during the celebration of 'Id al-Adha, the Muslim feast of Abrahamic sacrifice. The availability of powerful Moroccan hashish at some of these performances was also evidently an attraction. Since that time, the Jajouka musicians have engaged in several musical collaborations with Euro-American artists. These collaborations include recordings by jazz saxophonist Ornette Coleman (*Dancing in Your Head* in 1977) and the Rolling Stones (*Continental Drift* in 1989). Their recent concert tours have featured performances with jazz drummer Pete LaRoca and the klezmer band The Klezmatics. The Sufi connection of the Jajouka

group rests on their hereditary occupation as custodians and performers at the ancient tomb of Sidi Hmed Shikh, which is a local
center of pilgrimage with important healing functions held in weekly
Friday rituals.[22] The musicians, who have also in the past supplied
the Moroccan courts with performers of Andalusian music, are now
dependent on a new Western audience to replace their former tribal
patrons; a picture of Brian Jones hangs next to a photograph of the
king of Morocco in their clubhouse in Jajouka, and they have composed a song in his honor with the English refrain, "O Brian Jones,
Jajouka very stoned." Still, the Jajouka musicians derive their identity
from their performances at the saint's tomb, so in this way they
continue to invoke a Sufi connection.

There are many other traditions of Sufi music that continue to be
practiced in different regions. Some, but by no means all of these
traditions, have attracted the interest of Euro-American ethnomusi-
cologists and popular music producers. The music of the Moroccan
Sufi brotherhood of the Gnawa, which derives from West African
roots, is currently being advertised by an American producer as "very
bluesy, sort of like Malian music. . . . It's very warm and spiritual,
with a healing quality to it."[23] The Bauls, who are itinerant bards
reciting Bengali songs on Tantric and Sufi themes, have been recorded several times as an example of ecstatic singing in a folk tradition. There are highly refined developments of Andalusian Arabic
music that have been employed by Sufi orders for centuries in Morocco, in which different musical modes are linked to healing
through a complex physiological theory based on Greco-Arabic medicine. Egypt has a vital musical tradition of performance linked to
the *dhikr* rituals and saint's festivals of the Sufi orders; as Earle
Waugh has shown, Egyptian performers, such as Shaykh Yasin, are
amazingly popular both in person and through recordings, which include classical Arabic Sufi pieces, such as the poems of Ibn al-Farid.
In Iran, singers such as Shahram Nazeri have recorded powerful musical renderings of Rumi's Persian poetry, in styles ranging from

tambur-backed dervish choruses to classical court music (in compositions by 'Alizade) to European string orchestras. Pakistan's Folk Heritage Institute (Lok Virsa) has produced a series of books and recordings called *The Sufi Poetry Series* featuring musical performances in a variety of regional languages. Most of these musical traditions have been unconnected to dance. An exception is the practice of the Dances of Universal Peace, introduced by American Sufi leader Samuel Lewis, drawing upon dance forms and liturgies from a variety of traditions. While Sufi music is thus based on many different literary, musical, and symbolic idioms, the central element that allows us to call it Sufi music is the ritual use of the human voice to recite poetry directed to God, the Prophet Muhammad, and the Sufi saints. The mass reproduction of Sufi music for new audiences in the twentieth century and the performance of Sufi music and dance on concert stages have to some extent redefined this spiritual practice as an aesthetic event for spectators in which music takes priority over the word.

8
Sufism in the Contemporary World

Alas! The hidden secret will be public.

—HAFIZ (GHANI-QAZVINI, NO. 5)

As WE HAVE SEEN, the discovery by Europeans of something they called Sufism has satisfied a number of needs in Western culture over the past two centuries. Most importantly, creating Sufism as a new category of culture permitted it to be enjoyed and appropriated by Europeans (and Americans), precisely because it was separated from the newly emerging (and, to them, largely negative) category of Islam. This tendency has continued to the present day, especially in the realm of popular culture, where Sufism has been assimilated to generic New Age spirituality. Within Muslim countries, different ideological and political processes have also worked to create a special category of Sufism, which has now become a subject of intense dispute. Through the experience of colonialism and European-style education, Muslim modernists have been highly critical of Sufism, not on the grounds that it is foreign to Islam but because they see it as a medieval superstition and a barrier to modernity. Another perspective was that of European colonial authorities, who viewed Sufi masters and their followers as a powerful social force to be tamed or co-opted into the political system. In the post-independence period, the governments of formerly colonized states have made considerable efforts to appropriate the authority of Sufi shrines and orders into the overall program of the state. From yet another perspective, the movements that coalesced in the nineteenth century around Muslim reformists found Sufism to be highly problematic. The contemporary heirs of this tendency, usually grouped under the term *fundamentalism*, see Sufism as an enemy of Islam only slightly less threatening than Western secularism. Interestingly, both Orientalists and fundamentalists share (for somewhat different reasons) a "golden age" view of history, which lauds safely dead "classical" Sufis while scorning more recent examples of the tradition. All these debates have been made possible by the unprecedented publicization of Sufism through print and other media, a process that began in the nineteenth century. As a result, contemporary Sufi leaders have had to articulate their tradition in new ways that fit the present-day situation, whether in largely Muslim societies or as part of a new Sufism for the West.

As in previous chapters, it has to be acknowledged here that the subject of contemporary Sufism has grown to such an extent that it would require a full-length study to begin to do it justice. It would be necessary first of all to treat Sufism in each individual country where it flourishes (see "Sufism and the State," below), and in particular it would be desirable to survey the growth and development of Sufism in Western countries. Other writers have provided detailed chronological accounts of Sufism in America, with analyses of the subgroups derived from particular orders.[1] The examples in this concluding chapter are given as illustrations of the outstanding characteristics of contemporary Sufism rather than as an attempt at a comprehensive picture of the subject.

Sufism and Modernism

As an illustration of the modernist critique of Sufism, there is no better example than the poet and philosopher Sir Muhammad Iqbal

(1873–1938). Born in colonial northern India, Iqbal went to Europe for advanced study, where he encountered the works of modern thinkers such as Nietzsche and Bergson. While he was steeped in Persian literature and even taught Arabic for a time, he was convinced of the necessity of rethinking the Islamic heritage in view of the challenges presented by European thought. He expressed his views in a series of brilliant and provocative poems in both Persian and Urdu and in a set of lectures in English, published in 1930 as *The Reconstruction of Religious Thought in Islam*. Because of his advocacy of a separate state for the Muslims of British India, Iqbal is regarded today in Pakistan as the spiritual father of the country.

Iqbal was clearly engaged with individual Sufi writers, such as Rumi, who plays the role of guide in Iqbal's Dante-inspired tour of the heavenly spheres, the Persian *Book of Eternity*. Iqbal also creatively appropriated the thought of the Sufi martyr Hallaj in his construction of a modern theory of the dynamic self. But Iqbal rejected what he saw as the negative aspects of Sufism, which could be described as fatalism, passivity, and a false notion of the absorption of humanity in unity with God.

Iqbal's dissatisfaction with Sufism took the form of a devastating attack on the poetry of Hafiz in a passage of his 1915 Persian poem "Secrets of the Self":

> Beware of Hafiz the drinker,
> His cup is full of the poison of death.
> There is nothing in his market except wine—
> With two cups his turban has been spoiled,
> He is a Muslim but his belief wears the thread of an unbeliever.
> He gives weakness the name of strength,
> His musical instrument leads the nation astray.
> Go independent of the congregation of Hafiz,
> Beware of sheep and beware.[2]

Iqbal's poem generated an immense response, and the attack on Hafiz was vociferously protested. Several Indian authors wrote Persian poems in response to Iqbal's, defending the perspective of Sufi poetry. The controversy indicated the great reverence in which the poetry of Hafiz was held in India. In subsequent editions of the poem, Iqbal removed this offending section, in order to get a wider hearing for his message.

Iqbal's attack on Hafiz was emblematic of the modernist discomfort with mysticism, which was identified as quietist medieval obscurantism. For those who are enamoured with Western progress and modernity, it is easy to blame the mystically befuddled Sufi for the retrograde situation of Asian countries. A similar negative attitude towards Sufism was expressed by the Moroccan philosopher Mohamed Lahbabi.[3] It is striking to see how fully Iqbal's criticism of Sufism accorded with Orientalist theories. This may be at least in part due to Iqbal's association with British scholars such as Sir Thomas Arnold, his teacher at the Government College in Lahore, as well as his studies in Cambridge and Munich. Following the old notion that Sufism is just a recycled version of Plato, Iqbal uses exactly the same charge to reject Platonic idealism. He portrays Plato in "Secrets of the Self" as a sheep who tries to teach the tiger to be a passive and helpless vegetarian:

> Plato, the prime ascetic and sage,
> Was one of that ancient flock of sheep.
> He is a sheep in man's clothing,
> The soul of the Sufi bows to his authority.[4]

The message, directed to the Muslim reader, is that one should reject this sheeplike passivity and live up to one's true powerful nature. Iqbal was even more critical of the hereditary *pirs* descended from Sufi saints. They are no better than crows perching in the eagles' nests of great men of the past.[5] Again, it is difficult to distinguish the modernist critique of Sufism from the disparaging remarks made by Orientalists. For both, the "golden age" of Sufism may have been interesting, but the inheritors of this tradition are necessarily degenerate.

Because of the scientific posture of European scholarship, modernists in Muslim countries have tended to be impressed with the conclusions of Orientalism, whether expressed in English, French, German, or Russian. It is hard to overestimate the effect of the writings of scholars such as E. G. Browne, R. A. Nicholson, Ignaz Goldziher, and Louis Massignon; their studies of Islam and Sufism were published in Arabic or Persian translations and widely read by Muslim intellectuals. The critique of Orientalist scholarship had already been raised years before Edward Said's 1978 book *Orientalism*, as Muslim scholars witnessed unrecognizable and hostile portraits of their faith and their history put forth by Europeans (these objections, expressed in Arabic, Persian, or Turkish, were largely ignored in Europe). The reductionist approach to religion characteristic of secular ideologies such as Marxism has also furnished handy weapons with which to attack both classical and living Sufism. A particularly thorny topic for defenders of Sufism (as for Christians such as C. S. Lewis) was miracles. The author of an English biography of Shaykh 'Abd al-Qadir Jilani published in Lahore in 1953 addressed skeptical readers by simply inviting them to apply scientific standards to these mind-boggling events.[6] The defenders of Sufism replied to the threats of Orientalism and science on modern terms.

The Chishti leader Capt. Wahid Bakhsh Sial (d. 1995) is an example of a Sufi treating both Orientalists and Western scientists with their own medicine. In his English and Urdu writings he has systematically evaluated the theories and biases of European scholars of Sufism. On the one hand he has taken them to task for their tendency to separate Sufism from Islam. Over one third of his book *Islamic Sufism* is devoted to disproving "That Myth of Foreign Origin of Sufism."[7] On the other hand, he has appropriated the rhetoric of science and uses it to undermine secularists who criticize religion. The first paragraph of his book's introduction announces this strategy:

> Sufism and science are striving for the same destination. Science wants to know: How did the universe come into being and what is its nature? Is there any Creator? What is He like? Where is He? How is He related to the universe? How is He related to man? Is it possible for man to approach Him? Sufism has found the answers and invites the scientists to come and have that knowledge.

This is the rhetoric of authority, well established by the prestige of medicine, science, and engineering. In Europe since the time of Comte, this rhetoric has been used to make religion irrelevant. Like other Muslim apologists who appropriate the language of science, Capt. Wahid Bakhsh seeks to turn the tables.[8] While it has been possible for many Sufi leaders to accommodate their teachings in this way to the contemporary age, as will be shown below, modernism (whether religious or secular) is not comfortable with the spiritual authority, institutions, or practice of Sufism.[9]

The title of Capt. Wahid Bakhsh's book, *Islamic Sufism*, signals an intent to claim Islamic identity alongside the Sufi tradition. This emphatic joining of the two disputed terms occurs repeatedly in works written to defend Sufism, both in European languages and in Arabic script languages. Orientalists such as Nicholson had treated *tasawwuf* as a generic term "to denote any variety of mysticism."[10] Up to a point, Muslim authors initially accepted this category without question. Pakistani scholar B. A. Dar used the term *tasawwuf* in this sense in the title of an Urdu book on pre-Islamic mysticism, published in 1962 by the state-sponsored Institute for Islamic Culture; the book is based almost entirely on English-language scholarship from the early twentieth century.[11] A more recent Urdu study by another Pakistani scholar, Latif Allah, published in 1990 by the same Pakistani institute, explicitly challenges the concept of *tasaw-wuf* as generic mysticism. This author, who writes from a Chishti perspective, argues that Sufism is not something foreign added to Islam but is instead intrinsic to it; a new term (*sirriyat*, from *sirr*, secret) is coined as an equivalent for the English word *mysticism*.[12] For those who are critical of Orientalism and its modernist reflex among Muslims, establishing the Islamic identity of Sufism is an important goal.

Sufism and the State

By 1920, every Muslim country except four (Persia, Saudi Arabia, Afghanistan, and Turkey) had been conquered and colonized by foreign powers, mostly from Christian Europe. In a process that had begun well over a century earlier, colonial regimes extended their reach over the vast majority of Muslim populations around the world. In a number of areas, Sufi orders were the strongest local institutions that remained when local rulers had been overthrown by European arms. It is for this reason that Sufi orders were able to serve as centers of anticolonial resistance in a number of areas. Several such cases in Algeria, the Caucasus, and Sudan have been briefly mentioned already (above, chapter 1). To these one could add the example of the Sanusi order in Libya and the western Sudan, which fought for years against both the French and the Italians. Their leader, Shaykh Idris, was exiled to Egypt after World War I but was later with British assistance made king of Libya in 1951; until the rise of Muammar al-Qaddafi put an end to it, the modern Libyan kingdom had been built on the basis of a Sufi order. The semitheo-cratic states of Futa Jallon and Futa Toro in West Africa in the eighteenth and nineteenth centuries were further illustrations of the potential of Sufi orders to serve as a basis for social order and antico-lonial resistance. In Turkey, the final straw that precipitated the abolition of the dervish orders was a Kurdish revolt led by a Naqshbandi shaykh. Today in Chechnya, the independence movement invokes memories of nineteenth-century Sufi opposition to the Russian empire in mobilizing the current anti-Russian struggle.

Colonial administrators were therefore aware that the Sufi orders were well organized and highly motivated groups. Their fear of the power of the Sufi orders was realistic. Earlier rulers of Muslim societies had known that the intense bonds of loyalty between master and disciple could compete with royal authority. The Safavid empire, which ruled Iran from 1501 to 1732, came to power through a coalition of tribal groups based on allegiance to a Shi'i-oriented Sufi lineage. The strongly Sunni Ottoman rulers were deeply suspicious of Shi'i groups as a potential fifth column for the Safavids. When they suppressed the Janissary military corps in 1826, they also dealt a severe blow to the closely related (and Shi'i-oriented) Bektashi Sufi order. It is not surprising, therefore, that in the colonial period, Sufi orders could take on an oppositional role. By 1900, French colonial officials observed that their invasion and conquest of Algeria had actually strengthened the powerful Rahmaniyya Sufi order, which they regarded as the Algerian national church.[13]

As a necessary step in the administration of their territories, colonial governments regularly sponsored research studies of their subjects with a view to increasing the effectiveness of their rule. While the academic Orientalist establishments in European universities were generally content to study "classical" Sufi texts, colonial officials in the field dealt with current social realities. Occasionally, a trained Orientalist would be recruited by a colonial regime to prepare a field study of a Muslim society, as in the case of C. Snouck Hurgronje's study of the Achehnese, prepared for the Dutch East Indies government in 1894 following a series of revolts.[14] It was from these sources that the first semianthropological studies of Sufism and saints' shrines emerged. Much of the colonial study of Sufism is hidden away in official archives and bureaucratic publications. A good deal of it is still accessible in print, however, as for instance in the British colonial gazetteers of India and the French studies of North Africa. These accounts of current Sufism and saints' shrines are a combination of condescension and alarm. On the one hand, these groups could be viewed as backward and superstitious examples of inferior cultures. On the other hand, they might be dangerous. It is striking to see that the postcolonial bureaucracies of independent nations often perpetuate the very same attitudes.

The political attitude of colonial regimes towards Sufi groups is an interesting prefiguration of the depictions of modern fundamentalist groups in the mass media and military intelligence reports. That is, Sufi leaders then (like fundamentalist leaders now) were seen as fanatical leaders whose charisma inspired their followers with an irrational and blind devotion that made them capable of anything. This is a stereotype that has been known in the West ever since Marco Polo gullibly recounted stories in which the leader of the Assassins ordered enthusiastic followers to jump off cliffs to prove their obedience. The main difference is that nowadays ideology rather than charismatic leadership is seen as the source of fanaticism. The alarming implications of these stories should be a tip-off to their political usefulness. That is, if central political authority is able to portray its opposition as crazed followers of a dangerous cult, it lends an air of legitimacy and necessity to whatever steps the government finds necessary to repress the offending group. This is why the loudest warnings today against Islamic fundamentalism come from secular political regimes (Egypt, Israel, Algeria, Tunisia) interested in obtaining military aid from paranoid Western governments. The Western media, historically out of their depth in Muslim countries, assist this process by taking at face value the self-proclamations of fundamentalist leaders. In the nineteenth century, it was the anticolonial Sufi groups that were the focus of Western paranoia. It takes only a glance at the massive British propaganda directed at the messianic uprising of the Sudanese Mahdi in the 1880s to see the level of horror aroused by these "dervishes." It was rare to find a sympathetic account of a Sufi political leader—such as Tolstoy's admiring portrayal of a follower of Shaykh Shamil in *Hadji Murad*, based on his service in the Russian military force sent to pacify the Caucasus in the late 1850s.

There were other instances in which Sufi institutions were successfully co-opted into the colonial order. Important Sufi leaders in the Indian Punjab included hereditary custodians of Sufi shrines as well as teachers with strong networks of disciples organized along tribal lines.[15] By recognizing the hereditary *pirs* as local notables, British officials actually increased their authority and even appointed them to positions in the government; despite their official policy of neutrality towards religion, colonial bureaucrats ended up being closely involved in the administration and even the religious activities of many Sufi shrines. The British had to mediate and settle succession disputes at major shrines, in decisions that had serious repercussions in local politics. Some *pirs* advanced their political careers by using their influence with their followers to aid British military recruiting during World War I. Despite their close links to British rule, at the crucial moment Sufi leaders played a vital role in the success of the Pakistan movement. In independent Pakistan, Sufi leaders have continued to be active in electoral politics due to their strong rural power bases and networks of followers. A similar case of a Sufi group cooperating with a colonial regime is the Muridiyya order of Senegal, which through its extensive networks has controlled the peanut market both in the colonial period and after independence. Good relations with French officials and, later on, with the Senegalese bureaucracy have been important for the temporal success of this group.

Most Muslim-majority countries gained independence in the years following World War II, and the new regimes in many ways continued the policies of the colonial regimes that preceded them. Colonial governments had typically eliminated or neutralized other sources of authority, and they centralized all functions of government under their own control. Formerly colonized countries have inherited authoritarian government structures that did not welcome competing political forces. In many Muslim countries one can see special government bureaucracies devoted to controlling Sufi institutions. In Egypt, this takes the form of a bureau called the Majlis al-Sufiya or Association of Sufis, which lists and supervises some eighty "official" Sufi orders. As Islamicist Valerie Hoffman has shown, however, some of the most popular Sufi orders, such as the Sudan-based Burhaniyya with a membership of several million, are not recognized by the state.[16]

The attempt to control Sufi orders and institutions by the state should be seen in the context of nationalism. In Pakistan, political leaders such as Ayyub Khan and Z. A. Bhutto attempted to redefine Sufi shrines in terms of a national ideology. Festivals at the tombs of important Sufi saints are regularly graced by provincial governors and even the prime minister, who give speeches describing how these saints were forerunners of the Islamic state of Pakistan. On the bureaucratic level, this relationship is paralleled by assertion of the authority of the Department of Charitable Trusts over the operations and finances of major Sufi shrines. This same bureau is also responsible for a series of publications of official biographies of popular saints as well as devotional manuals, in this way indicating what constitutes officially approved forms of Sufism.[17]

Since Islam has been the principal issue of identity by which Pakistan was divided from India, it is interesting to see the contrasting way in which India deals with the Islamic heritage of its large Muslim minority. Typically this is done by praising Sufism as a form of religious tolerance, in contrast to what is described as the rigid bigotry of Islam. A recent study on the Sufis of Sind, published by the Ministry of Information of the Indian Government, argues that Sufis were not true Muslims because they were not fanatics; instead, they were advocates of secular nationalism, which happens to be the official policy of the Congress Party.[18] A 1994 film produced by the Indian Ministry of Information's Film Division, *The Lamp in the Niche*, assimilates Sufism to the category of Hindu *bhakti* devotion, with frequent quotations from the antisectarian verses of Kabir.

A special case in the twentieth century was the attempt of the Soviet regime to control Sufism. With an official policy of promoting atheism, the Soviet government tried to constrain all forms of religion, with tightly managed officially approved settings for a very small number of religious functionaries. A few Muslim officials were allowed to operate in the Central Asian regions, although Qur'ans were not available in translations, ostensibly to preserve the purity of the Arabic text. Despite the fact that Sufi gatherings and rituals were illegal, Sufism seems to have continued as the principal form of unofficial Islam in the Soviet Union, principally in the Caucasus and in Central Asia. Soviet Orientalists, who were required to undergo indoctrination in Marxist-Leninist ideology, had to stick to the official line when they discussed Sufism.[19] In the post-Soviet period, the Sufi shrines of Uzbekistan, particularly the tomb of Baha' al-Din Naqshband in Bukhara, have taken on considerable symbolic importance in the articulation of a new cultural and national identity.

It should not be forgotten that Sufism also has to be officially recognized by agencies of the United States government. Religion in the United States is defined principally by the courts, the Internal Revenue Agency, and the Immigration and Naturalization Service. Followers of a Turkish Sufi leader who wished him to stay in the U.S. asked me several years ago to write a letter on his behalf to the Immigration and Naturalization Service. In this letter, I had to indicate that he was an authentic religious teacher, so that he could qualify for a visa and later on a resident alien permit (green card) as a religious teacher. I was asked to make this certification based on the examination of an initiatic genealogy which gave the lineage of the shaykh in his order. There were a number of ironies and ambiguities inherent in asking an American scholar to judge whether a Turkish Sufi master was authentic. It was first of all the imposition of an American legal category to define a Sufi as religious from the viewpoint of the federal government. Second, the genealogy or "tree" document that I examined had been photocopied and then taped together in sections, so it was definitely a product of modern technology. Third, this Sufi teacher is legally prohibited from acting in this way in his home country, where his official profession is folk dance teacher; Sufism is still illegal in Turkey. Obviously, none of this has to do with the inner dynamics of Sufism, but it underlies the way in which Sufism is necessarily defined and controlled by the powers of the state, even in America.

It is important to keep in view these political and social aspects of Sufism. Those who consider mysticism a private affair and who view Sufism primarily through poetry or theoretical treatises may feel that military and economic activities do not fit the picture of inner mystical experience. From this point of view, any accommodation with political power constitutes a fall from purity. It is difficult, however, to reconcile such a purely otherworldly perspective with either the history or the teachings of Sufism. As one famous saying has it, "Sufism is all practical ethics (*adab*)." The prescriptive ethics that are bound up in Sufi rhetoric cannot be put into effect by isolated hermits. Sufis are constantly reminded of this by the model of the Prophet Muhammad, who plays for them the role of social and political leader as well as mystical exemplar. While there is certainly a tension between Sufism and the world, illustrated most dramatically by the repentance that is the beginning of the spiritual stations, Sufism is also very much a community affair that is hard to separate from the rest of life.

Sufism and Fundamentalist Islam

While Islamic fundamentalism is certainly the aspect of Islam most frequently discussed in the Western media, it is unfortunately not much better known than other aspects of Islamic culture. The vagueness with which these terms are thrown around makes the average reader suspect that they are synonymous; one would assume that all Muslims must be fundamentalists. While it is usually recognized that there are Christian fundamentalists as well (indeed, the term originated in Los Angeles early in this century), the press have nearly given Muslim fundamentalists a monopoly over the term. Since the term has a fairly negative air, probably dating from the time when it was associated with antievolutionist forces at the time of the Scopes trial, Muslims who are tarred with this brush rightly resent it. Nonetheless, if it is carefully defined, *fundamentalism* can be used as a descriptive term with a specific meaning in a variety of religious contexts. Bruce Lawrence defines it as an antimodernist ideology based on selective interpretation of scripture, used largely by secondary male elites in an oppositional role against the state.[20] It is important to note that antimodernist does not mean antimodern; fundamentalists are very much at home with modern technology and modern techniques of political struggle. Fundamentalists are instead opposed to the secularist ideology that has banished religion from public life; in being antimodernist they are being inescapably modern.

The relevance of fundamentalism for Sufism comes at the root of their belief systems. The selective interpretation of scripture that underlies the central authority of fundamentalism cannot afford to tolerate alternate interpretations. Since fundamentalists typically portray their interpretations as literal and hence unchallengeably true, any kind of psychological or mystical interpretation of the sacred text is a basic threat to the monopoly that they wish to claim over tradition. It has been pointed out before that Western journalists are too often content to accept the self-interpretation of Muslim fundamentalists as the sole authentic custodians of tradition. One would never guess from most media reports that fundamentalists usually constitute no more than twenty percent of any Muslim population and that in this respect they are likely to have the same proportion as fundamentalists in Christian, Hindu, or Buddhist societies.

Like the spin doctors who attempt to mold public opinion

through commentary, fundamentalist spokesmen attempt through their rhetoric of total confrontation to claim representation of Islam. For this effort to succeed, they must discredit and disenfranchise all other claimants to the sources of authority in the Islamic tradition. There is no stronger rival claim on these sources than in Sufism. Modern studies of Muslim fundamentalism rarely point this out, preferring instead to dwell on confrontation with European colonialism and the secular state as the proximate causes of this ideology. But the principal early fundamentalist movement, the Wahhabism that swept Arabia in the nineteenth century, had nothing to do with responses to Europe. While resistance to the Ottoman empire may have been a factor, there was a basic religious struggle going on between Wahhabis and Sufis for the control of central religious symbols. Fundamentalists articulated their goal as the domination of the symbol of Islam.

The remarkable thing is that many of the leaders of Muslim fundamentalism were raised in social contexts where Sufism was strong. Both Hasan al-Banna, founder of the Muslim Brotherhood in Egypt, and Abu al-'Ala' Maudoodi, founder of the Indo-Pakistani Jama'at-i Islami, were very familiar with the authority structures of Sufi orders from their youth. From their writings it is quite clear that they admired the organizational strength of Sufi orders, and they acted in relation to their followers with all the charisma of a Sufi master in the company of disciples. They did not, however, adopt any of the spiritual practices of Sufism, and in particular they rejected the notion of any saintly mediation between God and ordinary humanity. In an attempt to destroy the accretions of history and return to the purity of Islam at the time of the Prophet, fundamentalists rejected the ritual and local cultural adaptations of Sufism as non-Islamic. From a political point of view, one must acknowledge that fundamentalists had sized up their opposition well. No other group had such a powerful hold on Muslim society and spirituality as the Sufi orders and saintly shrines.

The notion of Islam promulgated in fundamentalist circles has more than a passing resemblance to fundamentalist forms of Christianity. In both cases, history and tradition are sacrificed in an attempt to recover the original purity and primitive authenticity of the religion as believed to be practiced by the founder. Religion becomes intensely doctrinal, and from being part of the texture of life it is turned into an objectified system that can be contrasted with other such systems. Fundamentalists object strenuously to the isolation of religion as a separate category, and it is for this reason that one constantly hears the refrain that "Islam is not just a religion; it is a way of life." This hopeful attempt to return to a prior golden age is unfortunately impossible. The rhetoric of fundamentalism has already accepted the notion of multiple religions as competing ideologies; the fundamentalist solution to this dilemma is simply to defeat all rivals. The average Muslim senses the extremism inherent in this situation. The term *Islamic* in Arabic is increasingly reserved (sometimes in tones of irony) for fundamentalists alone.

Many examples could be cited of conflict between fundamentalists and Sufis over the past two centuries, from the Indonesian *dakwa* movements to the persecution of Sufi orders in revolutionary Iran. One of the early examples was the series of debates held by Shaykh Ahmad ibn Idris, an extremely influential Sufi reformer in North Africa, when he was on pilgrimage in Arabia during the early Wahhabi period.[21] This kind of debate has continued to shape the lives of Muslims ever since. Several years ago I witnessed this kind of conflict when I was invited to give a talk at a state university about the Islamic origins of Sufism. My host was a Pakistani friend, a member of a Sufi order, who was studying for his Ph.D. in a technical field. The local Muslim student association was dominated by the Saudis, because they funneled a good deal of money into student scholarships and paid the expenses of the association. My friend had been blackballed because of his Sufi activities, which in the eyes of the Saudis made him worse than an infidel. Not fully aware of this situation, I proceeded to give a talk with a standard narrative about

the Islamic sources upon which Sufism is based; none of this is contested in current scholarship, and I have used it as preliminary material in a book on Sufism. At the conclusion of the lecture, which
was well attended, I was confronted by an insistent questioner who
presented his own point of view. "Every word that you have said,"
he informed me and the audience, "is false." From his perspective,
to suggest that there was anything Islamic about Sufism was sheerest
heresy. The newly purified symbol of Islam must have nothing to do
with saints, miracles, music, or the countless local customs and beliefs that give distinctive flavor to a host of Muslim cultures around
the world.

The Publication of the Secret

Perhaps the most remarkable aspect of the emergence of Sufism
as a topic in the nineteenth and twentieth centuries has been the
publicizing of a previously esoteric system of teaching through modern communications media. Today, Sufi orders and shrines in Muslim countries produce a continual stream of publications aimed at a
variety of followers from the ordinary devotee to the scholar. Just as
the recording industry democratized the private rituals of *sama'* for a
mass audience, the introduction of print and lithography technology
made possible the distribution of Sufi teachings on a scale far beyond
what manuscript production could attain. As has been noted in the
case of Ibn 'Arabi's Arabic works, when they first emerged into print
in the late nineteenth century, suddenly a work that had existed in
at most a hundred manuscripts around the world (and those difficult
of access) was now made easily available at a corner bookstore
through print runs of a thousand copies.[22] Evidence is still far from
complete, but indications are that in the principal locations for print
technology in Muslim countries in the nineteenth century (Cairo,
Istanbul, Tehran, and Delhi/Lucknow), the main patrons of publication, aside from governments, were Sufi orders.[23]

The publicization of Sufism occurred at precisely the time when Sufism was becoming an abstract subject, separated from Islam in Orientalist writings and condemned by reformists as a non-Islamic innovation. Some of these publications in turn respond directly to presentations of Sufism by Orientalists, fundamentalists, and modernists. In this category one can find not only editions of classical Sufi texts but also writings of contemporary Sufi leaders—including discourses, lectures and essays, biographies, prayer and meditation practices, and manuals for using talismans and charms bearing the names of God (*ta'widh*). Among these publications are also ready-made lineage documents, with blank spaces at the end for the would-be initiate and the master to inscribe their own names. Since all these books were available commercially, this new trend amounted to a mass marketing of Sufism on an unprecedented scale.

Through printed books, today one can gain access to Sufism through scholarly publications from Western-style universities, learned societies, and cultural centers sponsored by governments in many different Muslim countries. In format and style, these works are very much in the same tradition as European, academic Orientalism: European-style punctuation, footnotes, and editorial techniques have been largely adopted in Arabic-script publishing. In contrast to the elite monopoly on culture characteristic of the manuscript, book publication presupposes a mass audience created by public education and sustained by print capitalism. While access to manuscripts in the premodern period was rare and difficult and scribal errors required the comparison of different manuscripts, print makes books easy to acquire and standardizes their texts. Therefore, when an official at al-Azhar University in Egypt edits a classical Sufi text, it does not merely replicate the experience of an eleventh-century author for the modern reader. Carrying official authorization as part of Arabic "heritage" literature (the category corresponding to "classic"), the printed text now functions in new ways to defend Sufism from the polemics of both fundamentalists and Westernized secularists. In countries like Pakistan, where Arabic and Persian both function as "classical" languages, there has been a concerted effort to translate the whole curriculum of Arabic and Persian Sufi literature into Urdu. Like the classical Greek works of Aristotle and Euripides at Oxford bookstores, the Arabic Sufi works of Sarraj, Qushayri, and Suhrawardi are now to be found in Urdu versions on bookshelves in Lahore. Their eminence and learning makes them powerful allies in the defense of Sufism against ideological opponents.

Although little work has been done on this subject, biographical sources can furnish valuable information about the role of print media in the development of a modern form of Sufism. Here we can see, for instance, how the Chishti leader Dhawqi Shah (d. 1951) was a university graduate and a reporter for an English-language newspaper prior to becoming a Sufi. He continued to publish newspaper articles throughout his life, both in Urdu and in English. His writings deal with such modern topics as racial theory, fundamentalism, comparative religion, and the Pakistan nationalist movement. Most remarkably, his chief successor, Shaykh Shahidullah Faridi, was a British-born convert to Islam (originally named Lennard), who came to Pakistan after reading English translations of works on Sufism. His Urdu discourses, dictated in Karachi in the 1970s, are still available in print. The international distribution of printed books and periodicals was a necessary element in the lives of both men. The dramatic effects of print technology on subjects such as the Protestant Reformation and the development of nationalism have been frequently discussed, but the role of printing in the development of contemporary Sufism still needs to be investigated.

One particular form of publication seems especially valuable to reveal how Sufism has been practiced and disseminated in this century. Periodicals seem to have caught on fast with the introduction of printing. In South Asia it is clear that Urdu newspapers played an important role in the development of Muslim thought and self-consciousness. Arthur Buehler has shown how the modern Naqshbandi teacher Jama'at 'Ali Shah directed his movement through *Anwar-i sufiyya* (The Lights of the Sufis), a periodical aimed at Sufi devotees. Mandatory subscriptions for disciples combined with a rigorous train-travel program for Jama'at 'Ali Shah enabled him to use modern technology to keep in touch with a far-flung network of followers.[24] The Egyptian periodical *Ma'rifa* (Gnosis) published Arabic translations of articles by French esoterist Rene Guenon in the 1930s, thus providing a vehicle for the perennial philosophy school of thought in the Arab world. Today in America, English-language periodicals distributed by Sufi orders from Iran and other countries are a venue for both disciples and scholars.[25]

Another characteristically modern form of publication, the novel, also became popular in Muslim countries in the late nineteenth century. This literary form, which is intimately tied to both personal identity and social critique, has also been used for the expression of Sufism. In South Asia, the above-mentioned Dhawqi Shah wrote in 1920 a mystical novel in Urdu entitled *The Wine and the Cup*. The cultural hybridity of this book ranges from colonial Bombay to the imagined conversations of the Mughal emperor Shahjahan, with frequent quotations of Persian mystical poetry. It aroused the reluctant admiration of the Sufi-minded poet Akbar Ilahabadi, who remarked, "You have put the water of Zamzam [from Mecca] into a soda-water bottle!" The Chishti leader Hasan Nizami, who was attached to the shrine of Nizam al-Din Awliya' in Delhi, was also renowned for his Sufi-minded historical novels and other journalistic writings in Urdu. In Turkish, the novel *Nur Baba* by Yakup Kadri Karaosmanoğlu depicted a Bektashi dervish exercising a sinister influence over an upper-class Ottoman woman; its publication in 1922 is believed to have hastened the abolition of the dervish orders.[26] More recently, Turkish novelist Orhan Pamuk has incorporated extensive Sufi imagery into his writings, especially *The Black Book*. The Nobel Prize–winning Egyptian novelist Naguib Mahfouz has invoked Sufi figures, including the poet Ibn al-Farid, in works such as *The Thief and the*

Dogs.[27] In English, one can point to Sufi imagery in many of the
novels of Doris Lessing. Frank Herbert's science fiction novel *Dune*
is packed with obscure references to Sufism. In American Sufi circles,
the fictional quest narrative in novel form is an especially popular
vehicle for the discussion of Sufism.[28]

In the late twentieth century, the other form of publicizing Sufism has been through visual and electronic media. Most profession-
ally made films relating to Sufism have fallen into the category of
ethnographic or cultural documentary, although some governments
(Turkey, India, Uzbekistan) have produced films that appropriate
Sufi saints and Sufi-related culture as part of the national image.[29]
The availability of movie and video cameras has made it possible to
record the talks of Sufi teachers for several decades. This form of
visual recording seems to be used primarily for private circulation in
Sufi groups and for preservation of these talks for the future. But the
recent explosion of Sufi-related home pages on the Internet and in
on-line discussion groups indicates that Sufism is going to be a very
public part of the electronic age. The World Wide Web permits
anyone to set up a home page without having to seek authorization
from any particular religious hierarchy. It is accordingly receptive to
a cheerful anarchy and a generally antiauthoritarian attitude. The
principal divide that separates Sufi groups on the Internet is whether
or not they identify primarily with Islamic symbolism and religious
practice; while this was not even an option in the premodern period,
it is a major issue in debates about the nature of Sufism conducted
in Internet discussion groups. The Internet is also a vehicle for advertising books and recordings relating to Sufism, so it continues to
function as a marketing device.

The publicizing of Sufism through print and electronic media has
brought about a remarkable shift in the tradition. Now advocates of
Sufism can defend their heritage by publishing refutations of fundamentalist or modernist attacks on Sufism. In this sense the media
permit Sufism to be contested and defended in the public sphere as

one ideology alongside others. This is very much the case, for instance, in the publications of the Barelvi theological school in South Asia, which defend the devotional practices of Sufism against the scripturalist attacks of the Deoband school. At the same time more personal forms such as the novel allow for an intimate expression of individual spiritual aspirations, which can be communicated to a large audience through the empathy created by the novelistic narrative. Biographies and discourses can also create an intimate relationship between readers and Sufi masters; although this was also the function of those genres in manuscript form, the wide distribution of print greatly enlarges the potential audience. Through these modern public media, Sufism is no longer just an esoteric community constructed largely through direct contact, ritual interaction, and oral instruction. Now it is publicized through mass printing, modern literary genres, and electronic technology—with all the changes in personal relationships that these media entail.

New Styles of Sufi Leadership

In discussing the patterns of authority typical of premodern saints of the Chishti Sufi order of South Asia, Bruce Lawrence has pointed out eight recurrent paradoxes that sum up the kinds of qualities these saints seemed to possess:

1. Well born into an established Muslim family, the saint must yet be motivated to seek a Sufi master in order to improve the quality of his Islamic faith. There is an apparent absence of lower-caste trades among Indian Sufi masters, in contrast to their Iranian and Arab counterparts.
2. Educated in Qur'an, *hadith*, theology, and Sufi literature as well as poetry, the saint must be able to intuit the deepest truths behind, and often beyond, the written word.
3. Initiated by a shaykh whom he acknowledges to be the sole vehicle of divine grace for him, the saint must strive

to attain his own level of spiritual excellence, often through severe fasting and prolonged meditation.

4. Living in isolation from the company of others, the saint must constantly attend to the needs of his fellow Muslims or at least to those needs evidenced by his disciples and visitors to his hospice.

5. Married and the father of sons, he must be celibate in temperament and disposition.

6. Capable of performing miracles, he must be careful to suppress them on most occasions.

7. Prone to ecstasy, whether in silent solitude or abetted by music and verse while in the company of other Sufis, the saint must be able to recall and to perform his obligatory duties as a Muslim.

8. Avoiding the company of worldly people, merchants, soldiers, and government officials, including kings, he must live in proximity to them (that is, near a city) and stay in touch with worldly people through his lay disciples.[30]

Not every early Chishti saint possessed all of these qualities, but they may be taken as a catalogue of characteristics that might define the ideal type of Sufi saint.

Looking at patterns of leadership and authority in Sufism today, it is striking to see that many of the characteristics in the list just given may be found in contemporary Sufi leaders. The conditions of modern life have changed drastically, however, in every country of the world. The globalization of the economy has been paralleled by a globalization of culture that has redefined spiritual traditions such as Sufism. Sufi leaders, if they are not to choose privacy and obscurity, necessarily engage with what we call the modern world. There are thus a number of additional characteristics we can see in contemporary Sufism that would not have been found in premodern Sufis. As in the case of the characteristics of early Sufi leaders just mentioned, these additional modern qualities are not all found in every contemporary Sufi movement, but overall they furnish a distinctive profile of Sufism that can be commonly observed today—covering religious, scientific, technological, and sociocultural modes of modernity. Limitations of space do not permit a full enumeration of examples, but a few general remarks on each topic would be helpful.

Under the category of religion, one finds that contemporary Sufi groups are now called upon to make an explicit statement regarding the relation of the Sufi group with "mainstream" Islam, which may take the form of a nonrelation. In premodern Sufism it was rare that any option but Islam could even be articulated. On the level of theoretical and literary mysticism, one can find some rare instances of Jewish Sufism, such as Maimonides' grandson Obadiah ben Abraham (d. 1265), or the Christian Sufism of Ramon Llull (d. 1316). In both these cases the authors in question were powerfully affected by reading Arabic Sufi literature, which inspired them to write new works in the same vein addressed to their coreligionists. As far as Sufi orders are concerned, in India there were a few instances of premodern Hindus who were initiated by Chishti masters without having to convert to Islam, but these were extremely few in number and by no means typical. On less formal levels, many non-Muslims have had contact with Sufi saints and have been impressed by them on a personal level. Such was the case, for instance, with the Christians and Jews who attended the funeral of Rumi; during the later Ottoman centuries, many Christians and Jews interacted with Sufism in this manner. Occasionally Zoroastrians did the same in Iran. The same kind of relationship still holds today for many Hindus and Sikhs who visit Sufi shrines in India. All this was made possible by the inwardness of Sufism, which tends to make external boundaries less significant. But prior to the nineteenth and twentieth centuries, it was scarcely necessary for a Sufi, steeped in the Qur'an and the example of the Prophet Muhammad, to have to define him- or herself in terms of Islam. Once Islam had been narrowly defined as a legal and ideological system, however, the dual critique of Sufism by

Orientalists and fundamentalists forced Sufis to justify themselves in terms of scriptural sources. Certainly there had been criticism of particular Sufi practices or doctrines prior to this, but never had the entire inner dimension of religion been called into question.

Today, particularly in Western countries, Sufi groups have to position themselves in relation to Islamic identity. Some are rigorous in following Islamic law and ritual, and this insistence is often combined with adoption of the clothing and manners of the group's country of origin. Other groups are flexible for newcomers, on the theory that they can be gradually introduced to the outer dimension of religion later on after the inner aspect has been first absorbed. Yet other groups frankly relinquish Islamic law and symbolism, defining Sufism as the universal aspect of all religions. The most striking example of this universalist tendency is the life and legacy of Hazrat Inayat Khan, who came to the West in the early years of this century. Trained both as a musician and as a Sufi in the Chishti order, he traveled in Europe and America giving performances of classical Indian music. Faced with the need to articulate a religious position, he presented Sufism in terms of universal religion, detached from Islamic ritual and legal practice. The groundwork for this position had been partly established much earlier by European scholars who viewed Sufism as a mysticism comparable to any other. More importantly, there was a universalist dimension implicit in Sufism as there was in the Islamic tradition, which recognized that every people had been sent a prophet. In all Muslim societies, there were significant continuities with pre-Islamic cultures, which guaranteed that Islamic culture was never merely Islamic.

Other religious changes have seen Sufi leaders having to define themselves also in relation to other religious traditions, expanding beyond their traditional territories, and encountering other Sufi orders in a new kind of Sufi ecumenism. In pluralistic societies like America, Sufi leaders today are invited into the midst of eclectic gatherings of Zen masters, Tibetan lamas, Hindu yogis, Christian

monks, and Jewish Hasidim. They have in a number of cases established extremely positive relations with members of these other religious traditions. Proselytization has taken Sufi orders beyond their
historic homes to new regions; Pakistani Chishtis have found new
large followings in Malaysia, and Iranian Nimatullahis have established new centers in West Africa, Europe, and North America. An
especially striking phenomenon is the encounter of different Sufi
orders, fostered particularly by an annual Sufi conference held in
northern California under the auspices of the International Association for Sufism since 1994, where dozens of Sufi groups of different
origins gather for talks and *dhikr* performances. The Mevlevi order
with its characteristic dance also seems to serve as a kind of umbrella
for bringing together different Sufi groups to commemorate the
birth and death of Rumi, for instance. Social service organizations
have also been established by different Sufi groups to provide medi-
cal treatment and other forms of support to the public.

Another response to the religious dilemma has been the Traditionalist position, sometimes called the Perennial Philosophy, a response
to colonialism and modernism that has been adopted by European
converts to Islam and by intellectuals from Muslim countries as
well.[31] This school of thought, as represented by Rene Guenon,
Frithjof Schuon, and S. H. Nasr, proposes a vision of primordial divine tradition as the source of all religions, compared to which the
secular modern world is a deviation and a degeneration. Drawing on
Catholic traditionalism for its critique of modernism, members of
the Traditionalist school nevertheless generally view Islam as the
most viable religion today. This position makes it possible to view
Sufism in an ecumenical fashion as a particular example of universal
mysticism. The Traditionalist perspective has also proven attractive
to thinkers such as Aldous Huxley and Huston Smith. While the
Traditionalist school shares with less doctrinaire forms of universalist
Sufism an appreciation of other religions, its distinctive metaphysical

vision and its sharp confrontation with modernism set it apart from other perspectives associated with Sufism.

A different kind of Sufi reponse to modernism has been, as noted above, the adaptation of the rhetoric of science. Some Sufi leaders have taken the step of undergoing university training in the sciences, particularly in the professional discipline of psychology. Dr. Javad Nurbakhsh was formerly head of psychiatry at Tehran University. Psychology is a major element in the teachings of Pir Vilayat Khan, whose center at New Lebanon, New York, offers a wide range of seminars and training sessions. But the person who has made the most out of Sufism and psychology is Idries Shah, who has probably published more books having to do with Sufism than anyone else alive. Shah is not part of a traditional Sufi order but instead worked with J. G. Bennett in England, who in turn had developed the Sufi-related teachings of P. D. Ouspensky and G. I. Gurdjieff. He presents Sufism not as mystical Islam but as a psychological method for apprehending reality. His following resembles a Sufi order to the extent that he is regarded as the principal living authority for dispensing knowledge about Sufism. Some of his many writings, particularly the Mulla Nasruddin stories, represent not so much esoteric teaching as popular folklore. But psychology is not the only scientific discipline found among Sufis. Shaikh Fadlallah Haeri, an Iraqi-born leader whose main American center is in Texas, had a career as an engineer. Hazrat Shah Maghsoud Sadegh Angha, chief recent leader of the Iranian Oveyssi-Shahmaghsoudi order in California, was trained in America as a theoretical physicist and mathematician. His poetry includes not only the traditional themes of love and wine but also references to Einstein and relativity.

Beyond these religious and philosophical trends, one must notice the changes that technology and mass marketing have brought to Sufism. The earliest reference to popular poster art that I have seen in Sufi literature is an extremely critical remark by Shah Ghulam

'Ali, a Naqshbandi master who lived in India in the early nineteenth century; he was enraged when one of his disciples told him that pictures of saints (evidently printed) were available at the great mosque of Delhi.[32] Despite his reservations, this kind of mass-produced art is readily available at every saint's festival in South Asia today (see figure 4 on page 76). The media of print and film, discussed above, are obvious examples of how a reproducible technology can be adapted for reaching a mass audience, and tape recordings and compact disks have brought Sufi music to a large new audience. The Internet is adding a new dimension to the availability of spirituality. Audio tapes of oral teachings are also frequently circulated among the followers of a Sufi master. Some of this technology is used in ways that approximate to ritual. Certainly one can see how photographs of the Sufi master would be treated with respect. In certain groups one can acquire a locket containing a microfilm of an Arabic prayer dictated by a great shaykh, similar in its utility to the handwritten prayers or tiny Qur'ans that could be worn as amulets in earlier times. The followers of Bawa Muhaiyadeen videotaped as many of his talks as possible, with the result that thousands of hours of his discourses (in Tamil, with English translation) have been preserved. One videotape of him with a particularly important message regarding Sufi practice and prayer is replayed every year at the exact time when it was first delivered. A new symbolic element having to do with mass marketing is the logo, a copyrightable graphic design that serves to symbolize a Sufi group in its publications. Notable in this respect is the winged heart used in the publications of groups related to Hazrat Inayat Khan or the dervish axe used as a symbol by the Nimatullahi and other Iranian orders.

The biggest change to be faced by Sufism in the West is social and cultural, for this is the arena where nondoctrinal aspects of religion generally fall. Appreciation of the music and poetry of Sufism naturally leads to interest in the language of the home country (Arabic, Persian, Turkish, Urdu, Tamil). Distinctive traditional clothing may also be worn, if only on special occasions. Ethnic food provides an enjoyable access to community and opportunities for service. But the distinctiveness of Sufism as an imported spirituality carries with it a consciousness of cultural difference. Those who are willing to consider seriously a spiritual tradition from the Middle East or India are at least implicitly critical of homegrown alternatives. Even the most irenic Sufi teachers, Hazrat Inayat Khan for example, could be severe in their judgment regarding such typical modern Western vices as racism. But the most distinctive development of Sufism in the West is probably in the area of gender relations. Most Muslim societies where Sufism has been a living force have practiced some form of gender segregation. Female Sufi masters and saints, while known, have not been common in the past. But the social habits of the modern West are different, and it is not unusual to see men and women participating together in rituals, musical performances, and other gatherings held by Sufi orders. In some Sufi groups, women have quite naturally taken on positions of leadership. Just as American women are playing a notable and innovative role in the development of Buddhism in this country, so it may be expected that Sufism in the West will have to pay special attention to women's perspectives in order to succeed.

Considering all of the changes that have taken place in the social implementation of Sufi traditions in the past century or so, it is easy to see that there are differences from the old days. Sufism is attacked by modernists and fundamentalists, regulated by the state, publicized by the orders, and redefined in new religious, scientific, technological, and social terms. There are certainly some interpreters who are unhappy with these changes and who regard them as unfortunate concessions to bad times. One should be careful, however, about adopting the view that the golden age is located firmly in the past. This is a position that is peculiarly vulnerable to political agendas, whether it be the purism of the Orientalist who sees true Sufism only in texts, or the minimal concession of the fundamentalist, who praises early Sufis as good Muslims, while condemning all modern Sufism as a deviation from true Islam. Sufism, like Islam, is a debatable term, and it is caught in the cultural wars between the Euro-American and Muslim worlds, even as it functions as one of the few viable bridges between these cultures. At a time when Iran is one of the nations most hated by Americans, there is something more than ironic about the incredible popularity of the great Persian poet Rumi in America. Perhaps Sufism still conceals a mystery of the human heart that will help humanity go beyond the separative boundaries of the individual and collective ego. It is this sense of transcendence that contemporary Syrian sculptor Mustafa 'Ali attempted to convey in his piece entitled *Ibn 'Arabi, a Sufi for All Ages* (see frontispiece). Remembering the prescriptive ethical formulas used to define Sufism, we should give the final word to paradox and transcendence: "The Sufi is the one who is not."[33]

Notes

Preface

1. Jane I. Smith, *An Historical and Semantic Study of the Term 'Islam' as Seen in a Sequence of Qur'an Commentaries*, Harvard Dissertations in Religion, 1 (Missoula, Mont.: Scholars Press, 1975), esp. pp. 226–27.
2. William C. Chittick, *The Faith and Practice of Islam: Three Sufi Texts* (Albany: State University of New York Press, 1992), pp. 165–79. Chittick ends by defining Sufism simply as "being a good Muslim."
3. An indication of the immense bibliography on Sufism in European languages can be seen in *Les Voies d'Allah: Les ordres mystiques dans l'islam des origines a aujourd'hui*, ed. Alexandre Popovic and Gilles Veinstein (Paris: Fayard, 1996), and in the forthcoming multi-part article "Tasawwuf" in the new edition of *The Encyclopaedia of Islam* (Leiden: E. J. Brill).

Chapter 1: What Is Sufism?

1. Sir William Jones, "The Sixth Discourse, On the Persians," in *Works* (London, 1807), 3, 130–32.
2. Jones, "On the Mystical Poetry of the Persians and Hindus," in *Works*, 4, 220–21.
3. Colonel Sir John Malcolm, *The History of Persia, from the Most Early Period to the Present Time: Containing an Account of the Religion, Government, Usages, and Character of the Inhabitants of That Kingdom* (2 vols., London: John Murray, 1815), 2, 382.
4. Ibid., 2, 383.
5. Ibid., 2, 402.

6. Mountstuart Elphinstone, *An Account of the Kingdom of Caubul* (London, 1815; reprint ed., Karachi: Oxford University Press, 1972), 1, 273

7. John Leyden, "On the Rosheniah Sect, and its Founder Bayezíd Ansárí," *Asiatic Researches* 11 (1810), pp. 363–428. Leyden described the "philosophical ideas maintained by the Súfi sect" as the doctrine that only God exists, the principle of nonviolence, and the claim to attain divinity and prophecy (p. 379).

8. Lt. James William Graham, "A Treatise on Sufiism, or Mahomedan Mysticism," *Transactions of the Literary Society of Bombay* 1 (1819), quoting pp. 90–91.

9. Frid. Aug. Deofidus Tholuck, *Ssufismus, sive theosophia Persarum pantheistica* (Berlin: Ferd. Duemmler, 1821), pp. vi, n. 1; vii, n. 2.

10. Ibid., pp. 54, 70.

11. Ibn Khaldun, *The Muqaddimah: An Introduction to History*, trans. Franz Rosenthal, ed. N. J. Dawood, Bollingen Series (Princeton: Princeton University Press, 1969), p. 358; see also pp. 359–67.

12. As an example, see the article "Sufi" in Thomas Patrick Hughes, A *Dictionary of Islam* (London, 1885; reprint ed., Delhi: Oriental Publishers, 1973), pp. 608–22. This article nicely reproduces all of the theories and prejudices of nineteenth-century Orientalism.

13. 'Abd Allah Ansari, *Tabaqat al-sufiyya* (Generations of the Sufis), ed. Husayn Ahi (Tehran: Intisharat-i Furughi, 1362/1983), p. 7.

14. Shihab al-Din Abu Hafs 'Umar al-Suhrawardi, *'Awarif al-ma'arif* (Gifts of Gnosis), ed. 'Abd al-Halim Mahmud and Mahmud ibn al-Sharif (2 vols., Cairo: Matba'at al-Sa'ada, 1971), 1, 214.

15. Abu al-Qasim 'Abd al-Karim al-Qushayri, *al-Risala al-Qushayriyya* (The Qushayrian Treatise), ed. 'Abd al-Halim Mahmud and Mahmud ibn al-Sharif (Cairo: Dar al-Kutub al-Haditha, 1972–74), p. 20.

16. Ibid., pp. 550–57.

17. For examples, see Javad Nurbakhsh, *Sufism: Meaning, Knowledge, and Unity* (New York: Khaniqahi-Nimatullahi Publications, 1981), pp. 11–41.

18. 'Ali Hujwiri, *Kashf al-mahjub* (Unveiling the Concealed), ed. Ahmad 'Ali Shah (Lahore: Ilahi Bakhsh Muhammad Jalal al-Din, 1342/1923), p. 6.

19. Ibid., p. 32.

20. *Adab al-muluk fi bayan haqa'iq al-tasawwuf* (The Manners of Kings: Explaining the Realities of Sufism), ed. Bernd Ratke, Beiruter Texte und Studien, 37 (Beirut/Stuttgart: Franz Steiner Verlag, 1991), pp. 5–6.

21. Baha' al-Din Khurramshahi, *Hafiz nama: sharh-i alfaz, a'lam, mafahim-i kalidi wa abyat-i dishvar-i Hafiz* (The Book of Hafiz: Commentary on Terms, Names, Key Concepts, and Difficult Verses of Hafiz) (Tehran: Intisharat-i 'Ilmi u Farhangi, 1373/1995), no. 191, p. 1038, lines 1, 8; see also pp. 138–40 for parallel passages.

Chapter 2: The Sacred Sources of Sufism

1. Paul Nwyia, "Le Tafsir mystique attribue à Ga'far Sadiq," *Mélanges de l'Université Saint-Joseph*, 43 (1968), p. 37, reprinted in Abu 'Abd al-Rahman al-Sulami, *Majmu'a-i athar* (Collected Works), ed. Nasr Allah Purjavadi (2 vols., Tehran: Markaz-i Nashr-i Danishgahi, 1369–72/1991–4), 1, 48.

2. Abu Hamid Muhammad ibn Abi Bakr Ibrahim Farid al-Din 'Attar Nishapuri, *Kitab tadhkirat al-awliya'*, ed. Reynold Alleyne Nicholson (2 vols., 5th ed., Tehran: Intisharat-i Markazi, n.d.), 1, 136.

3. Abu al-Fadl Rashid al-Din al-Maybudi, *Kashf al-asrar wa 'uddat al-abrar* (The Unveiling of the Secrets and Provision for the Pious), ed. 'Ali Asghar Hikmat (10 vols., Tehran: Danishgah-i Tihran, n.d.), 3, 793–94.

4. See my "Mystical Language and the Teaching Context in the Early Sufi Lexicons," in *Mysticism and Language*, ed. Steven T. Katz (Oxford: Oxford University Press, 1992), pp. 181–201.

5. Abu Nasr 'Abdallah B. 'Ali al-Sarraj al-Tusi, *Kitab al-Luma' fi'l Tasawwuf* (The Book of Glimerings on Sufism), ed. Reynold Alleyne Nicholson (London, 1914; reprint ed., London, Luzac & Co., 1964), pp. 181–201.

6. Badi' al-Zaman Furuzanfar, *Ahadith-i mathnawi* (*Hadith* Sayings in the *Masnavi*), Intisharat-i Danishgah-i Tihran, 283 (Tehran: Chapkhana-i Danishgah, 1334/1956), no. 42, pp. 18–19 (citing *al-Jami' al-saghir*). This important reference work contains over seven hundred *hadith* sayings alluded to by Rumi in his *Mathnawi* (pronounced *Masnavi*).

7. Ibid., no. 70, p. 29 (cited by Sufis such as Najm al-Din Daya, but rejected by Ibn Taymiyya and others).

8. Ibid., no. 342, p. 113 (citing *Bihar al-anwar*).

9. Ibid., no. 301, p. 102 (citing Ahmad ibn Hanbal). A variation on this saying ends, "when Adam was between water and clay."

10. Ibid., no. 163, p. 63 (citing al-Bukhari).

11. For a commentary on this saying, see Henry Corbin, *Creative Imagination in the Sufism of Ibn 'Arabi*, trans. Ralph Manheim, Bollingen Series 91 (Princeton: Princeton University Press, 1969), pp. 272–81.

12. Furuzanfar, no. 346, pp. 114–15 (citing Ahmad ibn Hanbal, al-Bukhari, and Muslim).

13. Annemarie Schimmel, *Mystical Dimensions of Islam* (Chapel Hill: University of North Carolina Press, 1975). pp. 6, 142.

14. Jalal al-Din Muhammad Balkhi [Rumi], *Masnavi*, ed. with commentary by Muhammad Isti'lami (6 vols., Tehran: Zavvar, 1370/1991), 1, 9 (book 1, verse 6).

Chapter 3: Saints and Sainthood

1. Peter Brown, *The Cult of the Saints: Its Rise and Function in Latin Christianity* (Chicago: University of Chicago Press, 1982), pp. 56–64.
2. Qushayri, 2, 520–525.
3. Ruzbihan Baqli, *Sharh-i shathiyyat* (Commentary on Ecstatic Sayings), ed. Henry Corbin, Bibliotheque Iranienne, no. 12 (Tehran: Departement d'Iranologie de l'Institut Franco-Iranien, 1966), p. 10.
4. Qushayri, 2, 522.
5. A. J. Wensinck, *The Muslim Creed: Its Genesis and Historical Development* (Cambridge, 1932; reprint ed., New Delhi: Oriental Books Reprint Corporation, 1979), pp. 193, 224, quoting the Fiqh Akbar 2.
6. Michel Chodkiewicz, *Seal of the Saints: Prophethood and Sainthood in the Doctrine of Ibn 'Arabi*, translated by Liadain Sherrard (Cambridge : Islamic Texts Society, 1993).
7. Ruzbihan Baqli, *The Unveiling of Secrets: Diary of a Sufi Master*, trans. Carl W. Ernst (Chapel Hill, N.C.: Parvardigar Press, 1997), paragraph 5.
8. *Adab al-muluk*, p. 34.
9. Sulami, *Tabaqat al-sufiyya*, pp. 48–49
10. 'Attar, *Tadhkirat al-awliya'*, 1, 246.
11. Muhammad Dara Shikuh, *Sakinat al-awliya'* (The Ship of Saints), ed. Muhammad Jalali Na'ini (Tehran, 1344/1965), pp. 129–31. A fuller version of my translation was previously published in *Religions of India: In Practice*, ed. Donald S. Lopez, Jr., Princeton Readings in Religions (Princeton University Press, 1995), pp. 509–512.
12. 'Attar, *Tadhkirat al-awliya'*, 2, 122–23.
13. See my *Words of Ecstasy in Sufism*, (Albany: SUNY Series in Islam, SUNY Press, 1985), pp. 102–10.
14. Ibn 'Arabi, *al-Futuhat al-makkiyya* (The Meccan Openings), (4 vols., Beirut: Dar Sadir, n.d.), 1, 98–99.
15. Quoted from my "An Indo-Persian Guide to Sufi Shrine Pilgrimage," in *Manifestations of Sainthood in Islam*, ed. Grace Martin Smith, assoc. ed. Carl W. Ernst, (Istanbul: The Isis Press, 1994), pp. 60–61.
16. Advertisement for *Awliya' allah ke zinda kirishmat*, in *Karimi Islamibari taqwim Bumba'i 1408* (Bombay: Karimi Press, 1408/1988), inside back cover.

Chapter 4: The Names of God, Meditation, and Mystical Experience

1. Anthony Welch, *Calligraphy in the Arts of the Muslim World* (Folkestone, Kent: Dawson, 1979), p. 22.
2. Burhan al-Din Gharib, *Ahsan al-aqwal* (The Best of Sayings), comp. Hammad al-Din Kashani (Persian MS, Khuldabad), p. 111–12.

3. *The Way of Abu Madyan*, trans. Vincent J. Cornell, Golden Palm Series (Cambridge: The Islamic Texts Society, 1996), p. 74.

4. Burhan al-Din Gharib, p. 112.

5. Hughes, *A Dictionary of Islam*, p. 471

6. Shams al-Din Ahmad al-Aflaki al-'Arifi, *Manaqib al-'arifin* (Deeds of the Gnostics), ed. Tahsin Yazici (2 vols., Ankara: Turk Tarih Kurumu Basimevi, 1976–80), 1, 272.

7. G. C. Anawati and Louis Gardet, *Mystique musulmane: aspects et tendances—expériences et techniques* (4th ed., Paris: Librairie Philosophique J. Vrin, 1986), pp. 188–89.

8. Ibn 'Ata' Allah al-Sikandari, *Miftah al-falah wa misbah al-arwah* (The Key to Salvation and Lamp of Spirits) (Egypt: Matba'at Mustafa al-Babi al-Halabi wa Awladuh, 1381/1961), p. 4.

9. Ibid., pp. 28–29.

10. Ibid., pp. 34–36.

11. Ibid., p. 50.

12. For treatments of Sufi metaphysics and cosmology, see the writings of Henry Corbin, Seyyed Hossein Nasr, William Chittick, James Morris, Michel Chodkiewicz, and specialized articles such as those found in two volumes edited by Leonard Lewisohn: *Classical Persian Sufism from Its Origins to Rumi* (New York: Khaniqahi Nimatullahi Publications, 1993), and *The Legacy of Medieval Persian Sufism* (New York: Khaniqahi-Nimatullahi Publications, 1992).

13. Ruzbihan Baqli, *Maslak al-tawhid* (The Path of Unity), ed. Paul Ballanfat, §4.

14. Ibn 'Ata' Allah, p. 52.

15. *Abu Madyan*, trans. Cornell, p. 58.

16. Shaqiq al-Balkhi, *Adab al-'ibadat* (The Manners of Worship), in *Trois œuvres inédites de mystiques musulmans: Saqiq al-Balhi, Ibn 'Ata, Niffari*, ed. Paul Nwyia (2nd ed., Beirut: Dar el-Machreq Éditeurs SARL, 1982), pp. 17–20.

17. Abu Hamid al-Ghazali, *Ihya' 'ulum al-din* (Vivifying the Sciences of Religion) (Cairo: Dar al-Shu'ab, n.d.), 4, 2598.

18. See my "The Stages of Love in Persian Sufism, from Rabi'a to Ruzbihan," in *Classical Persian Sufism from Its Origins to Rumi*, ed. Leonard Lewisohn, pp. 435–55.

19. Louis Massignon, *Essai sur les origines du lexique technique de la mystique musulmane*, Études Musulmanes, 2 (new ed., Paris: Librairie Philosophique J. Vrin, 1968), p. 41. This has recently been translated as *Essay on the Origins of the Technical Language of Islamic Mysticism* (Notre Dame, Ind.: University of Notre Dame Press, 1994).

20. Paul Nwyia, *Exégèse coranique et langage mystique, Nouvel essai sur le lexique technique des mystiques musulmanes* (Beirut: Dar el-Machreq Éditeurs, 1970), pp. 170–73.

21. See al-Qushayri, *Principles of Sufism*, trans. B. R. von Schlegell (Berkeley: Mizan Press, 1990), an abridged translation consisting of the section on spiritual stations, arranged into forty-three chapters.

22. The best description of this system of meditation is found in Jamal J. Elias, *The Throne Carrier of God: The Life and Thought of 'Ala' ad-dawla as-Simnani* (Albany: State University of New York Press, 1995), esp. pp. 79–99, 119–46, upon which the following account (very much abbreviated) is based. See also Henry Corbin, *The Man of Light in Iranian Sufism*, trans. Nancy Pearson (Boulder: Shambhala Publications, 1978).

23. Muhammad Dhawqi Shah, *Sirr-i dilbaran* (The Secret of Beloveds) (4th printing, Karachi: Mahfil-i Dhawqiyya, 1405/1985), pp. 298–99.

24. Nuruddîn Abdurrahmân-i Isfarâyinî, *Le Révélateur des mystères: Kâshif al-Asrâr*, ed. and trans. Hermann Landolt (Paris: Verdier, 1986), p. 101 (Persian text), 44–45 (French translation), quoting Jibra'il Khurramabadi.

25. The complex argument and evidence upon which this paragraph is based are set forth in detail in the introduction to my forthcoming book *The Pool of Nectar: Islamic Interpretations of Yoga* (State University of New York Press).

26. Ibn 'Arabi, *Journey to the Lord of Power: A Sufi Manual on Retreat*, trans. Rabia Harris (Rochester Vt.: Inner Traditions, 1981), pp. 29–30.

27. Ruzbihan Baqli, *Kashf al-anwar*, §164, quoted in my *Ruzbihan Baqli: Mystical Experience and the Rhetoric of Sainthood in Persian Sufism*, Curzon Sufi Series (London: Curzon Press, 1996), p. 44.

28. Ruzbihan Baqli, *Kashf al-asrar* (The Unveiling of Secrets), §78. For samples of the vocabulary of mystical experience, see my *Ruzbihan Baqli*, pp. 32–35.

29. 'Abd al-Rahman Jami, *Nafahat al-uns* (Breezes of Intimacy), ed. Mahdi Tawhidipur (Tehran, 1336/1957), p. 479, quoting Najib al-Din Buzghush (d. 1280).

30. William Donkin, *The Wayfarers: An Account of the Work of Meher Baba with the God-Intoxicated, and Also with Advanced Souls, Sadhus, and the Poor* (San Francisco, 1969; reprint ed., Myrtle Beach, S.C., 1985).

31. Ruzbihan, *Sharh-i shathiyyat*, pp. 134–35. For a fuller discussion of ecstatic sayings, see my *Words of Ecstasy in Sufism*, SUNY Series in Islam (Albany: State University of New York Press, 1985).

Chapter 5: The Sufi Orders

1. Marshall G. S. Hodgson, *The Venture of Islam: Conscience and History in a World Civilization*, vol. 2, *The Expansion of Islam in the Middle Periods* (Chicago: The University of Chicago Press, 1974), p. 218.

2. O. Depont and Xavier Coppolani, *Les confréries religieuses musulmanes* (Algiers, 1897).

3. Muhammad ibn 'Ali al-Sanusi al-Khattabi al-Hasani al-Idrisi, *al-Silsabil al-ma'in fil-tara'iq al-arba'in* (Cairo: n.p., 1989), p. 6.

4. Suhrawardi, *'Awarif*, 1, 252. The word translated as inspires (*yulaqqinu*) in some manuscripts reads as impregnates (*yalqahu*).

5. Muslih al-Din Sa'di, *Gulistan* (The Rose Garden), 2.16, in *Kulliyyat* (Complete Works), ed. Muhammad 'Ali Furughi (Tehran: Sazman-i Intisharat-i Javidan, n.d.), p. 115.

6. The Arabic feminine termination -*iyya*—found in, for example, Qadiriyya—assumes the word *tariqa* or way, in the phrase *al-tariqa al-Qadiriyya*, the Qadiriyya way. One can also for convenience use the masculine form and speak of the Qadiri order.

7. Burhan al-Din Gharib, pp. 82–83.

8. For the following I draw upon the stimulating study by Ahmet T. Karamustafa, *God's Unruly Friends: Dervish Groups in the Islamic Later Middle Period, 1200–1550* (Salt Lake City: University of Utah Press, 1994).

9. The phrase is from Fazlur Rahman, *Islam* (2nd ed., Chicago: University of Chicago Press, 1979), p. 153.

10. J. Spencer Trimingham, *The Sufi Orders in Islam* (Oxford: Oxford University Press, 1971), pp. 2, 70–71.

11. Trimingham explicitly states that "the decline in the orders is symptomatic of the failure of Muslims to adapt their traditional interpretation of Islam for life in a new dimension" (pp. 256–57)—that is, the failure of Muslims to become totally Westernized. The most powerful critique of the notion of the decline of Islamic civilization was provided by Marshall Hodgson in *The Venture of Islam*, vol. 3, pp. 165–222.

12. Trimingham, pp. 261–63.

13. *Ruzbihan Baqli*, pp. 125–27.

14. I am grateful to Professor Arthur Buehler of Colgate University for this information.

15. Muhammad Taqi 'Ali Qalandar Kakorawi (d. 1290/1873), *al-Rawd al-azhar fi ma'athir al-qalandar* (The Manifest Exploration of the Deeds of the Qalandar) (Rampur: Matba'-i Sarkari, 1331–6/1913–8), p. 256, quoting Muhammad Akram Naqshbandi's *Manahij*.

16. The tensions over the succession to Nizam al-Din are discussed in *Eternal Garden*, pp. 118–23.

17. Bruce B. Lawrence, "Biography and the 17th-Century Qadiriyya of North India," in *Islam and Indian Regions*, ed. Anna Libera Dallapiccola and Stephanie Zingel-Ave Lallemant, Beiträge zur Südasienforschung, Südasien-Institut der Universität Heidelberg, 145 (Stuttgart: Franz Steiner Verlag, 1993).

18. For a fuller discussion of the problems surrounding the issue of conversion to Islam in relation to Sufism, see Carl W. Ernst, *Eternal Garden: Mysticism, His-*

tory, and Politics at a South Asian Sufi Center (Albany: State University of New York Press, 1992), pp. 155–68, and also Richard M. Eaton, *Islam and the Bengal Frontier* (Berkeley: University of California Press, 1993).

19. Shah Muhammad Rida Shattari Qadiri Lahuri (d. 1118/1706), *Adab-i muridi* (Manners of Discipleship), MS 5319 'irfan, Ganj Bakhsh library, Islamabad, pp. 108–14.

20. The comments that follow draw upon Suhrawardi, *'Awarif*, 1, 251–60.

Chapter 6: Sufi Poetry

1. François de Blois remarks that "the great majority of the quatrains that have come to be ascribed to 'Umar could not possibly be his. . . . In the Mongol period 'Khaiyam' is no longer a historical person but a genre." *Persian Literature, A Bio-bibliographical Survey*, begun by C. A. Storey, vol. 5, part 2, *Poetry ca. A.D. 1100 to 1225* (London: The Royal Asiatic Society of Great Britain and Ireland, 1994), p. 363.

2. The extent of the subject is revealed by Annemarie Schimmel, *As Through a Veil: Mystical Poetry in Islam*, Lectures on the History of Religions sponsored by the American Council of Learned Societies, New Series, no. 12 (New York: Columbia University Press, 1982).

3. Andras Hamori, *On the Art of Medieval Arabic Literature*, Princeton Essays in Literature (Princeton: Princeton University Press, 1974), pp. 31–77.

4. Th. Emil Homerin, " 'Tangled Words': Towards a Stylistics of Arabic Mystical Verse," in *Reorientations/Arabic and Persian Poetry*, ed. Suzanne Pinckney Stetkevych (Bloomington: Indiana University Press, 1994), pp. 190–98; Martin Lings, "Mystical Poetry," in *The Cambridge History of Arabic Literature*, *'Abbasid Belles-Lettres*, ed. Julia Ashtiany et al. (Cambridge: Cambridge University Press, 1990), pp. 235–64.

5. Louis Massignon, *Le Dîwân d'ál-Hallâj* (new ed., Paris: Librairie Orientaliste Paul Geuthner, 1955). See Schimmel, *Mystical Dimensions of Islam* (Chapel Hill, N.C.: University of North Carolina Press, 1975), pp. 70–71, for comments on Hallaj's poetry. Some verses by Hallaj are translated by Sells, *Early Islamic Mysticism: Sufi, Qur'an, Mir'aj, Poetic and Theological Writings* (Mahwah, N.J.: Paulist Press, 1997), pp. 302–303; Lings, pp. 245–48; *Words of Ecstasy*, pp. 27–28, 66, 69; Herbert Mason, "Three Odes of al-Hallâj," in Ilse Lichtenstadter, ed., *Introduction to Classical Arabic Literature* (New York: Twayne Publishers, 1974), pp. 316–321; Louis Massignon, *The Passion of al-Hallaj*, trans. Herbert Mason (4 vols., Princeton: Princeton University Press, 1982), 3, 337–339.

6. Massignon, p. 93; Husayn ibn Mansur al-Hallaj, *Sharh diwan al-Hallaj* (Commentary on the Poems of Hallaj), ed. Kamil Mustafa al-Shaybi (Beirut/Baghdad: Maktabat al-Nahda, 1394/1974), pp. 279–80.

7. Massignon, pp. 31–35; Shaybi, pp. 166–72.

8. See the examples translated by Cornell, *The Way of Abu Madyan*, pp. 150–75; one of these poems was checked with the oral version known by members of a Qadiri lodge in Marrakesh (p. 37).

9. Muhyi'ddın ibn al-'Arabí, *The Tarjumán al-Ashwáq, A Collection of Mystical Odes*, ed. and trans. Reynold A. Nicholson (London, 1911; reprint ed., London: Theosophical Publishing House Ltd, 1978).

10. Ibn al-'Arabi, *Tarjuman al-ashwaq* (The Interpreter of Longings), (Beirut: Dar sadir, 1386/1966), p. 10; my translation differs from that of Nicholson, p. 4.

11. Ibn al-'Arabi, *Tarjuman*, p. 39; see also Nicholson, no. 10, pp. 65–66.

12. Th. Emil Homerin, *From Arab Poet to Muslim Saint: Ibn al-Farid, His Verse, and His Shrine* (Columbia SC: University of South Carolina Press, 1994).

13. Abu al-Ma'ali 'Abd Allah ibn Muhammad ibn 'Ali ibn al-Hasan ibn 'Ali al-Miyanji al-Hamadani mulaqqab ba-'Ayn al-Qudat, *Tamhidat* (Preliminaries), ed. 'Afif 'Usayran, Intisharat-i Danishgah-i Tihran, 695 (Tehran: Chapkhana-i Danishgah, 1341/1962), p. 128.

14. This account draws upon Alessandro Bausani, *Storia della letteratura persana* (Milan, 1960), pp. 265–90.

15. Hamori, p. 67. For an example of mystical interpretation of secular Arabic wine poems on the theme of hangover, see *Ruzbihan Baqli*, pp. 73–74. Elsewhere (*Sharh-i shathiyyat*, p. 177), Ruzbihan quotes two lines from Abu Nuwas's famous verse, "Pour me wine, and tell me it is wine, / but don't pour secretly what can be public. // Permit it in my lover's name, but leave out nicknames, / for there's no good in pleasures if they're veiled."

16. de Blois, p. 273.

17. Shams al-Din Muhammad Hafiz Shirazi, *Diwan* (Bombay: 'Ali B'ha'i Sharaf-'Ali and Company Private Limited, 1377/1957), pp. 17–18.

18. Khurramshahi, pp. 40–90

19. Farid al-Din 'Attar Nishapuri, *Diwan*, ed. Sa'id Nafisi (Tehran: Kitabkhana-i Sana'i, 1339/1960), pp. 102–3; Jalal al-Din Muhammad Rumi, *Ghazaliyyat-i Shams-i Tabrizi*, ed. Mansur Mushfiq (Tehran: Bungah-i Matbu'ati Safi-'Ali-shah, 1338/1960), pp. 178–79.

20. Qasim Ghani, *Bahth dar athar wa afkar wa ahwal-i Hafiz* (Research on the Writings, Thought, and Life of Hafiz), vol. 2, *Tarikh-i tasawwuf dar islam wa tatawwurat wa tahawwulat-i mukhtalifa-yi an az sadr-i islam ta 'asr-i Hafiz* (The History of Sufism in Islam and its Different Developments and Changes from the Beginning of Islam to the Age of Hafiz) (Tehran: Kitabfurushi Zawwar, 1340/1961), p. ix (t).

21. Khurramshahi, p. 794.

22. See Michael Hillman, "Afterword," in *Hafez: Dance of Life* (Washington, D.C.: Mage Publishers, 1989), pp. 95–104.

23. See *Ruzbihan Baqli*, pp. 9–10, for details on the evidence for the connection of Hafiz and Ruzbihan.

24. Jami, *Nafahat*, ed. Isti'lami, pp. 611–12.

25. In a large anthology of Persian *ghazals* assembled in the 1940s in India for recitation in Chishti Sufi circles, the four most cited authors were Rumi, Hafiz, Ahmad-i Jam, and Jami. See Mushtaq Ilahi Faruqi, *Naghmat-i sama'* (Melodies of Music), (Karachi: Educational Press, 1392/1972).

26. A full account of Rumi's life is given by Annemarie Schimmel, *Triumphal Sun: A Study of the Works of Jalaloddin Rumi* (London: Fine Books, 1978), pp. 12–36.

27. William Chittick has pointed out the problems with interpreting Rumi via Ibn 'Arabi, in "Rumi and *wahdat al-wujud*," in *Poetry and Mysticism in Islam: The Heritage of Rumi*, ed. Amin Banani (New York: Cambridge University Press, 1994). For a convenient anthology of translations from Rumi's writings arranged by topic, see William Chittick, *The Sufi Path of Love: The Spiritual Teachings of Rumi*, SUNY Studies in Islamic Spirituality (Albany: State University of New York Press, 1983).

28. Fatemeh Keshavarz, *Reading Mystical Poetry: The Case of Jalal al-Din Rumi* (Columbia, S.C.: University of South Carolina Press, forthcoming in 1997).

29. Thanks to Peter Kaufman for suggesting this Latin version. Another effect would be found by substituting Italian: *piu desiderabile e dolce che'un bacio d'una vergine* (Carolyn Wood). For samples of the mixed language or macaronic verses found in Persian literature, see E. G. Browne, *A Literary History of Persia* (Cambridge: The University Press, 1964), 2, 44–46.

30. Jonathan Z. Smith, "Sacred Persistence: Toward a Redescription of Canon," in his *Imagining Religion: From Babylon to Jonestown* (Chicago: The University of Chicago Press, 1978).

31. For a recent scholarly translation, see Grace Martin Smith, trans., *The Poetry of Yunus Emre, A Turkish Sufi Poet*, University of California Publications in Modern Philology, 127 (Berkeley: University of California Press, 1993). A translation addressed to a more popular audience is *The Drop that Became the Sea: Lyric Poems of Yunus Emre*, trans. Kabir Helminski and Refik Algan (Putney, Vt.: Threshold Books, 1989).

32. The politics of the study of Ottoman literature have been admirably summarized by Victoria Rowe Holbrook, in *The Unreadable Shores of Love: Turkish Modernity and Mystic Romance* (Austin: University of Texas Press, 1994), pp. 13–31.

33. Samples of *tekke* verse can be seen in J. K. Birge, *The Bektashi Order of Dervishes* (London, 1937; reprint ed., London: Luzac Oriental, 1994), and in Nermin Menemencioglu, *The Penguin Book of Turkish Verse* (London: Penguin Books, 1978).

34. See Holbrook for a comprehensive study of Shaykh Ghalib.

35. See Mark R. Woodward, *Islam in Java: Normative Piety and Mysticism in the Sultanate of Yogyakarta* (Tucson: The University of Arizona Press, 1989).
36. For Sufi poetry in South Asia, see Schimmel, *As Through a Veil*.
37. See Annemarie Schimmel, *Pain and Grace: a Study of Two Mystical Writers of Eighteenth-Century Muslim India* (Leiden: E. J. Brill, 1976).

Chapter 7: Sufi Music and Dance

1. The best single study of Sufi music and dance is Jean During's *Musique et extase: L'audition mystique dans la tradition soufie* (Paris: Albin Michel, 1988). For developments in India see Bruce Lawrence, "The Early Chishti Approach to Sama'," in *Islamic Society and Culture: Essays in Honour of Professor Aziz Ahmad*, ed. Milton Israel and N. K. Wagle (New Delhi: Manohar, 1983), pp. 69–93.
2. Sa'di, *Gulistan*, II.26, p. 120. This passage is engraved in stone on one wall of the tomb of Sa'di in Shiraz.
3. Burhan al-Din Gharib, in Rukn al-Din ibn 'Imad al-Din Dabir Kashani Khuldabadi, *Shama'il al-atqiya'* (Virtues of the Devout), ed. Sayyid 'Ata' Husayn, Silsila-i Isha'at al-'Ulum, no. 85 (Hyderabad: Matbu'a Ashraf Press, 1347/1928–9), pp. 347–48.
4. Qushayri, p. 644.
5. Kashani, *Misbah al-hidayat*, p. 149.
6. Ibn 'Arabi, *Futuhat*, IV, 270.
7. For an account of Chishti rules for listening to music, see my *Eternal Garden*, pp. 145–54.
8. I am indebted to During for the following remarks, pp. 125–35.
9. This and the two preceding quotations are cited in *Shama'il*, pp. 356–58.
10. The best account of Chishti musical performance is Regula Burckhardt Qureshi's *Sufi Music of India and Pakistan: Sound, Context and Meaning in Qawwali* (Cambridge, 1986; reprint ed. with compact disc, Chicago: University of Chicago Press, 1995).
11. Regula Qureshi, " 'Muslim Devotional': Popular Religious Music and Muslim Identity under British, Indian and Pakistani Hegemony," *Asian Music* 24 (1992–93), pp. 111–21.
12. Thanks to my daughter Tess Ernst for supplying the correct categories for these musical groups. It is worth noting that another member of Pearl Jam, Jeff Ament, has formed a band called Three Fish (named after some stories told by Rumi); members of this band have traveled to Cairo and Istanbul to seek musical inspiration from the Sufi tradition.
13. Greg Kot, "Casting a Spell: Pakistani Musician Khan Propels a Powerful Concert Experience," *Chicago Tribune*, 26 August 1996, section C, p. 1.

14. Chris Nickson, "Trance Portation," *Wire Tapping* 97 (August 1996), p. 20.
15. During, pp. 168–206; Shems Friedlander, *The Whirling Dervishes: being an account of the Sufi order known as the Mevlevis and its founder the poet and mystic Mevlana Jalalu'ddin Rumi* (Albany, N.Y.: State University of New York Press, 1992); Walter Feldman, "Musical Genres and Zikir of the Sunni Tarikats of Istanbul," in Lifchez, pp. 187–202.
16. Lifchez, pp. 5, 101.
17. Lifchez, pp. 101–13.
18. An excellent selection of illustrations of dervishes may be seen in Yasar Nuri Ozturk, *The Eye of the Heart: An Introduction to Sufism and the Major Tariqats of Anatolia and the Balkans* (Istanbul: Redhouse Press, 1988). To these one should add the masterly portrait of a whirling dervish by the Orientalist painter Gerôme.
19. Pamela Sommers, "Dervishes: Out for a Spin," *Washington Post*, 14 November 1994, section D, p. 7.
20. For studies of the Alevi and Ahl-i Haqqmusical traditions, see two articles in *Manifestations of Sainthood in Islam*: Jean During, "The Sacred Music of the Ahl-i Haqqas a Means of Mystical Transmission," pp. 27–42, and Irene Markoff, "Music, Saints, and Ritual: Sama' and the Alevis of Turkey," pp. 95–110.
21. Robert Christgau, "That Old-Time Religion," *The Village Voice*, January 30, 1996, p. 62.
22. Philip D. Schuyler, "The Master Musicians of Jahjouka," *Natural History* 92 (October 1983), pp. 60 ff.
23. Randy Barnwell of Rounder Records, quoted by Bob Young, "Age-Old Traditions Fill the Music of Morocco at Longy," *The Boston Herald*, June 11, 1996.

Chapter 8: Sufism in the Contemporary World

1. See the detailed bibliographies in two broad survey articles by Marcia K. Hermansen: "In the Garden of American Sufi Movements: Hybrids and Perennials," in *New Islamic Movements*, ed. Peter C. Clarke (forthcoming), and "Hybrid Identity Formations in Muslim America: The case of American Sufi Movements," in *Muslims on the Americanization Path?*, ed. Yvonne Haddad and John Esposito (forthcoming). More focused studies have been contributed by Gisela Webb, in "Sufism in America," in *America's Alternative Religions*, ed. Tim Miller (Albany: State University of New York Press, 1995), and "Tradition and Innovation in Contemporary American Islamic Spirituality: The Bawa Muhaiyaddeen Fellowship," in *Muslim Communities in North America*, ed. Yvonne Haddad and Jane I. Smith (Albany: State University of New York Press, 1994). General surveys are given by Michael Koszegi, "Sufism in North America: A Bibliography," in J. Gordon Melton and Michael Koszegi, ed., *Islam in North*

America: A Sourcebook (New York: Garland Publishing, 1992), pp. 223–43, and Jay Kinney, "Sufism Comes to America," *Gnosis* 30 (Winter 1994), pp. 18–23.

2. Abu Sayeed Nur-ud-Din, "Attitude towards Sufism," in *Iqbal: Poet-Philosopher of Pakistan*, ed. Hafeez Malik (New York: Columbia University Press, 1971), p. 294, quoting Muhammad Anwar Harith, *Rakht-i Safar* (Travel Gear) (Karachi, 1952), pp. 117–19.

3. Trimingham, p. 252, n. 2.

4. Nur-ud-Din, pp. 292–93, quoting Muhammad Iqbal, *The Secrets of the Self*, trans. R. A. Nicholson (Lahore: Muhammad Ashraf, 1944), pp. 51, 56–57.

5. Muhammad Iqbal, "Disciples in Revolt," in *Poems from Iqbal*, trans. V. G. Kiernan (London: John Murray, 1955), p. 60.

6. S. A. Salik, *The Saint of Jilan* (Lahore, 1953; reprint ed., Chicago: Kazi Publications, 1985).

7. Capt. Wahid Bakhsh Sial Rabbani, *Islamic Sufism: The Science of Flight in God, with God, by God, and Union and Communion with God, Also showing the Tremendous Sufi Influence on Christian and Hindu Mystics and Mysticism* (Lahore: Sufi Foundation, 1984), chapter 5, pp. 112–249.

8. This message is also the burden of his Urdu treatise, Captain Wahid Bakhsh Siyal, *Mushahada-i haqq: islami ruhani sa'ins* (Contemplation of Truth: Islamic Spiritual Science) (Karachi: Mahfil-i Dhawqiyya, 1974).

9. The Chishti response to modernity is one of the topics of a forthcoming book, *Burnt Hearts: The Chishti Sufi Order* (London: Curzon Press), being prepared by Bruce B. Lawrence and myself.

10. R. A. Nicholson, "Sufiism," *Encyclopaedia Britannica* (11th ed., 1910), vol. 26, p. 31.

11. Bashir Ahmad Dar, *Tarikh-i tasawwuf qabl az Islam: Yunani, Yahudi, 'Isa'i, awr Chini tasawwuf ka tanqidi awr tarikhi ja'iza* (The History of Pre-Islamic Mysticism: An Analytical and Historical Survey of Greek, Jewish, Christian, and Chinese Mysticism) (Lahore: Idara-i Thiqafat-i Islamiyya, 1962).

12. Latif Allah, *Tasawwuf awr sirriyat: taqabuli mutal'a; tasawwuf ki asas, naw'iyyat, khususiyyat, awr tarikh ka tahqiqi ja'iza* (Sufism and Mysticism: A Comparative Study; A Research Survey of the Basis, Nature, Characteristics, and History of Sufism) (Lahore: Idara-i Thiqafat-i Islamiyya, 1990).

13. Julia A. Clancy-Smith, "The Man with Two Tombs: Muhammad ibn 'Abd al-Rahman, Founder of the Algerian Rahmaniyya, ca. 1715–1798," in *Manifestations of Sainthood in Islam*, p. 158.

14. C. Snouck Hurgronje, *The Achehnese* (Leiden: Luzac & Co., 1906).

15. For the following remarks I am indebted to David Gilmartin, *Empire and Islam: Punjab and the Making of Pakistan*, Comparative Studies on Muslim Societies, 7 (Berkeley: University of California Press, 1988), pp. 39–72.

16. Valerie J. Hoffman, *Sufism, Mystics, and Saints in Modern Egypt* (Columbia, S.C.: University of South Carolina Press, 1995).

17. Katherine Ewing, "The Politics of Sufism: Redefining the Saints of Pakistan," *Journal of Asian Studies* 52 (1983), pp. 251–68.

18. Motilal Jotwani, *Sufis of Sindh* (New Delhi: Government of India, Ministry of Information, 1986).

19. See the remarks of a Soviet-trained scholar about the difficulty of writing about Sufism and Islamic philosophy during the Soviet period, in Marietta Stepany-ants, *Sufi Wisdom* (Albany: State University of New York Press, 1994).

20. Bruce B. Lawrence, *Defenders of God: The Fundamentalist Revolt Against the Modern Age* (San Francisco: Harper & Row, 1989), pp. 100–101.

21. R. S. O'Fahey, *Enigmatic Saint: Ahmad Ibn Idris and the Idrisi Tradition*, Series in Islam and Society in Africa (Evanston, Ill.: Northwestern University Press, 1990).

22. Martin Notcutt, "Ibn 'Arabi in Print" in *Muhyiddin Ibn 'Arabi, A Commemorative Volume*, ed. Stephen Hirtenstein (Rockport, Mass.: Element, 1993), pp. 328–39.

23. Muhsin Mahdi, "From the Manuscript Age to the Age of Printed Books," in *The Book in the Islamic World: The Written Word and Communication in the Middle East*, ed. George N. Atiyeh (Albany: State University of New York Press/ Library of Congress, 1995), pp. 6–7. Mahdi suggests that the large followings of mystical orders made such publishing economically feasible.

24. Arthur F. Buehler, *Masters of the Heart: Naqshbandi Sufism and the Mediating Shaykh* (Charleston, S.C.: University of South Carolina Press, 1997).

25. In this connection one may mention the Ni'matullahi magazine *Sufi* and the Shahmaghsoudi magazine *Sufism: An Inquiry*.

26. Schimmel, *Mystical Dimensions of Islam*, p. 341.

27. Homerin, pp. 94–97.

28. Marcia Hermansen has made this point in the articles cited above, n. 1.

29. Several documentary films on Sufism are available for loan to educational institutions from the Non-Print Section, Undergraduate Library, University of North Carolina, Chapel Hill, NC 27599. Some of these include: *For Those Who Sail to Heaven* (about an Egyptian saint's festival at Luxor), *Saints and Spirits* (about Sufi shrines and spirit possession in Morocco), and two films about the Mevlevis, *Turning* and *Whirling Dervishes*.

30. Bruce B. Lawrence, "The Chishtiya of Sultanate India: A Case Study of Biographical Complexities in South Asian Islam," in *Charisma and Sacred Biography*, ed. Michael A. Williams (Chico, Cal.: Scholars Press, 1981), pp. 47–67.

31. See my review article, "Traditionalism, the Perennial Philosophy, and Islamic Studies," in *Middle East Studies Association Bulletin* 28 (1994), pp. 176–80.

32. Shah Ghulam 'Ali Dihlawi, *Makatib-i sharifa* (Noble Letters) (n.p. [Delhi?], 1371/1952; reprint ed., Istanbul: Waqf al-Ikhlas, 1989), pp. 66, 113.

33. Abu al-Hasan Kharaqani, in Jami, *Nafahat*, p. 298.

Select Bibliography

1. What Is Sufism?

Nasr, Seyyed Hossein. *Sufi Essays*. 2nd ed., Albany: State University of New York Press, 1991.

Schimmel, Annemarie. *Mystical Dimensions of Islam*. Chapel Hill: University of North Carolina Press, 1975.

2. The Sacred Sources of Sufism

Asani, Ali, et al. *Celebrating Muhammad: Images of the Prophet in Popular Muslim Poetry*. Columbia, S.C.: University of South Carolina Press, 1996.

Nurbakhsh, Javad. *Traditions of the Prophet: Ahadith*. New York: Khaniqahi-Nimatullahi Publications, 1981.

Schimmel, Annemarie. *And Muhammad Is His Prophet*. Chapel Hill: University of North Carolina Press, 1985.

Sells, Michael A. *Early Islamic Mysticism: Sufi, Qur'an, Mi'raj, Poetic and Theological Writings*. Classics of Western Spirituality. Mahwah, N.J.: Paulist Press, 1996.

3. Saints and Sainthood

'Attar, Fariduddin. *Muslim Saints and Mystics*. Translated by Arthur J. Arberry. London: Arkana, 1990.

Biegman, Nicolaas H. *Egypt: Moulids, Saints, Sufis*. The Hague: Gary Swartz/SDU Publications, 1990.

Chodkiewicz, Michel. *The Seal of the Saints: Prophethood and Sainthood in the Doctrine of Ibn 'Arabi*. Translated by Liadain Sherrard. Cambridge: Islamic Texts Society, 1993.

Cornell, Vincent. *The Dominion of the Saint: Power and Authority in Moroccan Mysticism.* Austin: University of Texas Press, forthcoming.

Nizam ad-Din Awliya. *Morals for the Heart.* Compiled by Hasan Dihlawi, translated by Bruce B. Lawrence. New York: Paulist Press, 1992.

Nurbakhsh, Javad. *Sufi Women.* 2nd ed., New York: Khaniqahi Nimatullahi, 1990.

Smith, Grace Martin, editor, and Carl W. Ernst, associate editor, *Manifestations of Sainthood in Islam.* Istanbul: Isis Press, 1994.

4. The Names of God, Meditation, and Mystical Experience

Bawa Muhaiyadeen, M. R. *The Asma'ul-Husna: Ninety-Nine Beautiful Names.* Philadelphia: Fellowship Press, 1979.

Corbin, Henry. *The Man of Light in Iranian Sufism.* Translated by Nancy Pearson. Boulder: Shambhala Publications, 1978.

Ernst, Carl W. *Ruzbihan Baqli: Mystical Experience and the Rhetoric of Sainthood in Persian Sufism.* Curzon Sufi Series. London: Curzon Press, 1996.

———. *Words of Ecstasy in Sufism.* SUNY Series in Islam. Albany: State University of New York Press, 1985.

Ibn 'Arabi. *Journey to the Lord of Power: A Sufi Manual on Retreat.* Translated by Rabia Harris. Rochester, Vt.: Inner Traditions, 1981.

Qushayri, al-. *Principles of Sufism.* Translated by B. R. von Schlegell. Berkeley: Mizan Press, 1990.

Ruzbihan Baqli. *The Unveiling of Secrets: Diary of a Sufi Master.* Translated by Carl W. Ernst. Chapel Hill, N.C.: Parvardigar Press, 1997.

5. The Sufi Orders

Ernst, Carl W. *Eternal Garden: Mysticism, History, and Politics at a South Asian Sufi Center.* SUNY Series in Muslim Spirituality in South Asia. Albany: State University of New York Press, 1992.

Ernst, Carl W., and Bruce B. Lawrence. *Burnt Hearts: The Chishti Sufi Order.* Curzon Sufi Series. London: Curzon Press, forthcoming.

Karamustafa, Ahmet T. *God's Unruly Friends: Dervish Groups in the Islamic Later Middle Period, 1200–1550.* Salt Lake City: University of Utah Press, 1994.

Karrar, Ali Salih. *The Sufi Brotherhoods in the Sudan.* Series in Islam and Society in Africa. Evanston, Ill.: Northwestern University Press, 1992.

Lifchez, Raymond, ed. *The Dervish Lodge: Architecture, Art, and Sufism in Ottoman Turkey.* Comparative Studies on Muslim Societies, 10. Berkeley: University of California Press, 1992.

Suhrawardi, Abu al-Najib al-. *A Sufi Rule for Novices: Kitab Adab al-Muridin.* Translated by Menahem Milson. Cambridge: Harvard University Press, 1975.

Trimingham, J. Spencer. *The Sufi Orders in Islam*. Oxford: Oxford University Press, 1971.

6. Sufi Poetry

Ghalib. *Poems*. Translated by Aijaz Ahmed with William Stafford and Adrienne Rich. New York: Hudson Review, 1969.

Homerin, Th. Emil. *From Arab Poet to Muslim Saint: Ibn al-Farid, His Verse, and His Shrine*. Columbia, S.C.: University of South Carolina Press, 1994.

Keshavarz, Fatemeh. *Reading Mystical Poetry: The Case of Jalal al-Din Rumi*. Columbia, S.C.: University of South Carolina Press, forthcoming in 1997.

Meisami, Julie. *Medieval Persian Court Poetry*. Princeton: Princeton University Press, 1987.

Schimmel, Annemarie. *A Two-Colored Brocade: The Imagery of Persian Poetry*. Chapel Hill: University of North Carolina Press, 1992.

Wilson, Peter Lamborn, and Nasrollah Pourjavady. *The Drunken Universe: An Anthology of Persian Sufi Poetry*. Grand Rapids: Phanes Press, 1987.

7. Sufi Music and Dance

Friedlander, Shems. *The Whirling Dervishes: Being an account of the Sufi order known as the Mevlevis and its founder the poet and mystic Mevlana Jalalu'ddin Rumi*. Albany, N.Y.: State University of New York Press, 1992.

Qureshi, Regula Burckhardt. *Sufi Music of India and Pakistan: Sound, Context and Meaning in Qawwali*. Cambridge, 1986; reprint ed. with compact disc, Chicago: University of Chicago Press, 1995.

Waugh, Earle H. *The Munshidīn of Egypt: Their World and Their Song*. Columbia S.C.: University of South Carolina Press, 1989.

8. Sufism in the Contemporary World

Hoffman, Valerie. *Sufism, Mystics, and Saints in Modern Egypt*. Columbia, S.C.: University of South Carolina Press, 1995.

O'Fahey, R. S. *Enigmatic Saint: Ahmad Ibn Idris and the Idrisi Tradition*. Series in Islam and Society in Africa. Evanston, Ill.: Northwestern University Press, 1990.

Trix, Frances. *Spiritual Discourse: Learning with an Islamic Master*. Conduct and Communications Series. Philadelphia: University of Pennsylvania Press, 1993.

Select Discography

Dhikr Ritual

Egypte: L'ordre Chazili, al-Tariqa al-Hamidiyya al-Chaziliyya. ARN 64211. Arion.

Maroc: Hadra des Gnaoua d'Essaouira. Produced by Pierre Toureille. C560006. Ocora Radio France.

Syria: Islamic Ritual Zikr in Aleppo. Produced by Jochen Wenzel. D 8013. UNESCO Collection.

Turquie: Ceremonie des derviches Kadiri. Produced by Ahmed Kudsi Erguner. CD-587. Disque VDE-GALLO, 1407 Donneloye, Switzerland. Tel. (4124) 331546, fax (4124) 331718.

Persian

Alizada, Husayn. *Raz o niyaz.* SITC-111. Shahram.

Nazeri, Shahram. *Atish dar nayistan.* Available from Navar.

Nazeri, Shahram. *Mutrib-i mahtab-ru.* Available from Navar.

Zul-Funun. *Bada-i guya.* Available from Navar.

North African

Master Musicians of Jajouka. Axiom 314–510 8572. Island Records.

Maroc: Anthologie d'al-Melhun. W 260016. Maison des Cultures du Monde, 101 Bd. Raspail, 75006 Paris, France. Tel. (1) 45.44.72.30.

Maroc–Moyen-Atlas: Musique sacree et profane. C559057, HM83. Produced by Pierre Toureille. Ocora Radio France.

Tazi, Ustad Massano. *Maroc: Musique classique andalouse de Fes.* Produced by Pierre Toureille. C559035. Ocora Radio France.

South Asian

Baloutchistan: Musiques d'extase et de guerison. Produced by Jean During. C 580017/18. Ocora Radio France.

Chisti, M. Saeed. *Qari Sage Miran.* Produced by John Matarazzo. IN5713. Interra Records Inc., 180 Varick St., New York, NY 10014.

Khan, Jafar Husayn. *Chant Qawwali de l'Inde du Nord.* Produced by Cherif Khaznadar. W 260048. Maison des Cultures du Monde, 101 Bd. Raspail, 75006 Paris, France. Tel. (1) 45.44.72.30.

Khan, Nusrat Fateh Ali. *Shahen-Shah.* 91300–2. Real World Records. Womad, Mill Lane, Box, Wiltshire SN149PN, UK.

Khan, Nusrat Fateh Ali. *En Concert a Paris*, vols. 2, 3-4-5. Produced by Pierre Toureille. C558659, C559072/073/074. Ocora Radio France.

Miah, Shahjahan. *Chants mystiques bauls du Bangladesh.* Produced by Cherif Khaznadar. W 260039. Maison des Cultures du Monde, 101 Bd. Raspail, 75006 Paris, France. Tel. (1) 45.44.72.30.

Nashenas. *Afghanistan: Classical Ghazals.* Auvitronics. UNHCR.

Sabri Brothers. *Greatest Hits of Sabri Brothers*, vols. 1–3. SIR CD-045, CD-046, CD-057. Serengeti Sirocco, Unit 4 Halles Business Centre, Pump Lane, Hayes Middlesex UB3 3NB, UK. Tel. 81-573 8827, fax 81-573 8831.

Sabri Brothers. *Ya Mustapha.* XENO 4041. Xenophile. Green Linnet Records, 43 Beaver Brook Road, Danbury, CT 06810.

Les Freres Sabri. *Musiciens Kawwali du Pakistan: Musique Soufi*, Vol. 3. Produced by Ariane Segal. ARN 64147. Arion.

Turkish

Qasimov, Alim. *Azerbaidjan: Musique et chants des ashiq.* Produced by Jean During. CD-613. Disque VDE-GALLO, 1407 Donneloye, Switzerland. Tel. (4124) 331546, fax (4124) 331718.

Kassimov, Alem. *Mugam d'Azerbaidjan*, vols. 1–2. Produced by Cherif Khaznadar. W 260012, W 260015. Maison des Cultures du Monde, 101 Bd. Raspail, 75006 Paris, France. Tel. (1) 45.44.72.30.

Mevlevi Ensemble. *Returning.* Produced by Kabir Helminski and Gerry James. CD-916. Interworld Music Associates, RD3 Box 395A, Brattleboro, VT 05301.

Toker, Bayram Bilge. *Bayram.* Produced by Karl Signell. CDT-122. Music of the World, P.O. Box 3620, Chapel Hill, NC 27515-3620.

Turquie: Musique Soufi. Produced by Pierre Toureille. C559017. Ocora Radio France.

Sources for Sufi Music

Kereshmeh, 12021 Wilshire Blvd., #420, Los Angeles, CA 90025. Tel. 310-451-3046, fax 310-260-3147, http://www.kereshmeh.com. Specializes in Persian music.

Navar Co., PO Box 392, North Hollywood, CA 91603. Tel. 818-988-8988, fax 818-762-2001. Specializes in Persian music.

Sufi Books, 227 West Broadway, New York, NY 10013. Tel. 212-334-5212, fax 212-334-5214.

World Music Institute, 49 W. 27th St., Suite no. 810, New York, NY 10001. Tel. 212-545-7536, fax 212-889-2771.

Index

251